Regression Inside Out

Linear regression analysis, with its many generalizations, is the predominant quantitative method used throughout the social sciences and beyond. The goal of the method is to study relations among variables. In this book, Schoon, Melamed, and Breiger turn regression modeling inside out to put the emphasis on the cases (people, organizations, and nations) that comprise the variables. By reanalyzing influential published research, they reveal new insights and present a principled way to unlock a set of more nuanced interpretations than has previously been attainable. The emphasis is on intuition and examples that can be reproduced using the code and datasets provided. Relating their contributions to methodologies that operate under quite different philosophical assumptions, the authors advance multimethod social science and help to bridge the divide between quantitative and qualitative research. The result is a modern, accessible, and innovative take on extracting knowledge from data.

Eric W. Schoon is Associate Professor of Sociology at The Ohio State University. His research interests include case-oriented and relational methods, sociological theory, and cultural dimensions of contentious politics. His work has appeared in outlets including *American Sociological Review*, *Journal of Politics*, *Social Forces*, and *Social Problems*.

David Melamed is Professor of Sociology and Translational Data Analytics at The Ohio State University. He is currently Co-Editor of *Sociological Methodology*. His research interests include the emergence of stratification and cooperation in complex systems. His work has appeared in *American Journal of Sociology*, *American Sociological Review*, and interdisciplinary venues.

Ronald L. Breiger is Regents Professor of Sociology at the University of Arizona. His interests include social network theory and methods and measurement issues in cultural and institutional analysis. He is the recipient of distinguished career awards from (respectively) the Methodology and Mathematical Sociology Sections of the American Sociological Association.

T0381643

Strategies for Social Inquiry

Editors

Colin Elman, *Maxwell School of Syracuse University*
John Gerring, *University of Texas, Austin*
James Mahoney, *Northwestern University*

Editorial Board

Bear Braumoeller[†], David Collier, Francesco Guala, Peter Hedström, Theodore Hopf, Uskali Maki, Rose McDermott, Charles Ragin, Theda Skocpol, Peter Spiegler, David Waldner, Lisa Wedeen, Christopher Winship

This book series presents texts on a wide range of issues bearing upon the practice of social inquiry. Strategies are construed broadly to embrace the full spectrum of approaches to analysis, as well as relevant issues in philosophy of social science.

Published Titles

John Gerring and Jason Seawright, *Finding Your Social Science Project: The Research Sandbox*

Jennifer Widner, Michael Woolcock and Daniel Ortega Nieto (eds.), *The Case for Case Studies: Methods and Applications in International Development*

Colin Elman, John Gerring and James Mahoney (eds.), *The Production of Knowledge: Enhancing Progress in Social Science*

John Boswell, Jack Corbett and R. A. W. Rhodes, *The Art and Craft of Comparison*

John Gerring, *Case Study Research: Principles and Practices, 2nd edition*

Jason Seawright, *Multi-Method Social Science: Combining Qualitative and Quantitative Tools*

Peter Spiegler, *Behind the Model: A Constructive Critique of Economic Modeling*

James Mahoney and Kathleen Thelen (eds.), *Advances in Comparative-Historical Analysis*

Diana Kapiszewski, Lauren M. MacLean and Benjamin L. Read, *Field Research in Political Science: Practices and Principles*

Andrew Bennett and Jeffrey T. Checkel (eds.), *Process Tracing: From Metaphor to Analytic Tool*

Nicholas Weller and Jeb Barnes, *Finding Pathways: Mixed-Method Research for Studying Causal Mechanisms*

Thad Dunning, *Natural Experiments in the Social Sciences: A Design-Based Approach*

Carsten Q. Schneider and Claudius Wagemann, *Set-Theoretic Methods for the Social Sciences: A Guide to Qualitative Comparative Analysis*

Michael Coppedge, *Democratization and Research Methods*

John Gerring, *Social Science Methodology: A Unified Framework, 2nd edition*

Regression Inside Out

Eric W. Schoon
The Ohio State University

David Melamed
The Ohio State University

Ronald L. Breiger
University of Arizona

CAMBRIDGE
UNIVERSITY PRESS

Shaftesbury Road, Cambridge CB2 8EA, United Kingdom

One Liberty Plaza, 20th Floor, New York, NY 10006, USA

477 Williamstown Road, Port Melbourne, VIC 3207, Australia

314–321, 3rd Floor, Plot 3, Splendor Forum, Jasola District Centre, New Delhi – 110025, India

103 Penang Road, #05–06/07, Visioncrest Commercial, Singapore 238467

Cambridge University Press is part of Cambridge University Press & Assessment, a department of the University of Cambridge.

We share the University's mission to contribute to society through the pursuit of education, learning and research at the highest international levels of excellence.

www.cambridge.org
Information on this title: www.cambridge.org/9781108841108

DOI: 10.1017/9781108887205

First published 2024

A catalogue record for this publication is available from the British Library

Library of Congress Cataloging-in-Publication Data
Names: Schoon, Eric W., author. | Melamed, David, author. |
Breiger, Ronald L., author.
Title: Regression inside out / Eric W. Schoon, The Ohio State University,
David Melamed, The Ohio State University, Ronald L. Breiger, University of Arizona.
Description: Cambridge, United Kingdom ; New York, NY, USA : Cambridge
University Press, 2024. | Series: Strategies for social inquiry |
Includes bibliographical references and index.
Identifiers: LCCN 2023035626 | ISBN 9781108841108 (hardback) |
ISBN 9781108887205 (ebook)
Subjects: LCSH: Regression analysis.
Classification: LCC QA278.2 .S35 2024 | DDC 519.5/36–dc23/eng/20231103
LC record available at https://lccn.loc.gov/2023035626

ISBN 978-1-108-84110-8 Hardback
ISBN 978-1-108-74488-1 Paperback

Contents

Part II   Action and Interaction

Part III   RIO as a Gateway

Figures

Tables

Acknowledgments

This book is the result of a collaboration that began at the University of Arizona. Ronald Breiger began working on his innovative approach to recasting regression modeling in relational terms around 2005, and in 2010, he invited Dave Melamed and Eric Schoon (then graduate students) to work with him, first as research assistants, then as full collaborators. Our first conference publication that called for "turn[ing] the conventional regression modeling 'inside out' to reveal a network of relations among the cases on the basis of their attribute and behavioral similarity" was Breiger and colleagues (2011). Over the next dozen years, the three of us worked together to continue to develop, refine, and explore the implications of turning regression models inside out.

We would like to express special thanks to the direct collaborators and coauthors with whom we have been privileged to work in developing and refining aspects of regression inside out, including Andrew P. Davis, Alessandro Lomi, Simone Rambotti, and Eunsung Yoon (with whom we have coauthored Chapter 4 of this book). Thanks to Simone also for coining the acronym RIO for our shared aspiration to turn regression modeling inside out. Additionally, we would like to thank our collaborators and coauthors who have worked with us in exploring and developing substantive applications: Gary Ackerman, Victor Asal, H. Brinton Milward, Lauren Pinson, and R. Karl Rethemeyer.

As with any work that has developed over such a long time, it is difficult to acknowledge everyone who has offered support, advice, or feedback on the ideas presented here. We will likely miss some people who have influenced this work, and for that we are sorry. That being said, we express our thanks to the following individuals. In the early days, Ron was the beneficiary of exceptional advice, support, criticism, and encouragement from Omar Lizardo and Kieran Healy. Jim Moody has been an unflagging source of astute insight, questioning, and inspiration. We have received additional valuable feedback, criticism, and encouragement over the years from Elisa Bienenstock, Matthew Brashears, Carter Butts, Christina Diaz, Patrick Doreian, the late Scott Eliason, Jeremy Fiel, Lane Kenworthy, Balázs Kovács, Erin Leahey,

John Levi Martin, Charles Ragin, and A. Joseph West, for all of which we are grateful. Additionally, we are grateful to Jason Beckfield, Charles Ragin, and Carsten Schneider, who shared replications materials from their published work with us, thereby meaningfully advancing our efforts to engage with substantively important research of exceptional quality.

We have benefited greatly from questions, critiques, and suggestions made by participants in conferences, colloquia, and workshops, including the 2005 Sunbelt Social Networks Conference, the Columbia University Networks and Time Seminar Series, the Duke University Network Analysis Center, Emory University's program in Quantitative Theory and Methods, the MaxPo Center on Coping with Instability in Market Societies (Paris, France), the Networks in the Global World conference (St. Petersburg, Russia), the NYU-Abu Dhabi Program in Social Research and Public Policy, the Quantifying Social Fields Conference at the University of California, Berkeley, the Stanford University Center for Education Research, and the Yale University Institute for Network Science.

We are grateful to the editors of the Strategies for Social Inquiry series, Colin Elman, John Gerring, and James Mahoney, for the support and encouragement they provided us throughout this project. Special thanks to them for exposing us to the critical insights and inspiration of Adam Slez and the late Bear Braumoeller, who participated along with the editors in an intensive book workshop the editors organized in September 2021, while we were in the midst of writing this book, and whose comments led to substantial improvements in our manuscript. We would especially like to thank Jim Mahoney for shepherding us through the early stages of the proposal process.

We thank John Haslam and his team at Cambridge University Press for their professional support. We also thank Christopher Kleps for his research assistance during the completion of this manuscript.

Elements of this work have been supported through funding from the Defense Threat Reduction Agency (HDTRA1-10-1-0017; Ronald Breiger, PI, 2010-2016) and the Intelligence Advanced Research Projects Activity (2018-17121900006; Eric Schoon, PI, 2018-2019).[1]

Finally, we would like to thank our families for the continual support and encouragement that made this book and the research that went into it possible. We dedicate this book to them.

[1] The views and conclusions contained herein are those of the authors and should not be interpreted as representing the official policies, either expressed or implied, of DTRA, ODNI, IARPA, or the US government. The US government is authorized to reproduce and distribute reprints for governmental purposes notwithstanding any copyright annotation herein.

1 Introduction

What can we learn from a regression model? This is the question that motivates *Regression Inside Out* (RIO). Regression is among the most widely used tools for data analysis. A workhorse of both academic and nonacademic research, it is a standard part of curricula in fields ranging from accounting to zoology. It can be used to explore data, test hypotheses, and bring statistical theory, discipline-specific theory, and data into dialogue (Belsley, Kuh, and Welsch 2004). A technical answer to the question, "what can we learn from a regression model?," is that we learn how average values of an outcome vary across subpopulations of observations that are defined by the values of a set of predictors (Cook and Weisberg 1999; Gelman, Hill, and Vehtari 2020). In a more practical sense, we routinely use regression models to learn a great deal about the world around us.

Over the past several decades, however, a growing chorus of scholars in the social sciences have raised concerns about *how* we learn from regression models. An early voice in this chorus was the pioneering quantitative sociologist Otis Dudley Duncan, who described a "syndrome" that he referred to as *statisticism*. Statisticism is

the notion that computing is synonymous with doing research, the naïve faith that statistics is a complete or sufficient basis for scientific methodology, the superstition that statistical formulas exist for evaluating such things as the relative merits of different substantive theories or the 'importance' of the causes of a 'dependent variable'. (Duncan 1984: 226)

To be clear, Duncan was not against regression analysis (as is evident from his own scholarship; see Goodman 2007). Rather, he was deeply concerned with how regression was used to conduct research and draw conclusions. This concern with how we learn from regression models has only grown in the decades since Duncan's prescient diagnosis (e.g., Abbott 1988; Berk 2004; Emirbayer 1997; Freedman 1991; Ragin 2006; Shalev 2007; Tong 2019).

For some observers, concerns about how we learn from regression are grounded in theory (Abbott 1988; Emirbayer 1997; Ragin 2000, 2006;

Shalev 2007). Regression imposes "homogenizing assumptions" (Ragin 2000: 5) that lead researchers to construe social reality in terms of what Abbott (1988) refers to as a *general linear reality*. Abbott explains that, far from simply summarizing how average values of an outcome vary across sub-populations of observations (as textbooks teach it), regression shapes how we think about, interpret, and understand the social world (Abbott 1988: 169). Ragin (2000) similarly observes that conventional approaches to quantitative research structure how analysts make sense of populations, cases, and causes in ways that constrain dialogue between theory and evidence, thereby limiting discovery. Taken together, these and other theoretically motivated critiques highlight how conventional regression analysis is not a neutral representation of empirical realities. Rather, regression imposes strong philosophical assumptions that guide how we think about the phenomena we study.

For others, concerns about how we learn from regression are grounded in practice (e.g., Berk 2004; Freedman 1991; Tong 2019). While issues with how practitioners use regression are quite varied, they tend to focus on a widespread overemphasis on model outputs (e.g., fitted values, coefficients, and variance) with insufficient attention to model inputs (e.g., data and "the ordering of data in time, space, or other characteristics" [Belsley et al. 2004: 4]). Observers point out that much of the focus of standard regression theory has to do with sampling fluctuations, and regression is routinely used to analyze data that fails to meet the assumptions that render these theories applicable (e.g., a representative sample from a known population). Consequently, conclusions are drawn from regression that are not supported by the data or by the method itself (see Berk 2007). Elaborating on how inattention to model inputs can create significant methodological problems, Tong (2019) argues that "formal, probability-based statistical inference should play no role in most scientific research" (p. 246). He makes the case that data are routinely used to guide model specification, and when they are, the inferential statistics that quantify uncertainty are biased. Other advocates of regression analysis who are concerned with how it is applied similarly cite routine failures to meaningfully consider how model inputs shape what we learn from regression. As Belsley, Kuh, and Welsch (2004) observe in their influential book on regression diagnostics,

In years past, when multivariate research was conducted on small models using desk calculators and scatter diagrams, unusual data points and some obvious forms of collinearity could often be detected in the process of 'handling the data,' in what was surely an informal procedure. With the introduction of high-speed computers and frequent use of large-scale models, however, the researcher has become ever more detached from intimate knowledge of [their] data. It is increasingly the case that the data employed in regression analysis, and on which the results are conditioned, are given only the most cursory examination for their suitability. (p. 4)

They make the case that thorough engagement with data and other model inputs is essential to good statistical practice.

To be clear, scholars voicing both theoretical and practical concerns with regression analysis recognize its value as a "formidable and effective method" (Abbott 1988: 169). Nonetheless, they emphasize the need for a more careful consideration of what we can actually learn from a regression model. They ask us to confront difficult questions, such as: How do the philosophical assumptions that undergird regression shape our understanding of the social world? To what extent do summaries of the relationships among variables apply to and inform our understanding of the specific observations in our data? How do we reconcile an intuitive understanding of causality as multiple and complex with an analytic focus on net effects? Or, more simply: What can we actually learn from a regression model?

Our goal in this book is to expand *what* we can learn from regression models by fundamentally rethinking *how* we learn from regression models. We do this by turning regression "inside out." As we elaborate in Chapters 2, 5, and 7, conventional regression analysis renders the cases, their relationships to one another, and their unique characteristics – all of which are key model inputs (Belsley et al. 2004) – invisible (Shalev 2007). By contrast, RIO makes the complexities of the cases (i.e., the rows of the data matrix) visible and puts them in dialogue with the variables. While RIO begins with a generalized linear model (GLM), it allows us to identify each individual observation's additive contribution to model outputs. Because the contributions are additive, we can move seamlessly between individual cases and the net effects produced by the GLM, comparing how individual cases or sets of cases shape the net effect. This clearly situates each case within the broader context represented by the overall model space. As we show throughout this book, this ability has both theoretical and methodological payoffs.

1.1   A Case-Oriented Approach to Regression Models

RIO is designed to allow us to look inside the regression model and gain a deeper understanding of how it represents the data. In doing so, RIO allows us to relax many of the restrictive philosophical assumptions embedded in regression analysis (Abbott 1988), which constrain dialogue between theory and evidence. This relaxing of assumptions is accomplished by analytically allowing for the complexities that emerge when observations are conceptualized as cases: spatially and temporally delimited phenomena of theoretical interest in their own right (Gerring 2017).

As noted earlier, the thrust of standard regression theory focuses on sample fluctuation. Regression is designed to identify population-level trends based on a representative subset of that population (Berk 2004). When analyzing a sample that meets the baseline assumptions for inference in a regression model, individual observations are entirely interchangeable, or more technically, they are exchangeable (Kutner, Nachtsheim, and Neter 2004). For example, if we are interested in assessing how attitudes toward gerrymandering affect the probability that voters in the United States will elect a Democrat or Republican president, it makes no difference whether we (the three authors) or you (the reader) are personally included in the sample, how we feel, or what we prefer. What matters is how the data were sampled. If the data were sampled properly, we can summarize how the conditional distribution of voter preferences varies based on attitudes toward gerrymandering and use those summaries to draw conclusions about the relationship between these variables in the population as a whole.

Yet, regression is often applied in contexts where the goal is to draw conclusions about a given set of cases rather than a population based on a representative sample. Consider, for example, almost all analyses where countries are the unit of analysis. We might use regression to examine the effects of a nation's regime type on interstate war (e.g., Schultz 1999), the determinants of status in the international system (e.g., Bezerra et al. 2015), or the effects of regional integration on poverty (Beckfield 2006). However, the observations in these analyses are not exchangeable. Consequently, it would be statistically and substantively untenable to take a representative sample of countries and use that sample to make inferences about all countries in the world. Moreover, unlike when we are drawing conclusions about population-level trends, the results of an analysis of countries are meaningful only to the extent that they can be related to tangible outcomes for real cases. Particularly in comparative international research, it is (perhaps surprisingly) common to find zones in a distribution with no observed data (Rosenberg, Knuppe, and Braumoeller 2017). Consequently, the results of a linear regression might produce values that have no observable empirical basis. These same limits and considerations are equally applicable to other, smaller units of analysis. A focus on cases can be found in regression analyses with observations ranging from individuals (Ragin and Fiss 2017) to corporations (McKendall and Wagner 1997), and beyond.

Cases necessarily introduce complexities. When observations are theoretically and substantively exchangeable, differences from one case to the next are simply factored into the error term and are substantively irrelevant beyond any possible trends in the error term. However, when observations are theoretically or substantively meaningful, differences from one case to the next can imply substantively or theoretically important differences in associations between variables, distinct causes of an outcome, or any number of other forms of complexity (Abbott 1988; Mahoney and Goertz 2006; Ragin 2006, 2014b). Consider, for example, an analysis of the relationship between social capital and school achievement. A regression model can show that social capital obtained through families improves children's academic achievement more than social capital obtained through school (Dufur, Parcel, and Troutman 2013). However, attention to case-level variation may reveal that different sources of social capital have different impacts from one student to the next, or that social capital does not matter at all for some students but matters a great deal for others. Similarly, a regression model might show that organizations engaged in political violence are more likely to participate in illicit drug economies when they control territory (Asal, Rethemeyer, and Schoon 2019; Cornell and Jonsson 2014). However, attention to case-level variation may reveal that the reasons groups participate in illicit drug economies are not simply the inverse of the reasons that they do not, such that participation is driven by economic need while lack of participation is driven by an absence of opportunity. These possibilities are rendered invisible (or, theoretically impossible) within the bounds of the general linear reality (Abbott 1988; Rambotti and Breiger 2020; Shalev 2007). However, by accounting for how individual cases contribute to net effects, turning our regression model inside out allows us to explore such discontinuities at the level of cases and subsets of cases. Thus, rather than rejecting "general linear reality," our aim in this book is to show how to get more out of it.

Shalev (2007) offers a similar example in research on comparative social policy. He notes that a well-established finding in comparative welfare state research is that there are two subtypes of European welfare states that are known to spend a great deal: Social Democracies and Christian Democracies (see Kersbergen 2003; Korpi and Shalev 1980). Discussing the effects of regime types on spending, he writes,

[T]his presents no problem for the standard additive regression model provided that the effects are equivalent and unrelated – if for instance a strong social-democratic party could be expected to have the same effect whether or not it governed in coalition with a Christian-Democratic party. However, the Austrian experience suggests that this is unlikely since historically, the black half of the 'red-black' [Christian Democratic/Social Democratic] coalition severely constrained its welfare state development. (Shalev 2007: 265)

Here, the unique features of Austria suggest an interactive effect, but it is not clear whether such an interaction would be statistically significant in a net effect model given the unique features of the Austrian case.

It is RIO's ability to account for these kinds of complexities at the level of cases that allows us to relax many of the restrictive assumptions built into the GLM. Most straightforwardly, it allows us to avoid the homogenization of cases that is inherent in conventional regression (Ragin 2000). More broadly, however, this relaxing of assumptions extends further. Consider Abbott's (1988) elaboration of the philosophical assumptions that are embedded in GLMs. As he notes, when we use regression models to represent social reality, we are required to transpose social life onto the algebra of regression models. He continues:

Such representational use assumes that the social world consists of fixed entities (the units of analysis) that have attributes (the variables). These attributes interact, in causal or actual time, to create outcomes, themselves measurable as attributes of the fixed entities. The variable attributes have only one causal meaning (one pattern of effects) in a given study, although of course different studies make similar attributes mean different things. An attribute's causal meaning cannot depend on the entity's location in the attribute space (its context), since the linear transformation is the same throughout that space. For similar reasons, the past path of an entity through the attribute space (its history) can have no influence on its future path, nor can the causal importance of an attribute change from one entity to the next. All must obey the same transformations. (p. 170)

Abbott notes that some methods – such as demographic methods, sequence analysis, and network analysis – relax these basic assumptions of general linear reality. Demographic models, for instance, relax the assumption of fixed entities with variable attributes by allowing entities to move, appear, disappear, merge, or divide over time. Sequence analysis, in contrast, relaxes nearly all the assumptions, while network analysis relaxes assumptions of independence (both independence among observations and independence from context).

RIO's grounding in the GLM binds it to the assumption of fixed entities with variable attributes. However, its orientation toward cases allows us to relax the remaining assumptions. By focusing on how individual cases shape the linear model, we can account for discontinuities in the meanings of particular variables. These effects depend on an entity's location in the attribute space, which we can see by breaking down and mapping that attribute space (see Chapters 2, 3, 7, and 9), situating individual cases in relation to one another and to the variables. Moreover, a focus on cases allows us to account for the past path of an entity through the attribute space and explore how that history influences its future path forward. This can be done either by incorporating substantive knowledge into our interpretation of the location of cases in the attribute space, or by mapping the trajectory of individual cases across the model space over time. We illustrate this latter possibility in Chapter 7 (see Figure 7.12c), showing how a break in the plotted trajectory of an individual case across the attribute space corresponds with a major historical event that shifted its relationship to the variables in the model. Finally, a focus on cases allows us to explore and account for the possibility that the causal importance of an attribute changes from one entity to the next.

In short, by turning regression models inside out, we are able to get more out of the summaries of conditional distributions that are represented by conventional model outputs and engage with the complexity that often undergirds the social realities that regression represents. RIO is still firmly grounded in regression and statistical thinking (Tong 2019). Yet, by shifting how we learn from a regression model – turning attention toward the empirical relationships among cases rather than limiting our focus to the relationships among variables – we can dramatically expand what we are able to learn from a regression model.

1.2   A Methodological Gateway

By allowing us to relax many of the philosophical assumptions of conventional regression analysis, RIO opens the door to incorporating insights from, and contributing insights to, methodologies that operate under quite different philosophical (i.e., conceptual and epistemological) assumptions. Because of regression's ubiquity in the social sciences, it is routinely used as a benchmark when enumerating defining features of other seemingly disparate methodological approaches. Distinctions between qualitative and quantitative methods in the social sciences typically associate quantitative approaches with the logic of regression and contrast this logic with qualitative approaches that are case-oriented and highly sensitive to the influence of individual observations (see, e.g., Mahoney and Goertz 2006). Similarly, in *The Comparative Method*, Charles Ragin's foundational introduction of qualitative comparative analysis (QCA), Ragin often contrasts QCA with regression to emphasize key elements of the comparative approach (see also Ragin 2000, 2006, 2009; Ragin and Fiss 2017). In his *Manifesto for a Relational Sociology*, Emirbayer (1997) contrasts relational approaches to what he refers to as substantialist approaches. He identifies methods common to these approaches, situating regression among the substantialist approaches in contrast to methods of network analysis.

In these and other instances, comparisons between regression and other methods often imply technical differences along with conceptual differences. However, the technical differences are often not as great as they appear at first blush. Breiger (2000) illustrates this through his comparison of correspondence analysis and lattice analysis (two fundamentally relational methods) with the quantitative approach developed by James Coleman (1994) in his *Foundations of Social Theory* (a fundamentally substantialist approach). He shows that there is "a remarkable homology – at the level of formal practices, if not indeed in their 'very spirit' – between the mathematical techniques" (p. 95). Subsequent research (e.g., Breiger 2009; Breiger and Melamed 2014; Breiger et al. 2011, 2014; Pattison and Breiger 2002; Rambotti and Breiger 2020) shows how the mathematical techniques associated with network analysis, configurational comparative analysis, and regression all share similar homologies.

Similarities in the formal practices undergirding these methods provide an opportunity to bring them into dialogue and highlight how the barriers that have motivated many to draw distinctions between regression and other analytic tools are more philosophical than methodological. As we illustrate in Chapters 8 and 9, the fact that RIO allows us to relax many of the assumptions of regression provides us with an opportunity to incorporate other philosophies and assumptions into our thinking as we apply and interpret regression models.

In addition to expanding how we interpret and engage with regression, the mathematical homologies between regression and other methodologies also stand to enhance multimethod research that incorporates regression analysis. The standard design for multimethod research relies on triangulation, which involves asking the same question using different methods and comparing the findings of each (e.g., Jick 1979; Tarrow 1995). However, as Seawright (2016) argues, there are no standards for drawing conclusions when two methods yield conflicting answers. He thus advocates for an integration-oriented approach. Rather than using each method to validate the other, he recommends bringing the two into conversation so that each method enhances the other. RIO stands to contribute to such efforts, offering a way of bringing regression into closer dialogue with many of the (typically case-oriented) methodologies commonly employed to complement regression in multimethod research. Whether this means assessing how case studies fit in relation to an overall regression model (Chapter 7), bridging the gap between set-theoretic and correlational approaches to analysis (Chapter 8), or incorporating insights from field theory (Chapter 9), looking inside a regression model allows us to better assess how results from other methods (which are typically assumed to be disparate) are situated in relation to the results of a regression.

1.3   Understanding versus Improving Models

In the literature on regression models, cases are discussed mostly in the context of regression diagnostics. In that context, the aim is to identify a small number of cases that do not fit the model, and therefore imply a different model (with different cases). While the analytic framework of RIO builds on known methods for regression diagnostics, RIO's intended purpose is quite distinct from their typical goals, which are oriented toward improving regression analysis by formulating new models. As the preceding discussion indicates, the intended purpose of RIO is to provide new ways of learning from – interpreting, engaging with, and thinking via – regression models. We highlight this distinction because it provides a necessary orientation for readers moving forward.

While we view diagnostics as a critical step in any regression analysis, the question of how to fit a better model is quite distinct from the question of how to interpret and understand the model at hand. Over the past decade, standard textbooks on statistical methods have increasingly incorporated thorough discussions of regression diagnostics (e.g., Gelman et al. 2020), and there are many excellent texts devoted entirely to developing and/or explaining methods for improving model fit, detecting collinearities, correcting for biases, and many other necessary tasks for estimating an analytically robust regression model (e.g., Belsley et al. 2004; Berry 1993; Fox 2019; Pregibon 1981; Velleman and Welsch 1981). Despite important and exciting innovations in regression diagnostics specifically, and statistical modeling more generally, making sense of regression outputs is generally treated as well-trod ground and left to introductory texts.

Because RIO builds on the GLM, we assume that any user will have already fit a model, and it is our hope that this will have been done in dialogue with appropriate tests and assessments to ensure that the model itself is the best possible representation of the data. As we show in Chapter 6, turning a regression model inside out may lead an analyst to respecify their model. However, the value added by turning a regression model inside out extends farther than identifying a better model. Put differently, the aim of regression diagnostics is to learn about problematic cases, while the aim of RIO is to learn more about how the cases and the variables co-constitute the regression output (i.e., the coefficients and standard errors).

Keeping this distinction in mind will help to situate some of the facets of RIO that we discuss. For example, if we identify a single observation as being highly influential using conventional diagnostics like Cook's distance (Cook 1977) or DFBETA (Belsley et al. 2004), RIO will likely identify that observation as having a large additive contribution to one or more regression coefficients, and/or to the variance. However, simply having a large additive contribution to one or more regression coefficients or the variance does not imply that dropping that case will meaningfully alter our model, as it typically does when such cases are identified using conventional diagnostics. The reason for this is, with RIO, each case's contribution is based on the given model. If we drop one case or alter a variable, the model itself changes, and so do the relationships. Thus, RIO does exactly what is advertised: it allows us to look at what is going on inside our given regression model. It is worth noting that understanding what is going on inside our regression model may lead us to revise the model, but that is not our primary goal.

Despite these differences, throughout this book, we often compare RIO with methods employed for the purposes of regression diagnostics. This is because diagnostics is the only area of conventional regression analysis where individual observations are taken seriously. Given that our focus is on cases (which are typically conceptualized as observations in the data matrix, but can be represented by multiple observations, as we show in Chapters 5 and 7), the methods used in regression diagnostics provide a useful counterpoint for us to illustrate how a case-oriented approach to regression contrasts with the treatment of cases in conventional, variable-oriented regression, where individual cases (or sets of cases) are only considered to the extent that they risk violating assumptions used to draw conclusions about the relationships among variables.

1.4   Plan of the Book

As sociologists, we are writing from the perspective of the social sciences. The examples that we use as illustrations throughout the book are all drawn from the social sciences (specifically from sociology and political science), as are many of the theoretical and conceptual considerations that we address. However, we believe that RIO will prove useful for researchers in any field where the GLM is a commonly used methodological tool, including the biological, physical, and computational sciences as well as professional fields such as law, medicine, management, policy, education, criminology, and many others.

The approach presented here can be applied by anyone with a practical familiarity with the GLM. The only assumption we make about the level of technical knowledge or expertise that readers should have to make sense of this book is that the readers have a working understanding of multiple regression. Some of the chapters in this book (e.g., Chapters 3 and 4) are oriented specifically toward readers interested in the more advanced technical aspects of RIO. The remaining chapters, however, are designed to speak more broadly to anyone who has computed a regression model and tried to make sense of it.

RIO is divided into three sections. The first section (Chapters 2–4) introduces the foundations of the method. In Chapter 2, we introduce the logic and basic mathematics of RIO using ordinary least squares (OLS) regression. We use this chapter to demonstrate the range of analytic possibilities that emerge from looking inside a regression model. We ground our discussion in a detailed reimagining of a published regression analysis: Lane Kenworthy's (1999) study of the effects of social-welfare policies on poverty. We use Kenworthy's analysis as a didactic touchstone in later chapters (specifically, Chapters 4, 7, and 9), building on the analyses presented in Chapter 2.

Chapters 3 and 4 are more technical. Chapter 3 details how the procedures outlined in Chapter 2 generalize to other forms of the GLM. We illustrate how the link function enables linearization, allowing our approach to apply to the entire family of the GLM. We illustrate this specifically with logistic, Poisson, and negative binomial regression. Additionally, we demonstrate how a relatively straightforward modification of the linear model makes it possible to generalize to Fixed Effects models as well. In Chapter 4, we consider how we can turn the standard errors and variance of the model inside out. We discuss some of the challenges associated with identifying additive case-level contributions to the errors and outline two distinct approaches to making this assessment. We also discuss the utility of turning errors inside out, and emphasize the descriptive nature of any conclusions that might be drawn from these measures of uncertainty.

The second section (Chapters 5 and 6) illustrates some of the substantive value-added of RIO. These chapters will be of particular interest for researchers who plan to use RIO to better engage with their regression models. Having introduced the concepts and mathematics of RIO, Chapter 5 demonstrates some of the analytic and substantive payoffs of turning regression models inside out by applying the material introduced in Chapters 2–4 in reanalyses of three exemplary empirical research studies. Our first application is a reanalysis of regression models published by Jason Beckfield (2006), which examines the effects of regional integration on poverty. In this example, we demonstrate how RIO can be used to account for the effect of cases when those cases are represented by multiple observations. The second illustration focuses on the economic determinants of health across 20 wealthy nations, turning published regression models by Simone Rambotti (2015, Rambotti and Breiger 2020) inside out to demonstrate how a focus on cases' contributions to the overall regression model yields novel substantive insights. For our third illustration, we use General Social Survey (GSS) data to look at the determinants of dog ownership. We show how we can incorporate clustering algorithms to identify subsets of cases and explore the unique contributions of these sets to identify different "stories" told by the regression model. These three examples all rely on different forms of the GLM (fixed-effects and random-effects, OLS, and logistic, respectively) and all highlight unique features and substantive benefits of RIO.

In Chapter 6, we explain how RIO can be used to detect statistical interaction terms. As noted earlier in this chapter, the purpose of RIO is not to improve a model. However, exploring what is going on inside our models can yield valuable insights that do lead to respecification. Here, we show how accounting for the relationships among cases allows us to identify systematic discontinuities in the effects of certain conditions across those cases. We show how these discontinuities imply statistical interaction effects, and present two ways of identifying statistical interaction terms. Using Monte Carlo simulations, we show that our approach to detecting statistical interactions identifies statistically significant interaction effects in the data 1,000 out of 1,000 times.

The final section explores how RIO can act as a gateway between regression and other distinct methodological approaches. Chapter 7 turns attention to case selection, which methodologically stands at the core of case study research. A growing collection of scholarship has devoted attention to algorithmic case selection, which relies on quantitative indicators to identify cases for in-depth analysis. Building on an overview of several common types of case studies, we show how RIO can both inform and advance existing approaches to algorithmic case selection that align with these forms, yielding deeper insights into the relationships among cases, as well as relationships among cases and variables.

Chapter 8 shows how RIO can serve as a gateway to configurational comparative analysis. Configurational comparative methods are designed to facilitate systematic, cross-case comparison while at the same time treating individual cases holistically. This case-orientation makes it possible to account for the kinds of complexities that are inherent in cases, while still providing a foundation for broad comparison. The most formalized and widely known approach to configurational comparative analysis is QCA, a set-theoretic approach to social research that is designed to facilitate the identification of necessary and sufficient conditions (Ragin 2014b; Rihoux and Ragin 2008; Schneider and Wagemann 2012). Using QCA as our reference point, we detail key dissimilarities between the logics, mathematics, and goals of QCA versus regression. We then explain and illustrate how RIO can bridge these divides, making it possible to account for many of the forms of complexity that are commonly associated with QCA, and facilitating greater dialogue between the two approaches in multimethod research.

Chapter 9 shows how the foundation of RIO in the geometry of the regression model (introduced in Chapter 2) can serve as a gateway to field-theoretic approaches to data analysis. In particular, we focus on geometric data analysis (GDA), a formal approach and family of techniques fundamental to the varieties of field theory developed by social theorists including, most influentially, Pierre Bourdieu (Lebaron 2009; Lebaron and Le Roux 2018; Rouanet, Ackermann, and Le Roux 2000). We show how our geometric thinking yields precise algebraic results with any number of independent variables (dimensions). New results include a novel decomposition of "leverage" (the cells on the diagonal of the Hat matrix), showing the leverage of each case as a function of each predictor variable in the regression model. Then we reanalyze a dataset on the average savings rate across 50 countries. These data, originally published as a didactic example by Belsley, Kuh, and Welsch (2004), are a classic example in regression diagnostics, and provide an excellent basis for illustrating how RIO can serve as a gateway to field theory, while also substantially recasting and broadening the analysis of diagnostics to include the study of the structuring of the entire network among the cases that underlie every regression model.

In Chapter 10, we conclude by reviewing our main thesis: turning RIO allows an analyst to bring cases to the fore, making it possible to better account for, and explicitly engage with, the kinds of complexities that cases introduce into any analysis. In summary, RIO is a method for learning about how the cases and the variables co-constitute each other, and what that implies for an estimated regression model. It enables analysts to look "under the hood" of a regression model to see associations in the space of the model. The insights gained by doing so can improve understanding of processes, draw connections between disparate methodologies, and sometimes lead an analyst to formulate another model altogether.

1.5   Reproducibility and Replication Materials

There are two resources we highlight for readers that can render this material more accessible. First, we have developed a package – `rioplot` – for the R software environment that includes four functions. The functions implement the methods we discuss throughout the book. Most importantly, the `rio.plot` function is a flexible way to visualize a model object, including both the cases and the variables in the same space. As of this writing, the R package is hosted on Github and may be obtained as follows: `devtools::install_github("dmmelamed/rioplot")`.   Aside from the functions, the R package includes the data we analyze throughout the book.

The second resource we point out is the companion website at Open Science Framework: https://osf.io/yb4np/. Here you will find R scripts that reproduce the results we report throughout the book. We hope access to those materials makes the methods in general more accessible.

Part I

Turning Regression Inside Out

2 OLS Inside Out

Unfortunately, too many people like to do their statistical work as they say their prayers – merely substitute in a formula found in a highly respected book written a long time ago.
– Hotelling et al. (1948: 103; as quoted in Kennedy 2002: 572)

As we detailed in Chapter 1, turning regression inside out allows us to explore how the observations of our data shape the outputs of our regression model. This facilitates a case-oriented approach to regression that makes it possible to move beyond the central tendency of our data and see specifically how each individual observation is contributing to the coefficients and standard errors. Bringing cases to the fore opens a range of analytic possibilities that allow us to gain greater insights from our regression model than are possible in the context of conventional regression analysis.

In this chapter, we introduce the foundations of RIO and illustrate some of the range of ways that RIO enables us to learn more from our regression models than a conventional approach to regression allows. We begin with a focus on OLS regression because it is the most widely known and accessible form of the GLM and should be familiar to anyone who has taken a statistics class. For the time being, we also bracket the question of variance in RIO. In Chapter 3, we show how the same procedures introduced in this chapter can be generalized to other forms of the GLM, and in Chapter 4, we provide a detailed discussion of turning variance inside out. However, beginning with a focus on turning the OLS coefficients inside out allows us to illustrate the logic of RIO in an intuitive and accessible way.

The foundations of RIO rely on both matrix multiplication and the singular value decomposition (SVD). While an understanding of matrix multiplication and SVD is not necessary for understanding what RIO can do, it is necessary for understanding how RIO works. Both matrix multiplication and SVD are straightforward to understand and are referenced throughout this book. Readers unfamiliar with these techniques may wish to read Appendices A (on Matrix Multiplication) and B (on the SVD) before reading this chapter. Readers familiar with these techniques will have sufficient background knowledge to understand the inner workings of RIO.

We introduce the mathematics, logic, and analytic possibilities of RIO via a concrete empirical example. We take this approach in an effort to make this initial introduction both tangible and accessible. Our application centers on a reanalysis of data drawn from a widely cited study by Lane Kenworthy (1999), which addresses the question: do social welfare policies reduce poverty? In his study, Kenworthy examines the effects of social welfare policy extensiveness on poverty reduction across 15 affluent industrialized nations over three decades (1960–1991) using OLS regression.

We focus on this example for three reasons. First, we believe that it provides an exemplary application of OLS in a context where the cases are of inherent interest. Second, the small number of observations makes it possible to present and grasp the overall relationships among cases and variables and see the substantive benefits of RIO. Third, Lane Kenworthy himself has been a prominent, conscientious research leader who gains insight from regression models while being mindful of the restricted nature of regression modeling as it is usually practiced. Too often, he writes, regressions are both the starting point and the ending point of the analysis (Kenworthy 2007). What should be done? As Kenworthy writes,

I would like to see more papers in which regression is used to inform discussion of cases. What do the regression results tell us about why country A or regime-type B turned out as it did or changed in the way it did? Discussion of cases can then, of course, be used to question and/or further explore the regression results. (p. 349)

In other work (Hicks and Kenworthy 2003a), Kenworthy follows this prescription, using case-oriented techniques to identify a dimensional space within which cases (welfare states) can be mapped, in order to study "identities and consequences" of welfare state regimes. We thus understand Kenworthy as being a proponent of the type of approach that we develop here. It is for these same reasons that we revisit this example in Chapters 4, 7, and 9, using it as an empirical touchstone for substantively meaningful and intuitive illustrations.

2.1   Regression by the Book

We begin by setting the stage for our empirical example. As noted at the start of this chapter, the aim of Kenworthy's (1999) analysis is to assess the impact of social welfare policies over the period 1960–91 on poverty rates in

Table 2.1 Independent and dependent variables, taken from Kenworthy (1999)

Nation	ISO3	Matrix **X** Transfers	Matrix **X** Pretax/ transfer Poverty	Matrix Z_X Transfers (scaled)	Matrix Z_X Pretax/ transfer Poverty (scaled)	Y Posttax/ transfer Poverty	Z_Y Posttax/ transfer Poverty (scaled)
Australia	AUS	7.3	23.3	−1.38	−0.01	11.9	0.38
Belgium	BEL	19.3	26.8	1.51	0.4	6.0	−0.46
Canada	CAN	9.5	22.5	−0.85	−0.1	6.5	−0.39
Denmark	DNK	13.5	26.4	0.11	0.35	5.9	−0.48
Finland	FIN	10.4	11.9	−0.63	−1.32	3.7	−0.79
France	FRA	17.8	36.1	1.15	1.47	9.8	0.08
Germany	DEU	14.8	15.2	0.43	−0.94	4.3	−0.71
Ireland	IRL	10.5	39.2	−0.61	1.83	29.4	2.87
Italy	ITA	14.5	30.7	0.36	0.85	14.3	0.72
Netherlands	NLD	21.5	22.1	2.05	−0.14	7.3	−0.28
Norway	NOR	13.4	9.2	0.09	−1.63	1.7	−1.08
Sweden	SWE	14.6	23.7	0.38	0.04	5.8	−0.49
Switzerland	CHE	9.4	12.5	−0.88	−1.25	3.8	−0.78
United Kingdom	GBR	10.1	29.6	−0.71	0.72	16.8	1.07
U.S.A.	USA	8.8	21.0	−1.02	−0.27	11.7	0.35
Mean		13.027	23.347	0.00	0.00	9.260	0.00
SD		4.142	8.666	1.00	1.00	7.015	1.00

1991 for 15 of the most affluent democratic nations.[1] These nations are listed in Table 2.1. His analysis consists of cross-sectional OLS regression models.

The dependent variable in Kenworthy's analysis is a national-level measure of poverty in 1991 after taxes and government transfers are taken into account.[2] Examples of government transfers include cash welfare benefits and "near-cash" programs (such as food stamps in the United States). Taxes include personal income and employee payroll taxes. Kenworthy labels the dependent variable "posttax and posttransfer poverty rates." From here forward, we refer to it more simply as "post-pov," the poverty rates after taxes

[1] These nations were members of the Organization for Economic Cooperation and Development (OECD) with populations of at least 3 million in 1991. Three of the 18 nations meeting this criterion – Austria, Japan, and New Zealand – could not be included due to lack of adequate availability of data on poverty (Kenworthy 1999: 1123). The 15 nations included in the study are named in our Table 2.1.
[2] Data on poverty rates were not available for the year 1991 for each nation. Kenworthy (1999: 1126) makes use of data for the year closest to 1991 for each country.

are paid and transfers are completed. For each nation, poverty is measured as the percentage of individuals in households with posttax and posttransfer incomes (adjusted for household size) that are below 40% of the U.S. median posttax, posttransfer income.

To assess the effectiveness of social welfare policies, an analogous measure of poverty in each nation in 1991 *prior* to the provision of government transfers and the payment of taxes is defined as an independent variable. From here forward, we label this variable as "pre-pov," and in Table 2.1, we report the values Kenworthy gives for this measure.

Kenworthy's study formulates three separate OLS regression equations, each making use of a distinctive measure of national-level social welfare policy extensiveness.[3] Very similar results are found in each of the three regression equations. Here, we focus on just one equation for didactic purposes. The measure of welfare policy extensiveness we focus on is government transfers, which are monies that the government of each respective nation pays out as benefits for sickness, old age, family allowances, social assistance grants, and so forth. Government transfers are given as a percentage of each nation's gross domestic product (GDP), averaged over the years 1960 to 1991 (see the column labeled "Transfers" in Table 2.1).

In addition to government transfers and pretax, pretransfer poverty rates, Kenworthy employs a third independent variable for each nation in each of his regression equations: GDP per capita, measured at the beginning (1960) of the three-decade period in which he is interested. This predictor variable is crucial for Kenworthy's theorization, among other reasons because some analysts argue that increased welfare expenditures serve to decrease GDP, which in turn abets an *increase* in poverty. However, a consistent finding of Kenworthy (1999) is that GDP per capita has an insignificant effect on post-pov, no matter which measure of social welfare policy extensiveness is used. In Chapters 7 and 9 (on regression modeling as a gateway to case selection and to field theory, respectively), we revisit this example and demonstrate how our approach allows us to see the role of this variable (GDP per capita). Here, however, we ignore it for the sake of simplicity.

Kenworthy (1999: 1131) reports his regression results for the original variables as well as for variables measured in standard form. For didactic purposes, we will focus on standardized coefficients. To obtain standardized versions of each variable, we subtract the column mean from the value of

---

[3] Policy extensiveness is one of the key independent variables in Kenworthy's study – a measure of how much each nation is spending to enhance social welfare.

each observation in that column and divide the difference by the column standard deviation. The resulting z-scores (labeled "scaled" scores) are also shown in Table 2.1.

2.2   Turning OLS Inside Out

We will use a "simple regression" example to introduce our case-oriented approach to regression. We will consider one independent variable, pre-pov. After building intuition about how our approach works in this elementary context, we will then proceed to our perspective on multivariate OLS.

A main take-away from our discussion will be to understand each regression coefficient not only as a statement about relations among variables, but also as a sum across contributions from the cases. This key aspect of our approach is trivial to see for simple regression, but less trivial when examining multiple regression coefficients (Section 2.2.2) and when considering other generalized linear models (Chapter 3).

2.2.1   Simple Regression

Our dependent variable is post-pov, which is our label for Kenworthy's measure of poverty after taxes and transfers have been taken into account. We will measure this variable in standard form (see the final column of Table 2.1), and we will denote these 15 numbers as Z_y. Our single independent variable, which we denote Z_x, is pre-pov, also measured in standard form (with values given in the second column under "matrix Z_x" in Table 2.1). Because our variables are expressed in standard form, the intercept for the regression of Z_y on Z_x is 0. The regression slope (also known as the regression coefficient), b, is

$$b = \frac{\sum Z_{X_i} Z_{Y_i}}{\sum Z_{X_i}^2} = \frac{10.8038}{14} = 0.7717 \tag{2.1}$$

If we "adjust" the scores for pre-pov (Z_x) by dividing each score by its sum of squares, then (2.1) is identical to

$$b = \sum \left(\frac{Z_X}{\sum Z_X^2} \right) Z_Y = 0.7717 \tag{2.2}$$

We can interpret the regression coefficient (as is usual) as a statement about the variables: countries that have high poverty before taxes and transfers tend to have high poverty after these processes take place. As Kenworthy (1999: 1129) writes, the welfare state, "is inherently reactive, coming into play after the distribution of primary (pretax/pretransfer) income has been established" and pre-pov sets strong "limits to how much the welfare state ... can accomplish in reducing poverty."

Our approach begins to get interesting, however, when we turn this regression model "inside out" to examine this same bivariate relationship from the point of view (so to speak) of the cases. Specifically, we may interpret the regression coefficient as a sum across the cases! (Similar interpretations will apply to regression coefficients in a large galaxy of more general regression models, as we show in this book.) Ignoring the first summation sign in (2.2), we have, for each of the 15 countries, a "contribution" to the regression coefficient that is the product of the Z_y score and the "adjusted" Z_x score for each case. These "contributions" sum to the regression coefficient (0.7717). These contributions are shown in Table 2.2. (To use GBR as an example, from the row for the United Kingdom in Table 2.1, we have (0.72 / 14) * 1.07 = 0.055 as shown in Table 2.2.)

Figure 2.1 plots the outcome variable (Z_y) against the adjusted predictor, $Z_x / \sum Z_x^2$. Moreover, each country in the figure is represented by a circle proportional to the size of its contribution. Using Figure 2.1, we can illustrate

Table 2.2 Contributions to regression coefficient, simple regression

ISO3	Pre-pov
AUS	−0.0001
BEL	−0.0132
CAN	0.0027
DNK	−0.0121
FIN	0.0748
FRA	0.0081
DEU	0.0475
IRL	0.3751
ITA	0.0435
NLD	0.0029
NOR	0.1257
SWE	−0.0014
CHE	0.0696
GBR	0.0554
USA	−0.0067
Sum	0.7717

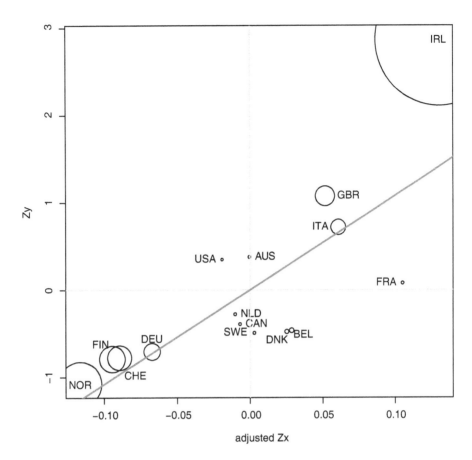

Figure 2.1   Scatterplot of Z_Y and adjusted Z_X. (Circles proportional to size of contribution of each country to the regression coefficient)

what the contributions mean. Each axis is centered on 0. A country at the origin (with coordinates [0,0] in Figure 2.1) would be average on both poverty measures, with respect to the 15 countries studied by Kenworthy in his 1999 paper. Countries above and to the right of the origin – including France, Italy, the UK, and (especially) the Republic of Ireland – have above-average poverty before taxes and transfers, as well as afterward. We can see that Ireland's contribution to the regression coefficient is just under half of the total (0.3751 of the regression coefficient of 0.7717; see Table 2.2).

Each country's contribution to the regression coefficient has a geometric representation in Figure 2.1 as a rectangle having as opposite corners the origin and that country's location in the Figure. For example, Ireland's coordinates on adjusted Z_X and Z_Y, respectively are 0.131 (i.e., 1.83/14) and 2.87 (see Table 2.1).

The distance to Ireland along the Z_X axis of Figure 2.1 is (1.83/14) = 0.13 (or 0.13066 to more decimal places), and the distance along the Z_Y axis is 2.87 (or 2.87105 to more decimal places). The size of the rectangle is (1.83/14) * 2.87 = 0.3751 (if enough decimal places are kept), which is Ireland's "contribution" as reported in Table 2.2. In brief: each contribution is the area of a rectangle.

Countries in the opposite quadrant – those below and to the left of the origin – also contribute to increasing the magnitude of the regression coefficient. But they do so for a different reason. They have less poverty than average both before and after taxes are paid and welfare payments are transferred. The sum of the contributions of three nations – Norway, Finland, and Switzerland – is about 35% of the magnitude of the total regression coefficient (which is the sum of the contributions of all 15 nations, a coefficient of 0.7717).

Nations in the two remaining quadrants have contributions that tend to attenuate the regression coefficient. Belgium, for example, is above average on poverty before taxes and transfers, but below average afterward. This is in contrast to the United States, which has less poverty than average prior to taxes and transfers, but more poverty than average afterward. Does this imply that Belgium has an effective welfare state with relatively large transfers (as a percentage of GDP), or that the United States has a relatively ineffective welfare state? We can't answer this question on the basis of the two variables in the breathtakingly simplistic bivariate model that we are presently considering. Furthermore, the contribution of Belgium to the regression coefficient (dampening it by 0.0132, or adding −0.0132 to it; Table 2.2) is negligible, and similarly for the United States (a contribution of −0.0067). This information is suggestive, and while our primary goal is not diagnostic, it highlights how we can use a map (like Figure 2.1) of case contributions to a regression coefficient to suggest that we specify a new regression model with an additional variable.

While our approach does allow identification of outliers (such as Ireland in Figure 2.1), we are particularly interested in looking for sets (or clusters) of countries that occupy similar positions in the multivariate space. As illustrated in the preceding paragraphs, some nations have high poverty both before and after intervention of taxes and transfers (Ireland, the UK, Italy); some have low poverty both before and after intervention (Norway, Finland, Switzerland, Germany); some have less poverty after intervention than before (Belgium, Denmark, Sweden), while others have more poverty after intervention than prior to it (United States, Australia). The regression coefficient is – literally – just a summation over this potentially rich range of conditions that pays no heed to the contours of the scatterplot mapping. The simple bivariate example that we use here is too elementary for us to gain major new insights, but even in this example, we can see suggestions of our motivation for digging *beyond* the regression coefficient itself, to see how that coefficient is constituted by the cases that comprise it.

As to the technical aspects of our approach in this elementary example, we have done nothing that should have surprised any reader who has ever studied the regression model, however cursorily. In fact, this illustrates another facet of our approach to turning regression inside out. Namely, that everything we do with the regression model has been, so to speak, "hiding in plain sight" all along. We simply choose to focus on facets of the model that are not seen or brought to bear in the usual analyses. We ask the reader to keep this point about our approach "hiding in plain sight" in mind as we increase the level of technical sophistication of our discussion, while pointing to new insights that we discover.

2.2.2 Multiple Regression Inside Out

We will now introduce our approach to multiple regression. Our discussion here, which is based on having two independent variables, generalizes in a straightforward way to multiple OLS regression with any number of predictor variables. For continuity with Section 2.2.1, we retain post-pov as our outcome variable, and we use both pre-pov and transfers as the independent variables. As mentioned above, Kenworthy (1999) considers "transfers" to be a key measure of welfare state extensiveness, defined as monies (as a percentage of GDP) that the government of each respective nation pays out as benefits for sickness, old age, family allowances, social assistance grants, and so forth (see the column labeled "Transfers" in Table 2.1). Are countries with more extensive welfare states (higher "transfers") more effective at reducing poverty, after primary income (before taxes and transfers) is taken into account? That is the motivating question for the following analysis.

The standardized regression coefficients, along with related information often appearing on the usual printouts produced by standard statistical software, are shown in Table 2.3. These coefficients are essentially the same as Kenworthy reports on the basis of his OLS regression model, which also included the nonsignificant measure of GDP per capita.[4] Additionally, the

---

[4] The standardized regression coefficients that Kenworthy reports for transfers and pre-pov (respectively) are −0.44 and +0.78. The respective t-values are −3.049 and 5.273. The p-values are 0.01 and <0.001. The multiple R^2 is 0.7733, and the adjusted R^2 is 0.7166. Each of these values from Kenworthy's equation with three independent variables (Kenworthy 1999: 1132) is very close to the results reported in our Table 2.2 for our two-variable model.

Table 2.3 OLS regression of Z_Y on the variables in Z_X

Variable	Coefficient	t-value	p-value
Transfers	−0.3953	−2.788	0.02
Pre-pov	0.8419	5.938	<0.001

Note: Multiple $R^2 = 0.7469$; adjusted $R^2 = 0.7079$

Table 2.4 Predicted $\widehat{Z}_y$ for OLS regression of Z_Y on the variables in Z_X

	$\widehat{Z}_y$
AUS	0.5420
BEL	−0.2633
CAN	0.2543
DNK	0.2515
FIN	−0.8614
FRA	0.7834
DEU	−0.9607
IRL	1.7813
ITA	0.5738
NLD	−0.9298
NOR	−1.4100
SWE	−0.1158
CHE	−0.7076
GBR	0.8869
USA	0.1754
Mean	0.0000
SD	0.8642

predicted values for each nation on the dependent variable (the "Y-hat" values, or $\widehat{Z}_y$) are given in Table 2.4; these are the values on post-pov that we predict for each case as the sum of products of that case's Z-scores on the two respective predictor variables (Table 2.1) times the regression coefficient for each respective variable (Table 2.3).

Our interpretation of Table 2.3, which follows common interpretive practice, emphasizes three points. First, poverty before taxes and transfers (pre-pov) is the more important determinant of poverty after taxes and transfers (post-pov), such that a nation that is one standard deviation above average on pre-pov is modeled to be 0.84 standard deviations higher on poverty posttax and posttransfer poverty. Kenworthy (1999: 1129, quoted also in Section 2.2.1) writes of his essentially identical finding: "[This] underscores the limits of how much the welfare state – which is inherently reactive, coming into play after the distribution of primary (pretax/pretransfer) income has been established – can accomplish in reducing poverty."

Second, net of pre-pov, nations that have higher expenditures on government transfers *do* have lower rates of poverty after transfers have been made and taxes paid. A nation that is one standard deviation above average on Transfers has on average a posttax, posttransfer poverty rate that is 0.3953 standard deviations lower, controlling for its pretax, pretransfer status. In answer to the research question that motivated Kenworthy's study, increased social welfare policy extensiveness *does* lead to reduced poverty rates posttax and posttransfer, with respect to the nations and time period under study. Third, although the aim here is not to develop a theory or a full explanation of poverty, this simple two-variable model accounts for 71% of the variation in posttax, posttransfer poverty rates for this very small sample of nations (after adjusting for degrees of freedom).

In addition to using OLS regression, Kenworthy provides exemplary additional analyses of the sensitivity of his results to potential outliers and to alternative thresholds for his poverty measures. While we do not review these additional analyses here, the sensitivity analyses show that his findings are robust.

As we turn Kenworthy's multiple regression model inside out, we begin with an overview of OLS regression. Equation 2.3 shows predicted values from the standard regression model in matrix form, where **b** is a vector of regression coefficients, **X** is the matrix of independent variables (which may be scaled to be in standard or Z-score form), and $\hat{\mathbf{y}}$ (which may also be scaled) is the vector of predicted values on the outcome.

$$\hat{\mathbf{y}} = \mathbf{Xb} \tag{2.3}$$

To compute the regression coefficients, we use the usual matrix formula[5]

$$\mathbf{b} = \left[(\mathbf{X}^{\mathsf{T}}\mathbf{X})^{-1}\mathbf{X}^{\mathsf{T}} \right]\mathbf{y} \tag{2.4}$$

Let us take a moment here to relate this equation for multiple regression coefficients to our previous examination of simple bivariate regression. If our data matrix (**X**) has n rows (one for each case) and p columns (one for each

---

[5] See standard textbooks (of which one excellent example is Draper and Smith 1998) for a comprehensive treatment of regression in matrix terms. Appendix A provides a brief introduction to matrices and matrix multiplication.

independent variable) – here n is 15 countries and p is 2 independent variables – then the matrix product in brackets in Equation 2.4 has p rows.[6] To compute the regression coefficients, we multiply each of these rows in turn by the outcome variable, y. Then, the sum of each row is the respective multiple regression coefficient for its respective variable. Prior to summing, though, each row contains the multiple regression "contributions by case to a multiple regression coefficient" that are analogs to the case contributions discussed in Section 2.2.1 (on bivariate regression). In fact, the material in brackets in Equation 2.4 looks very much like the "adjusted Z_X" of Equation 2.2. This tells us that the fundamental regression formula (Equation 2.4) is in fact a summation across case-wise weights. But in practice, researchers ignore this and work only with the sums (the regression coefficients). We want to change this research practice, because the sums (regression coefficients) mask so much information about what is going on among the cases, and how the cases comprise the variables! This is another way in which our case-oriented approach to multiple regression has been "hiding in plain sight" in the usual regression model. We choose to look at, and to work with, the case contributions that are embedded inside the usual regression formula.

In our applications in this chapter, we will consider both the independent variables (the columns of matrix $\mathbf{X}$) and the dependent variable (the vector $\mathbf{y}$) to be in standard form (mean 0, standard deviation 1).

Moving from variables to cases, we seek to ascertain each case's additive contribution to the overall regression coefficients. To obtain this, we simply replace $\mathbf{y}$ with a diagonal matrix that has $\widehat{\mathbf{Z}_y}$ (Table 2.4) as the main diagonal and zeroes in all other cells. We refer to this matrix as $\widehat{\mathbf{Y}}$ in Equation 2.5.[7] The vector $\mathbf{1}$ is a column vector of 1's (in our example, $n = 15$, so $\mathbf{1}$ is a column of 15 1's).

$$b = \left(\mathbf{X}^T\mathbf{X}\right)^{-1}\mathbf{X}^T\widehat{\mathbf{Y}}\mathbf{1} \qquad (2.5)$$

Table 2.5 presents each case's contribution to the overall regression coefficient using the scaled (Z-score) versions of our dependent and independent variables from Table 2.1. As the reader can see, each row of $\left(\mathbf{X}^T\mathbf{X}\right)^{-1}\mathbf{X}^T\widehat{\mathbf{Y}}$

---

[6] The matrix product in brackets was called the matrix of *catchers* by Mosteller and Tukey (1977) and is "the single most useful matrix for computing regression diagnostics" (Velleman and Welsch 1981: 237).

[7] Alternatively, we could decompose the identical regression coefficients in OLS models if the diagonal of the matrix we call $\widehat{\mathbf{Y}}$ consisted of the observed values on the dependent variable (the last column of numbers in Table 2.1), instead of the predicted values (Table 2.4). However, for models that generalize OLS (see Chapter 3), the link function must be used; in this example, the link is merely an identity matrix.

Table 2.5 OLS regression coefficients as sums across cases

	Transfers (scaled)	Pre-pov (scaled)
AUS	−0.0552	0.0096
BEL	−0.0280	−0.0025
CAN	−0.0156	0.0010
DNK	0.0010	0.0062
FIN	0.0254	0.0768
FRA	0.0515	0.0732
DEU	−0.0422	0.0720
IRL	−0.1229	0.2546
ITA	0.0087	0.0332
NLD	−0.1421	0.0348
NOR	−0.0395	0.1714
SWE	−0.0032	0.0002
CHE	0.0341	0.0572
GBR	−0.0546	0.0554
USA	−0.0126	−0.0012
Column Sums	−0.3953	0.8419

sums to the overall regression coefficients presented in Table 2.3. We refer to the cell values in the above matrix as the "contributions" of the cases to the regression coefficients, or as the "intensities" (Rambotti and Breiger 2020), as each case's contribution reflects the intensity of association of each observation with each variable (Breiger and Melamed 2014).

To enhance intuition on the meaning of the "contributions" to multiple regression coefficients such as those in each column of Table 2.5, we return to the matrix product $(\mathbf{X}^T\mathbf{X})^{-1}\mathbf{X}^T$ in brackets in Equation 2.4. Each row of that matrix may be computed equivalently in the following way:

- Take one independent variable (e.g., Transfers), and regress it on all other independent variables in the multiple regression equation. (In our example, there is only one other independent variable, pre-pov.)
- Compute the residuals from the above regression.
- Define the "adjusted residuals" by dividing each case's residuals by a single number: the sum of squares of all the residuals.
- These "adjusted residuals" comprise the row in $(\mathbf{X}^T\mathbf{X})^{-1}\mathbf{X}^T$ (Equation 2.4 and 2.5) for the selected variable (in our example, for the variable Transfers).

- Multiply the adjusted residuals by $\hat{\mathbf{y}}$ from the multiple regression equation. This gives us the "contributions" such as those reported in each column (respectively) of Table 2.5.
- Summing the contributions gives us each (respective) regression coefficient (as in Table 2.5).

We will make use of the above steps when we plot against the adjusted residuals (in Section 2.3.1 and in our discussion of Figure 2.2).

2.3   Geometry of the Regression Model

The same results as those reported above can be obtained via the matrices produced using the SVD of the data matrix, and this approach is often preferable because it deepens the analyst's usual understanding of the geometry of the regression model. For any real-valued matrix $\mathbf{X}$, such as any of the data matrices used in regression analyses in this book, its SVD produces a set of dimensions (matrix $\mathbf{U}$, with one column for each dimension) that characterize the row-space of matrix $\mathbf{X}$, and a set of dimensions (matrix $\mathbf{V}$) for the column-space of $\mathbf{X}$. For the data matrices that concern us in regression analyses, typically there is one dimension in the SVD for each variable, so the number of dimensions (d) equals the number of variables (p). Crucially, however, any two dimensions of the row-space $\mathbf{U}$ are orthogonal (represented geometrically by vectors "at right angles" to each other), as are any two dimensions of the column-space $(\mathbf{V})$. If $\mathbf{X}$ has n rows and p columns, matrix $\mathbf{U}$ is of size $n \times d$, and matrix $\mathbf{V}$ has dimension $p \times d$. Finally, each dimension is associated with a weight ("singular value"), and these d weights are given in a diagonal, $d \times d$ matrix denoted $\mathbf{S}$. All three matrices – $\mathbf{U}$, $\mathbf{S}$, and $\mathbf{V}$ – are produced by the SVD.

Any data matrix $\mathbf{X}$ is precisely identical to its decomposition into a row space (the orthogonal dimensions of matrix $\mathbf{U}$) and a column space (the independent dimensions of matrix $\mathbf{V}$), with the dimensions appropriately weighted:

$$\mathbf{X} = \mathbf{U}\mathbf{S}\mathbf{V}^{\mathrm{T}} \tag{2.6}$$

In presentations of an SVD, the dimensions are ordered according to the magnitudes of the respective weights (singular values) on the diagonal of matrix $\mathbf{S}$, which thus has values ordered from highest to lowest. If all d dimensions are used in Equation 2.6, then the data matrix $(\mathbf{X})$ is reproduced exactly by the dimensional representation. If only the first d' dimensions are used ($d' < d$), then Equation 2.6 produces (by the Eckart–Young theorem) the least-squares estimate of matrix (**X**) that uses d' dimensions (see, e.g., Martin and Porter 2012).

Table 2.6 a–c presents the values for **U**, **S**, and **V** for the data matrix (Z_X in Table 2.1) in our example. (See Appendix B for an introduction to the concepts of SVD used here, as well as for how to use simple arithmetic to compute the numbers in Table 2.6.)

Table 2.6a–c SVD matrices for Z_X (Kenworthy 1999)

a) Matrix **U** (15 nations × 2 dimensions)

	Dimension	
	[,1]	[,2]
AUS	−0.242	−0.287
BEL	0.333	0.233
CAN	−0.165	−0.157
DNK	0.081	−0.050
FIN	−0.340	0.143
FRA	0.457	−0.067
DEU	−0.089	0.285
IRL	0.212	−0.508
ITA	0.210	−0.103
NLD	0.331	0.456
NOR	−0.269	0.359
SWE	0.073	0.071
CHE	−0.370	0.078
GBR	0.003	−0.298
USA	−0.225	−0.156

b) Matrix **S** (2 dimensions × 2 dimensions)

	Dimension	
	[,1]	[,2]
[1,]	4.061	0.000
[2,]	0.000	3.393

c) Matrix **V** (2 dimensions × 2 variables)

	Variable	
	Transfers	Pre-pov
[1,]	0.707	0.707
[2,]	0.707	−0.707

Table 2.7 Transpose of matrix $\mathbf{VS^{-1}U^T}$ for OLS of posttransfer poverty

Nation	ISO3	$\mathbf{VS^{-1}U^T}$ Transfers	Pre-pov
Australia	AUS	−0.102	0.018
Belgium	BEL	0.107	0.009
Canada	CAN	−0.062	0.004
Denmark	DNK	0.004	0.024
Finland	FIN	−0.030	−0.089
France	FRA	0.066	0.093
Germany	DEU	0.044	−0.075
Ireland	IRL	−0.069	0.143
Italy	ITA	0.015	0.058
Netherlands	NLD	0.153	−0.037
Norway	NOR	0.028	−0.122
Sweden	SWE	0.028	−0.002
Switzerland	CHE	−0.048	−0.081
United Kingdom	GBR	−0.062	0.062
U.S.A.	USA	−0.072	−0.007

By substitution of the definition of the SVD (Equation 2.6) into Equation 2.5, we see that an equivalent way to compute the regression coefficients (compare Equation 2.5) is

$$b = \mathbf{VS^{-1}U^T}\widehat{Y}\mathbf{1} \tag{2.7}$$

where $\mathbf{U}$, $\mathbf{S}$, and $\mathbf{V}$ are defined in Appendix B on SVD and given in Table 2.6, $\widehat{Y}$ is a diagonal matrix with (in our example) $\widehat{\mathbf{Zy}}$ (given in Table 2.4) on its diagonal and 0's elsewhere, and $\mathbf{1}$ is a 15×1 vector of 1's. From this equation, we again see that the regression coefficients are sums across the rows (cases) of this $p \times n$ (variables by cases) matrix,

$$\mathbf{VS^{-1}U^T}\widehat{Y} \tag{2.8}$$

whose entries are identical to those in Table 2.5. The matrix $\mathbf{VS^{-1}U^T}$ is given in Table 2.7.[8] This matrix is identical to $[(\mathbf{X^TX})^{-1}\mathbf{X^T}]$, which appeared earlier in Equation 2.4. Why then go to the trouble of using the SVD? Our

---

[8] For example, for Australia, the first number given in Table 2.7 is −0.102. When multiplied by Australia's predicted value on the outcome variable (0.5420, from Table 2.4), the result (except for minor rounding error) is −0.0552 (the first number in Table 2.5), which is the "contribution" of Australia to the multiple regression coefficient for transfers.

answer is that the SVD allows us to understand the geometry of the regression model, and to apply that model, in new and important ways that are just not in the playbook of standard analytical moves.

2.3.1   Visualizing the Model Space

Using the SVD to calculate case-level contributions provides multiple opportunities for deeper insights, including the ability to visualize various aspects of the model space. We will start by showing how we can visualize each case's contribution to the overall regression coefficient, illustrating this with the coefficient for Transfers. We begin by reviewing our bullet-point discussion at the end of Section 2.2.2, but applied here to gaining insight into the SVD. We regress Transfers on pre-pov (our other independent variable from Table 2.1) and then compute the residuals. These residuals indicate the extensiveness of Transfers net of pre-pov, and we label these residuals *trans.resids*. These residuals are given in Table 2.8 (column 1). We scale the residuals by dividing each value by the sum of squares (13.588, given at the bottom of column 1). This yields "adjusted" residuals, shown in column 2. Note that these values are identical to the values of $\mathbf{VS^{-1}U^T}$ given previously for variable Transfers in Table 2.7. Hence, the regression of $\mathbf{Z_y}$ (given in Table 2.4) on "trans.resids" (Table 2.8, column 1) should have a slope identical to the *multiple* regression coefficient for Transfers (−0.3953; see Table 2.3). And this is indeed the case, as shown in the scatterplot of Figure 2.2. The regression slope in Figure 2.2 is −0.3953, identical to the multiple regression coefficient for transfers given in Table 2.3.[9]

From Figure 2.2, we can visualize the contributions made by each case to the regression coefficients obtained using Equations (2.5) and (2.7) and presented in Table 2.5. Using the Republic of Ireland (IRL) to illustrate, Figure 2.2 allows us to visualize its contribution to the multiple regression coefficient of −0.3953. The coordinates for point IRL are −0.935 on "Transfers (residualized from pre-transfer poverty"; see Table 2.8, column 1) and 1.7813 on "Predicted Poverty" (Table 2.4). If we form a rectangle in the scatterplot that has these coordinates (for the point IRL) and the origin (0,0) as its opposite corners, the (signed) area of this rectangle is (−0.935 × 1.7813)/13.558 = −0.1229 (except for slight rounding error), which is precisely Ireland's contribution to the multiple regression coefficient for Transfers, as shown in Table 2.5. This is the multiple-regression

---

[9] A related approach, "partial plots" (an x-y plot that displays information about a single regression coefficient that appears in a multiple regression equation) is reviewed by Velleman and Welsch (1981, p. 235).

Table 2.8 Residualized transfers

	trans.resids	Adjusted trans.resids
AUS	−1.382	−0.102
BEL	1.444	0.107
CAN	−0.834	−0.062
DNK	0.052	0.004
FIN	−0.399	−0.030
FRA	0.891	0.066
DEU	0.595	0.044
IRL	−0.935	−0.069
ITA	0.205	0.015
NLD	2.071	0.153
NOR	0.380	0.028
SWE	0.373	0.028
CHE	−0.653	−0.048
GBR	−0.835	−0.062
USA	−0.972	−0.072
Sum	0.000	
Sum of squares	13.558	

Note: Column 1 presents residuals from regressing Transfers on Pre-pov; column 2, values from column 1 divided by its sum of squares.

version of the point we made about bivariate regression (Section 2.2.1): each contribution of a case to a multiple regression coefficient is the area of a rectangle in a scatterplot of appropriately transformed variables.

Figure 2.2 allows us to gain deeper insights into the effects of Transfers than a conventional interpretation of its multiple regression coefficient. With respect to the multiple regression coefficient for the effect of Transfers on predicted posttax, posttransfer poverty, the two largest contributions (both negative) come from the Netherlands (−0.1421; see Table 2.5) and from Ireland (−0.1229; computation described above; also given in Table 2.5). Because the contributions are additive, these two nations together contribute a total of −0.2650 to the multiple regression coefficient of −0.3953 (Table 2.5, bottom row), representing 67% of the overall effect. However, as Figure 2.2 shows, these two cases occupy opposing quadrants, indicating antipodal positions in the model, and indeed they are substantively quite dissimilar. Ireland is (like the English-speaking countries found in the same quadrant) quite stingy with welfare transfer benefits (net of pretax,

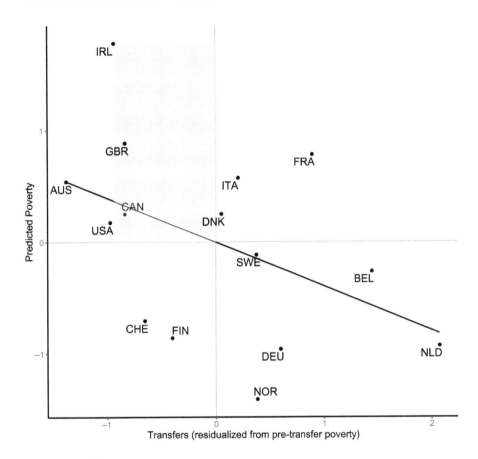

Figure 2.2   Scatter plot of $\widehat{Z}_y$ and trans.resid

pretransfer poverty), and it also has an exceptionally high rate of posttax, posttransfer poverty. To the contrary, the Netherlands is the most generous nation in this sample in providing welfare transfer benefits (net of pretax, pretransfer poverty) and has a (relatively) very low rate of poverty after transfers have been completed and taxes paid. Both cases contribute very strongly to the negative sign and magnitude of the multiple regression coefficient, but they evince opposing profiles.

Visualizing the relationships among cases not only allows us to make sense of substantive differences across cases (for more on this, see Chapter 7 on case selection), it also allows us to identify sets of cases that exhibit substantive similarities. For example, the five English-speaking countries[10] that

---

[10] The Republic of Ireland has two languages with official status, Irish and English. Canada has two official languages, English and French.

comprise Quadrant 2 (but no other countries) in Figure 2.2 share a profile (like Ireland's and that of the United States) of stinginess on welfare benefits (net of pretax, pretransfer poverty rates) and high poverty rates following taxes and transfers. This is consistent with what Gøsta Esping-Andersen (1999) identified as a particular species of welfare regime (a type labeled "liberal" in the classic sense of market-driven), characterized precisely by stingy benefits and little poverty reduction (as seen in Figure 2.2) as well as by means tests for assistance. Indeed, Esping-Andersen (1999) labeled four of the five nations in Quadrant 2 of our Figure 2.2 as evincing a "liberal" welfare regime (Australia, Canada, Great Britain, and the United States), while Ireland remained unclassified in his scheme (see also Hicks and Kenworthy 2003a, 2003b).

2.3.2 Clusters of Cases

Turning regression inside out allows us to identify the contribution to the multiple regression coefficient of a single case. But it also allows us to identify the contribution of clusters of cases. For example, taking the five English-speaking countries (quadrant 2 of Figure 2.2) as a cluster, summing their individual contributions (Table 2.5, column 1), shows that these nations that largely fit the "liberal" welfare regime as Esping-Andersen characterized it have a total contribution of −0.2609. The negative sign reflects their positioning as having a smaller welfare state (they are to the left of Figure 2.2) while also evincing greater poverty (they are toward the top of Figure 2.2). The contribution of this cluster of cases to the multiple regression coefficient is 66% (i.e., −0.2609/−0.3953; the contribution of the outlier, Ireland, alone is less than half of this cluster-specific contribution).

Observations such as this one support our contention that our case-oriented approach to regression analysis can address concerns such as Kenworthy's (2007: 349, quoted earlier), speaking to questions such as, "What do the regression results tell us about why country A or regime-type B turned out as it did or changed in the way it did?" While a conventional reading of the regression coefficients renders the cases invisible, turning the model inside out and visualizing the relationships among cases vis-à-vis the model coefficients facilitates direct dialogue between case-level substantive insights and conventional model outputs.

The contribution to a multiple regression coefficient of a subset (or "cluster") of multiple cases (such as the −0.2609 discussed just above) is not the same as estimating separate regression models for clusters of cases separately.

However, the analogy is a useful point of departure for pinning down the difference. Consider the expression

$$\frac{\sum_s (x_s y_s)}{\sum_t x_t^2} \qquad (2.9)$$

where s indicates a subsample of the model space (i.e., the cases within a cluster of cases, or even any single case), t refers to the total sample space, $\mathbf{x}$ is an independent variable that has been residualized from the other independent variables, and y is the linear prediction (e.g., $\hat{\mathbf{y}}$ in the case of OLS) from the model we are considering. As Breiger and Melamed (2014: 269) explain, "If $s = t$ (no clustering), then the above expression summed across the cases is identical to the ... regression coefficient for variable x." However, if s represents a subset (or cluster) consisting of multiple cases, then the expression above represents the "contribution" of the cluster. While the denominator stays the same regardless of whether we are looking at a subset or the individual cases in the entire dataset, the numerator of the equation changes. This means that we are looking at the effect of the subset (multiple cases, or even a single case) relative to the variance ($\Sigma \mathbf{x}^2$) of the entire sample space, as opposed to just the variance within a specific cluster. As we show in later chapters, these contributions allow researchers to examine and potentially account for various forms of heterogeneity among cases.

2.4 Regression Coefficients and Fitted Values inside a Field of Cases and Variables

In addition to visualizing the contributions of cases to individual regression coefficients, RIO also allows us to visualize the entire regression model by constructing a diagram that situates regression coefficients and $\hat{\mathbf{y}}$ values inside a joint field of cases and variables, thereby facilitating a field-theoretic approach to understanding relationships among cases and variables (for more on this, see Chapter 9). To do this, we begin by forming a 15×2 matrix consisting of the independent variables in standardized form (i.e., government transfers and pretax, pretransfer poverty), then adjoining as the third column the $\widehat{\mathbf{Z}_\mathbf{y}}$ values from the multiple regression equation (Table 2.4). We then perform an SVD of this 15×3 table, referring to the SVD components as $\mathbf{U}^*$, $\mathbf{S}^*$, and $\mathbf{V}^*$

Table 2.9 Singular value decomposition of a 15 × 3 matrix consisting of transfers (scaled), pre-pov (scaled), and the $\widehat{Z}_y$ from Table 2.4

	a) Matrix U*				b) U* times S* = Matrix US*		
	Dimensions				Dimensions		
	[,1]	[,2]	[,3]		[,1]	[,2]	[,3]
AUS	0.084	0.366	−0.072		0.404	1.429	0.000
BEL	0.015	−0.406	−0.840		0.070	−1.587	0.000
CAN	0.026	0.227	−0.099		0.126	0.885	0.000
DNK	0.089	−0.035	−0.004		0.426	−0.137	0.000
FIN	−0.319	0.186	−0.011		−1.536	0.727	0.000
FRA	0.328	−0.325	0.000		1.579	−1.270	0.000
DEU	−0.281	−0.100	0.089		−1.355	−0.392	0.000
IRL	0.534	0.136	0.122		2.571	0.532	0.000
ITA	0.208	−0.106	−0.034		1.002	−0.413	0.000
NLD	−0.165	−0.539	0.397		−0.796	−2.106	0.000
NOR	−0.448	−0.001	−0.188		−2.159	−0.005	0.000
SWE	−0.012	−0.101	0.017		−0.060	−0.395	0.000
CHE	−0.285	0.249	−0.037		−1.374	0.972	0.000
GBR	0.239	0.177	−0.191		1.153	0.691	0.000
USA	−0.010	0.274	−0.157		−0.050	1.069	0.000

	c) Matrix S*				d) Matrix V*		
	Dimensions				Dimensions		
	[,1]	[,2]	[,3]		[,1]	[,2]	[,3]
[1,]	4.816	0.000	0.000	Transfers	−0.039	−0.956	0.289
[2,]	0.000	3.907	0.000	Pre-pov	0.757	−0.218	−0.616
[3,]	0.000	0.000	0.000	$\widehat{Z}_y$	0.653	0.195	0.732

to distinguish them from the components of the previous SVD. The diagonal of matrix S* will have only two nonzero entries because regression modeling ensures that the $\widehat{Z}_y$ values are a linear combination of the independent variables.[11] Thus, only the first two columns of U* and V* need concern us.

---

[11] As Le Roux and Rouanet (2004b) discuss, the singular value decomposition, its use in principal components analysis (PCA), and more generally the framework of geometric data analysis (GDA), are closely related to regression. Of particular relevance to our discussion here: fitted values from a multiple linear regression of an outcome variable on the set of all predictor variables (i.e., the variable $\widehat{Z}_y$ that we discuss in the text) is closely related to the concept of supplementary variable that is often used in PCA (Le Roux and Rouanet 2004b).

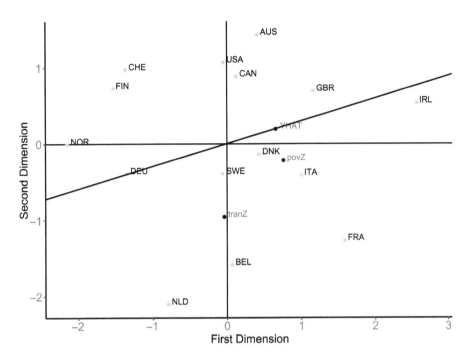

Figure 2.3   Plot of the overall model space, as represented by **US*** and **V***

We postmultiply **U*** by **S***, calling the result **US***, which scales the dimensions of the row space (**U***) by the singular values in **S***. Computed values of **U***, **S***, **US***, and **V*** are provided in Table 2.9. Again, only the first two columns of **US*** are nonzero. We then plot both the nations (dimensions **US***) and the variables (**V***) in a joint, two-dimensional space. The result is Figure 2.3. In this figure, we have also drawn a line from $\widehat{\mathbf{Z}}_y$ (labeled in the figure as "YHAT") through the origin.

2.4.1 Multiple Regression Coefficients

In Figure 2.4, we project each independent variable to the line connecting $\widehat{\mathbf{Z}}_y$ ("YHAT") to the origin. By the definition of a projection, a right angle is formed. We show the distance of each projected point to the origin by a thick black line and a thick gray line (respectively) in Figure 2.4.

Remarkably, the multiple regression coefficients (-0.3953 for Trans, $.8419$ for pre-pov) appear in Figure 2.4 as proportional to the lengths of the gray and black lines, respectively. Using elementary geometry, we can compute

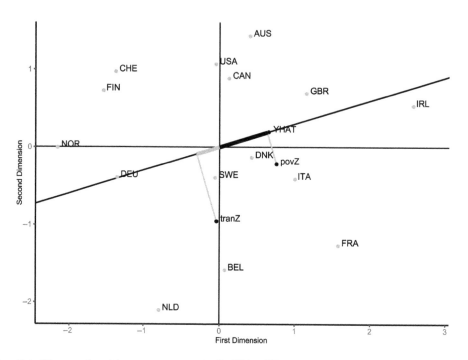

Figure 2.4   Plot of the overall model space, as represented by **US*** and **V***, coefficients as distances to the origin

the distance of the projection of any point p_i to the line connecting YHAT to the origin by using the formula

$$\text{projection}(i) = \frac{\sum p_i p_{\text{YHAT}}}{d_{\text{YHAT}}} \qquad (2.10)$$

The coordinates of point YHAT in Figure 2.4 (0.653, 0.195) are given in Table 2.9 in the $\widehat{Z_y}$ row of matrix **V***. The distance of point YHAT from the origin (d_{YHAT}) is therefore the square root of $0.653^2 + 0.195^2$, which equals 0.6811. The coordinates of tranZ in Figure 2.4 (−0.039, −0.956) appear in the Transfers row of matrix **V***. Then, Equation 2.10 is

$$\frac{(-0.039 \times 0.653) + (-0.956 \times 0.195)}{0.6811} = \frac{-0.2120}{0.6811} = -0.3112$$

This tells us that the length of the gray line in Figure 2.4 is 0.3112. The negative sign indicates that tranZ is on the opposite side of the origin from YHAT.

By a similar application of Equation 2.10, we find that the length of the black line in Figure 2.4 is + 0.6628. The ratio of these projections – that is, the ratio of the length of the black line to the length of the gray line – is

$$\frac{\text{distance of projection of Pre}-\text{pov}}{\text{distance of projection of Transfers}} = \frac{0.6628}{-0.3112} = -2.1298$$

For the multiple regression coefficients (Table 2.3), the corresponding ratio is identical!

$$\frac{b_{2.1}}{b_{1.2}} = \frac{0.8419}{-0.3953} = -2.1298$$

To summarize Figure 2.4: a key aspect of our approach to turning OLS regression inside out is that the regression coefficients appear inside a diagram that includes cases and variables.

In fact, the multiple regression coefficients (Table 2.3) may be computed directly from matrix $\mathbf{V^*}$ (Table 2.9):

$$\begin{bmatrix} -0.039 & -0.956 \\ 0.757 & -0.218 \end{bmatrix} \begin{bmatrix} 0.653 \\ 0.195 \end{bmatrix} \Big/ (1-d_{\text{YHAT}}^2) = \begin{bmatrix} -0.3953 \\ 0.8419 \end{bmatrix}$$

If our multiple regression equation has more than two independent variables, the geometry of the above equation still holds, even though we cannot draw four-dimensional (or higher) diagrams.

2.4.2 Fitted Values

Figure 2.5 projects each of the 15 nations to the same line connecting YHAT to the origin that was the main axis of the previous figure. The distance of each projected point from the origin is given in Table 2.10. Projected points that fall on the opposite side of the origin from $\widehat{Z}_y$ have distances given a negative sign.[12] The key result here (dual to that of the previous paragraph) is that the projection of distances (Table 2.10) is correlated perfectly (+1.000) with the $\widehat{Z}_y$ values in Table 2.4. In fact, the fitted value for any country (Table 2.4) is d_{YHAT} times that country's projected distance (Table 2.10), where (as shown above), $d_{\text{YHAT}} = 0.6811$. Thus, the $\widehat{Z}_y$ values from the multiple regression appear inside the same diagram (Figure 2.5) that includes the cases, the variables, and the multiple regression coefficients.

[12] The reader may verify distances given in Table 2.10 for nations similarly to the way illustrated for variables in the previous section. Consider, for example, Norway (NOR) in Figure 2.5. Norway's coordinates are (−2.159, −0.005) as given in matrix $\mathbf{US^*}$ in Table 2.9. The coordinates of YHAT are (0.653, 0.195) as given in matrix $\mathbf{V^*}$ in the same table. Applying Equation (2.10), the distance of the projection of Norway (i.e., the distance from the origin to where the line emanating from NOR in Figure 2.5 hits the line from YHAT) is −2.070. This distance is reported for NOR in Table 2.10. This distance is proportional to the fitted value for Norway from the multiple regression equation (−1.4100, from Table 2.4), and the constant of proportionality is $d_{\text{YHAT}} = 0.6811$.

Table 2.10 Distances of nations' projections

Nations	Distances of Projections
AUS	0.796
BEL	−0.387
CAN	0.373
DNK	0.369
FIN	−1.265
FRA	1.150
DEU	−1.411
IRL	2.616
ITA	0.843
NLD	−1.365
NOR	−2.070
SWE	−0.170
CHE	−1.039
GBR	1.302
USA	0.258

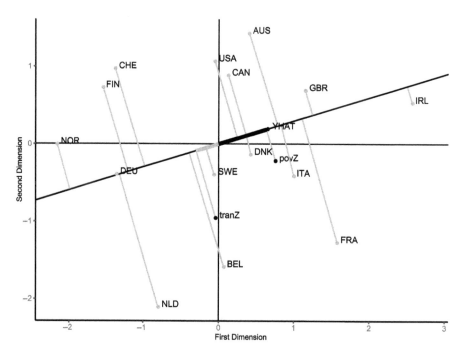

Figure 2.5   Plot of the overall model space, as represented by **US*** and **V***, $\widehat{Z}_y$ values as distances to the origin

2.4.3   Positionings of Cases and Variables

The diagrams in Figures 2.4 and 2.5 are precise visualizations of relations among cases and variables with respect to the regression model (in two dimensions). The regression model itself also appears in these diagrams, which visualize both the regression coefficients and the predicted values of the dependent variable.[13] In addition to capturing the multiple regression coefficients and the fitted values from the regression equation, these diagrams allow us to identify clusters or communities among the cases based on their similarity, and jointly among cases and variables. For example, Figures 2.4 and 2.5 show us that Canada and the United States are very close to each other in the OLS model space. Specifically, if we draw a line from Canada to the origin, and one from the United States to the origin, the angle formed by these two lines is very small, and therefore the cosine of the angle is very large. Computing the cosine among these two rows (for Canada and the United States) in matrix US* (data given in Table 2.9), the cosine is +0.98. This shows that Canada and the United States are highly similar across the predictor variables in this study. We can also read from these figures that Britain has a very negative association with providing welfare transfer benefits. If we were to draw a line from Great Britain to the origin, and one from Transfers to the origin, the angle would be found to be obtuse, suggesting a negative cosine of fairly high magnitude.[14] As we show in greater detail in Chapter 7, this ability to incorporate relations among the cases and variables and assess their similarity is particularly valuable for situating case studies in relation to the results of regression analyses.

The fact that proximity in our diagrams indicates similarity based on the model specification facilitates exploratory analysis, which can be done

---

[13] The diagrams in this chapter can be visualized precisely in two dimensions because we restrict our analysis to only two predictor variables. If we have more than two predictor variables, the algebra underlying the diagrams is the same as here, generalizing precisely to any number of predictors in a multidimensional space. For multiple regression with three or more predictor variables, the two-dimensional diagrams of this algebra become approximations (much as the first two dimensions of a principal components analysis provide an approximation to the full dimensional structure). Breiger and Melamed (2014) work with diagrammatic approximations such as these in a study encompassing 395 organizations (as "cases") and 5 predictor variables.

[14] This statement, assessing the degree of similarity among different "modes" of the data array (a nation and a variable), is true as stated in the text. Precise comparisons, however, require a slightly different diagram, as was anticipated by Goodman (1996). From Table 2.9, we compute the square root of matrix S*, calling it $S^{*\frac{1}{2}}$. Using this and matrices U* and V* of Table 2.9, we compute $US^{*\frac{1}{2}}$ and $VS^{*\frac{1}{2}}$. The cosine of Great Britain's row in $US^{*\frac{1}{2}}$ and the row for Transfers in $VS^{*\frac{1}{2}}$ is computed to be −0.5917. The distance from the origin of GBR's row in $US^{*\frac{1}{2}}$ is 0.6310 and the distance from the origin of the row for Transfers in $VS^{*\frac{1}{2}}$ is 1.8924. Now the product $0.6310 \times 1.8924 \times -0.5917$ is −0.7066, which is the observed-data value for Great Britain on Transfers (rounded to −0.71 at the intersection of GBR's row and the scaled Transfers column in Table 2.1).

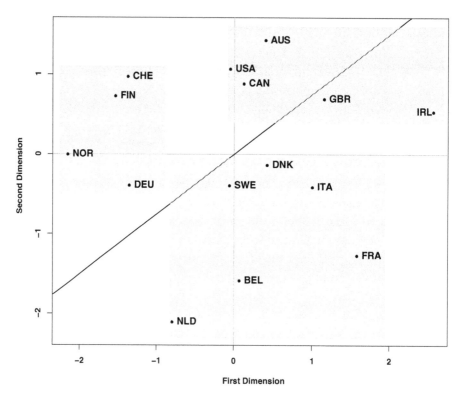

Figure 2.6   Plot of the overall model space, as represented by **US*** and **V***, k-means three-cluster solution

deductively (as we have shown, focusing on cases like Canada and the United States, which we know or theorize to be similar, or on cases and variables like Great Britain and Transfers, which we know to be dissimilar). We can also apply inductive tools to identify subsets of the data (for an additional illustration, see Chapter 5). While this can be done in a variety of ways, one possibility is to use clustering algorithms to identify subsets of cases. To illustrate, we performed a clustering (using the k-means algorithm) on the first two dimensions of the nations in matrix **US*** (Table 2.9).[15] We preferred a three-cluster solution, which is illustrated in Figure 2.6.[16]

---

[15] Why not cluster, instead, on the data matrix (Table 2.2, first two columns)? The reason is that geometric representation of each case (a row of data matrix **Z**) is usually given by the Mahalanobis distance of this vector from the origin. We note, however, that this is identical to the Euclidean distance of the corresponding row of matrix **U** (or the product of matrices **U** and **S**) from the origin. With linear models, it is more straightforward to cluster rows of **U**, rather than rows of the data matrix, for this reason. On these points, see Skillicorn (2006) and van de Geer (1971).

[16] For further discussion of clustering algorithms, their uses, drawbacks, and merits, see Chapters 5 and 6.

Table 2.11 Values above or below the mean (+1 or −1), for each variable, with nations grouped by the three clusters

	Transfers	Pre-pov	$\widehat{Z}_y$
Cluster 1			
Australia	−1	−1	1
Canada	−1	−1	1
Ireland	−1	1	1
United Kingdom	−1	1	1
U.S.A.	−1	−1	1
Cluster 2			
Finland	−1	−1	−1
Germany	1	−1	−1
Norway	1	−1	−1
Switzerland	−1	−1	−1
Cluster 3			
Belgium	1	1	−1
Denmark	1	1	1
France	1	1	1
Italy	1	1	1
Netherlands	1	−1	−1
Sweden	1	1	−1

Straightaway, we can see that the five English-speaking liberal welfare regime countries identified in our previous discussion of Figure 2.2 again are clustered together. However, the similarities among cases within the remaining clusters are less clear. To better understand the logics behind all three clusters, we looked at whether the nations in each cluster were above or below average on the two independent variables (Table 2.1) and $\widehat{Z}_y$ (Table 2.4). The result is in Table 2.11.

The clustering of nations in model space along with the relative (dis)affiliation of clustered nations with variables (Table 2.11) suggests a logic that is not a part of conventional regression modeling interpretation, although it underlies such modeling. We see in Table 2.11, for example, that the five "liberal" nations in Cluster 1 are all below average ("stingy") on welfare transfer payments, and also all are above average on predicted posttax, posttransfer poverty $\left(\widehat{Z}_y\right)$. Moreover, these five nations are the only ones with these two qualities. All four nations in Cluster 2 share low poverty rates both pre- and posttax and transfer. Moreover, they are the only four nations with these traits. Cluster 3 seems on its face to be more heterogeneous. And yet, all six of these nations are above average ("generous") with welfare transfer payments, and all (with the exception of the Netherlands) have relatively high poverty rates prior to transfers and taxation.

As this simple exercise illustrates, the regression model rests on a context of nations clustered by an institutional logic of welfare. Researchers on welfare regimes (e.g., Hicks and Kenworthy 2003; Shalev 2007) have made much progress in theorizing this logic. The innovation of our approach using RIO is to demonstrate that a field-theoretic representation of this kind of institutional logic is a part of the regression model, but one that is to our knowledge ignored (with respect to regression modeling) outside of the work we have reviewed in this chapter.[17]

2.5   A Matrix of Profile Similarity

Our approach to visualization allows for an explicitly relational way of understanding the relationships among cases and variables as defined by the regression model. Extending this line of thinking allows us to understand these relationships in network-analytic terms. Previously (in Section 2.3) we introduced the SVD of the matrix of independent variables, and we showed how the multiple regression coefficients, as well as the contribution of each case to each coefficient, could be estimated. Now we point out that the row space (matrix U in Table 2.2) from the SVD has some special properties that will be helpful to us.

The matrix product of U with its transpose, $U * U^T$, which we abbreviate as UU^T, is an $n \times n$ matrix of profile similarity among the cases. This matrix is referred to in mathematical statistics as the projection matrix, and it is known to students of regression diagnostics as the Hat matrix (Belsley et al. 2004).[18] Indeed, the diagonal of this matrix is often used (either directly, or adjusted in various ways) to identify highly influential and/or problematic observations. Cells not on the diagonal of the Hat matrix are typically ignored by regression analysts.

---

[17] Geometric data analysis (GDA, in particular multiple correspondence analysis) is an analytical perspective and a set of techniques that are central to the field theory of Pierre Bourdieu (as discussed at greater length in Chapter 9). GDA has provided inspiration to our project of attempting to see regression modeling in a new way: as both rooted in, and identifying analytically, the study of social fields.

[18] The Hat matrix is usually written $X(X^TX)^{-1}X^T$. By substituting the definition of Singular Value Decomposition (Equation [2.6]), this expression is seen to be identical to UU^T, as authors including Belsley, Kuh, and Welsch (2004) show.

In turning OLS inside out, we have a particular attitude about the Hat matrix $(\mathbf{U}\mathbf{U}^T)$, a matrix that is most often used to identify one, or a very small number, of problematic observations. When researchers employ regression diagnostics, the assumption seems to be that most of the observations are well-behaved, and the task is to find a few that, against this well-behaved background, may appear odd. In contrast, we begin by searching for macro clusters of cases, and we look for distinctive influence among these clusters (as just illustrated in our discussion of Figure 2.6). We are not the first to recognize the importance of off-diagonal entries in the Hat matrix (Gray and Ling 1984), but we use those entries in a comprehensive way to formulate a case-oriented dual to the usual regression modeling of the variables.

The Hat matrix has an interesting decomposition,

$$\mathbf{U}\mathbf{U}_{ij}^T = d_i d_j \cos\left(\mathbf{U}_{[i,]}\mathbf{U}_{[j,]}\right) \tag{2.11}$$

where d_i is the square root of the ith diagonal cell of the Hat matrix (and similarly for d_j), and $\cos(\mathbf{U}_{[i,]}, \mathbf{U}_{[j,]})$ is the cosine of rows i and j of matrix $\mathbf{U}$. We can represent the cases geometrically as points in a multidimensional space, with d_i the distance of the ith point from the origin (and similarly for d_j),[19] and the cosine measuring the angle between the lines connecting points i and j (respectively) to the origin. For the example that we have been carrying through in this chapter, we report the cosine matrix in Figure 2.7, with the nations arranged according to the clusters discussed above (Figure 2.6). As the key on the right-hand side of the figure indicates, cells close to black represent cosines close to +1, and cells close to white represent cosines close to −1.[20]

We see in Figure 2.7 that the three clusters identified from k-means clustering on matrix $\mathbf{U}$ are highly similar internally. For those familiar with network analysis, this plot should bear a striking similarity to those produced using blockmodeling, community detection, or other similar approaches to pattern discovery in networks (e.g., Rosvall et al. 2019; White, Boorman, and Breiger 1976). With this in mind, we might say that we have identified network communities of nations on the basis of their profile similarity across the variables used in this study. At the same time, with respect to outliers, we might depart from the usual discussions (which are focused on identifying a

---

[19] The magnitude of a cell on the diagonal of the Hat matrix, for example $\mathbf{H}(i,i)$, is the square of the distance of the ith row of $\mathbf{U}$ from the origin.

[20] For example, in the first row of Figure 2.7, the cosine of Belgium (with the Netherlands, Finland, Norway, Switzerland, Australia) is (+0.94, −0.53, −0.03, −0.68, −0.97), respectively. Cosines are computed from rows of matrix $\mathbf{U}$ in Table 2.6a.

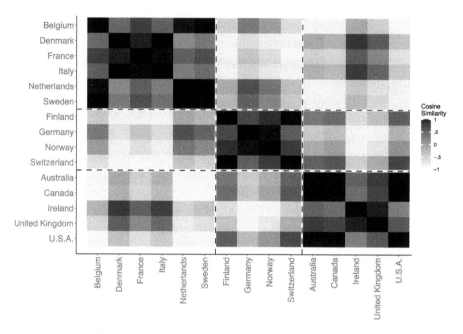

Figure 2.7   Depiction of cos (**UU**ᵀ)

small number of outliers) by noticing that each of our three macro clusters (Figure 2.6) seems to be an outlier with respect to the other clusters, and that this appears to be especially so with respect to the first two clusters as listed in Figure 2.7.

The network interpretation of the Hat matrix within the regression context is further reinforced by the common observation (e.g., Belsley, Kuh, and Welsch 2004) that matrix (or network) $\mathbf{UU}^{\mathrm{T}}$, postmutiplied by the vector of observed values $(\mathbf{Y})$, yields the vector of predicted values $(\widehat{\mathbf{Y}})$. Thus (for example), the predicted value of the ith case in the typical regression model is identical to the weighted sum of observed values of all cases, weighted by the similarity (in $\mathbf{UU}^{\mathrm{T}}$) of each respective case to case i. We build further on these observations in Chapter 9.

2.6 Summary

In this chapter, we introduced the mathematics, logic, and some of the analytic possibilities that come from turning regression models inside out. In Appendices A and B, we provided a basic introduction to key mathematical operations that are necessary for understanding how RIO works: matrix multiplication and SVD. While not necessary for understanding what RIO can do, these sections provide useful background and help to contextualize some of the discussion and notation that appears throughout the chapters that follow.

After reviewing these operations, we introduced RIO in the context of OLS regression in dialogue with a subset of data published by Kenworthy (1999). Along with introducing the underlying mathematics for turning OLS inside out, this application allowed us to provide tangible illustrations of how RIO can offer new insights into the workings of the most straightforward regression models. We showed how RIO allows us to identify each observation's additive contribution to each overall regression coefficient. We demonstrated how RIO allows us to visualize the model space such that the relationships among cases, variables, and the output of the regression model (regression coefficients, fitted values of the predictor variables) are all represented in a single diagram. Finally, we introduced the idea of conceptualizing the row-space of the regression model as a matrix of profile similarity: a network where relationships are defined by similarities among nodes or cases.

The material presented in this chapter provides a foundation for all subsequent chapters. We build on the mathematics introduced in this chapter to show how RIO can be generalized to other forms of the GLM (Chapter 3), and to model variance (Chapter 4). We then demonstrate how the procedures introduced here can yield novel substantive insights (Chapter 5), facilitate inductive identification of statistically significant interaction terms (Chapter 6), and provide a gateway to methodologies that are typically understood as distinct or incommensurate with regression analysis (Chapters 7–9).

3   Generalizing Regression Inside Out

In Chapter 2, we provided a detailed overview of how to turn OLS regression models inside out. By extension, linear probability models (Woolridge 2010: 454–55) for binary responses can be turned inside out using those methods as well. However, as noted in Chapter 1, Regression Inside Out (RIO) extends to the entire GLM. In this chapter, we discuss how RIO can be generalized beyond OLS to other forms of the GLM. We begin by describing why we need to adjust RIO to account for noncontinuous outcomes and explain a straightforward approach to doing so. We then illustrate how this approach to generalizing RIO allows us to turn logistic, Poisson, negative binomial regression, and random intercept mixed models inside out. We then discuss fixed effects models for continuous outcomes, which involve a simple modification of an OLS model.

3.1   Generalizing RIO

When estimating a regression model, it is important that the outcome distribution have the possibility of being within the range of the fitted values.[1] If your dependent variable has a range from 1 to 100, then the fitted values should have the possibility of falling between 1 and 100. Similarly, if you have a binary outcome, the fitted values should not exceed the 0–1 thresholds of the observed response. There are some consequential byproducts of having fitted values that do not match the distribution of the outcome. Substantively, fitted values that fall outside the threshold of the observed values make little sense. Thus, if you fit an OLS model to a binary response,

---

[1] RIO is agnostic about which link function readers use. If using a linear probability model, the content in Chapter 2 is sufficient to turn that model inside out. When the link function is anything but an identity link, we need to adjust the methods and this chapter focuses on that methodological generalization (see Ai and Norton 2003; Mize 2019).

the fitted values can exceed the 0–1 thresholds of the observed response. Analytically, the distribution of the residual is unlikely to be normal. This is because the outcome can only take two values (0 and 1), while the fitted values are continuous. This results in an inefficient estimation of the parameter values (Allison 2009).

Robust estimation of standard errors and modeling a convenient transformation of the outcome are common solutions to the problem noted above (Woolridge 2010: 454–57). For example, in the case of a binary response, there are two common transformations. The most common approach is to model the log-odds of the outcome (Long 1997). This results in logistic regression. The log-odds fit the range of the fitted values while the binary, untransformed response does not. A less common approach is to assume that the binary response has an underlying latent distribution, with a threshold above which a "1" is observed and below which a "0" is observed.[2]

More generally, when assuming an outcome variable is not continuous, analysts use a *link function* to ensure that the range and distribution of the fitted values match the assumed range and distribution of the response. Again, in the context of a binary outcome, the logit of a binary response is a continuous function, making the range of the left-hand side of the equation the same as the right-hand side. Count-distributed outcomes can only be positive – hence the log link is commonly used when modeling a count outcome (Hilbe 2011). This is true regardless of the assumed distribution on the outcome (e.g., Poisson, negative binomial).

As detailed in Chapter 2, RIO relies on a linear relationship between the predictors and the fitted values from the model. In the case of a continuous outcome, the linear relationship is built into the model. The link function in OLS regression is the identity link, meaning that no transformation of the linear predictors is required to generate the fitted values. This is also true in a linear probability model – the relationship between the predictors and the fitted values is linear here too. In the case of regression with a noncontinuous outcome – specifically in regression models with a link function that is not the identity link – the relationship between the predictors and the fitted values is no longer linear. The linear predictors are transformed by the link function to derive the fitted values from the model. The nonlinearity in link functions breaks the linear correspondence between the predictors themselves and the fitted values.

---

[2] In the context of binary responses, we focus our subsequent discussion on logistic regression since it is by far the most prevalent.

There is a simple solution that allows us to generalize RIO across the GLM, which is to use the linear predictors themselves. That is, rather than use the predicted values in the context of a regression model with a link function, the linear predictors are preferred because it maintains the one-to-one correspondence between predictors and the variable representing the outcome.[3] In the sections that follow, we show how this is done using multiple forms of the GLM.

3.2   Logistic Regression

When the outcome is binary, researchers often assume the outcome is binomially distributed and use the logit link function. This results in the run-of-the-mill logistic regression model. Equation 3.1 presents the generalized linear model (Neter et al. 1996). This is general notation, where logistic regression is defined by the function itself. The outcome is the sum of a mean response $f(X_i,\beta)$ given by the nonlinear response function and the error term (ε_i). In the case of logistic regression, the nonlinear response function is given in Equation 3.2. The right-hand side of 3.2 is the logistic function of the linear predictors, which transforms the fitted response to be within the interval [0,1].

$$Y_i = f(X_i,\beta)+\varepsilon_i \tag{3.1}$$

$$Y_i = \frac{1}{1+e^{-(X_i\beta)}} \tag{3.2}$$

We can illustrate this with a textbook example. Hilbe (2011) models the number of affairs that married people have had as a function of several predictors. The predictors include self-reports of how happy the marriage is, respondent religiosity, and the length of the marriage. For our analysis, we use dummy variables to denote a happy marriage (=1) and whether the respondent is religious (=1). Length of marriage is represented by dummies for being married at least 7, 10, or 15 years, with less than 7 as the reference category. Here we binarize the outcome such that 0 corresponds to no extramarital affairs, and 1 corresponds to any number of extramarital affairs. Later in this chapter, we model this outcome as a count.

---

[3] Practically, it is often easier to submit the fitted values to the inverse of the link function to derive the linear predictors (software will sometimes provide the fitted values, but not the linear predictors).

Table 3.1 Summary of a logistic regression predicting whether the respondent has had an extramarital affair

	Full rank regression coefficients	Products in **V** (full rank)
Happy marriage[1]	−0.869***	−0.193
	(0.205)	
Religious[2]	−0.870***	−0.193
	(0.214)	
Married at least 7 years[3]	0.568	0.126
	(0.311)	
Married at least 10 years[3]	0.797*	0.177
	(0.323)	
Married at least 15 years[3]	0.779***	0.173
	(0.243)	
Constant	−0.653**	−0.145
	(0.226)	

Note: $*p < 0.05$, $**p < 0.01$, $***p < 0.001$. $N = 601$.
[1] Reference category is Unhappy marriage.
[2] Reference category is Not Religious.
[3] Reference category is less than 7 years.

Table 3.1 presents the results of a logistic regression using this model specification. We find that those who have happy marriages or are religious are less likely to have an affair. We also find that those who have been married for 10 or more years are more likely to have had an extramarital affair. To turn this regression model inside out, we append the linear predictors to the design matrix (i.e., the predictor variables and a column of 1's [the constant]), and then take the SVD. The product between the part of the column space matrix (**V**) corresponding to the predictor variables and the part of the column space matrix corresponding to the linear predictors has a one-to-one correspondence with the regression coefficients. These products are also shown in Table 3.1. Importantly, the regression coefficients are perfectly correlated with the products from the column space matrix $\mathbf{V}(r = 1.00)$. As such, we use these dimensions to plot the variables and illustrate the model.

Figure 3.1 presents a plot of the logistic regression model. Specifically, we are plotting the first two dimensions or columns of **V** (the column space matrix) from the SVD of appending the linear predictors to the design space matrix from the model in Table 3.1. In this case, **V** has seven columns, corresponding to the five predictors, the constant, and the linear predictions. We have projected a line through the linear predictors and the origin, along with

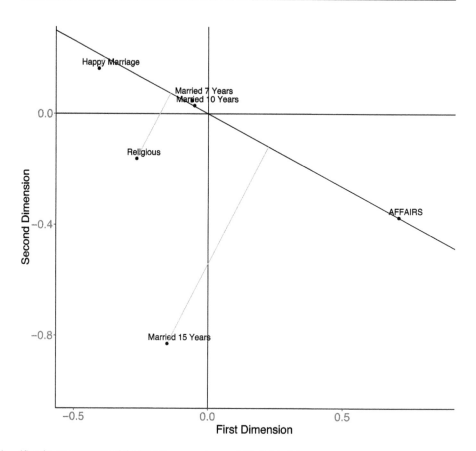

Figure 3.1   Visual representation of the logistic regression model in Table 3.1

lines from each predictor to the line running through the origin and the linear predictors. As in Chapter 2, the distances in the column space matrix are
perfectly associated with the estimated regression coefficients. We plot the
model space by focusing on the first two leading dimensions.[4]

Computing the SVD of a matrix consisting of the linear predictors and
the design matrix thus allows us to construct plots of the regression space.
As with other dimension reduction techniques (e.g., correspondence analysis, multidimensional scaling), the leading dimensions explain the most
variation, but not all of it. In this case, there are a total of seven dimensions, but we are only illustrating the first two. Researchers could, of course,

---

[4] If one estimates the logistic regression coefficients using fewer dimensions (i.e., as in principal
components logistic regression), then the two-dimensional plot is a perfect reflection of the underlying
model coefficients.

examine more than just the first two dimensions. In complicated models, more dimensions may be needed to really grasp what is going on inside of the regression model. We recommend plotting the weights from the SVD to determine the number of important dimensions. Additionally, as we show in Chapter 2, it is also possible to incorporate the positions of cases into these plots. This simply requires appending the product of matrices $\mathbf{U}$ and $\mathbf{S}$ from the SVD to $\mathbf{V}$.

In addition to plotting the relationships among variables (and cases), we can also compute each observation's contribution to the overall logistic regression coefficients. Again, for OLS, this requires a linear solution to the regression coefficients, but postmultiplying by a diagonal matrix of the outcome instead of treating it as a vector. Equation 3.3 presents the linear solution to the logistic regression coefficients, where $\mathbf{X}$ is the design matrix, $\mathbf{W}$ is a diagonal matrix with $\hat{\pi}_i\left(1-\hat{\pi}_i\right)$ as entries ($\hat{\pi}_i$ refers to the ith observations predicted probability), and $\mathbf{z}$ is the working or pseudo-response, defined as $X\hat{\beta}+W^{-1}r$, with $\mathbf{r}$ referring to the residuals (Hosmer and Lemeshow 2000: 129). To transform 3.3 into a variables-by-cases matrix whose rows sum to the overall logistic regression coefficients, we postmultiply by $\mathbf{Z}$ instead of $\mathbf{z}$, where $\mathbf{Z}$ is a diagonal matrix with z_i as entries.

$$\mathbf{b} = \left(\mathbf{X}^T\mathbf{W}\mathbf{X}\right)^{-1}\mathbf{X}^T\mathbf{W}\mathbf{z} \tag{3.3}$$

3.3   Poisson and Negative Binomial Models

The same logic that allows us to turn logistic regression inside out can be used to generalize to other types of regression models as well. Here, we illustrate this using Poisson and Negative Binomial models using the same data on extramarital affairs. The affairs outcome is originally a count variable measuring the number of extramarital affairs. We binarized it above to illustrate logistic regression, but we can also model affairs as a count assuming that it follows both a Poisson and a negative binomial distribution. In both cases, we use the log link, which is the most common link function in the social sciences for a count distributed outcome. Again, this allows us to both visualize the count regression models, and to decompose the coefficients by individual cases. We do both with the same model specification as above, just altering the assumed distribution on the outcome.

Results from a Poisson regression model are presented in Table 3.2. Just as we did with the logistic regression, turning this Poisson regression

Table 3.2 Summary of a Poisson regression predicting the count of extramarital affairs

	Full rank regression coefficients	Products in **V** (full rank)
Happy marriage[1]	−0.776***	−0.143
	(0.069)	
Religious[2]	−0.941***	−0.173
	(0.079)	
Married at least 7 years[3]	0.734***	0.135
	(0.116)	
Married at least 10 years[3]	0.989***	0.182
	(0.115)	
Married at least 15 years[3]	1.010***	0.203
	(0.091)	
Constant	0.463***	0.085
	(0.086)	

Note: $^*p < 0.05$, $^{**}p < 0.01$, $^{***}p < 0.001$. $N = 601$.
[1] Reference category is Unhappy marriage.
[2] Reference category is Not Religious.
[3] Reference category is less than 7 years.

model inside out entails simply appending the linear predictors (i.e., the log of the fitted values) to the design matrix, and taking the SVD. Again, the corresponding distances in the column space matrix **V** from the predictors to the fitted values are also presented in Table 3.2. As in OLS and logistic regression, the estimated coefficients are perfectly associated with these distances ($r = 1.00$). As such, we again plot the two leading dimensions or vectors in **V** in Figure 3.2. The figure illustrates the relatively strong and negative effects of being in a happy marriage or being religious on extramarital affairs.

The linear solution to the Poisson regression coefficients is also defined in Equation 3.3, except that both **W** and **z** are defined differently. For Poisson regression, **W** is a diagonal matrix of fitted values and **z**, the working response, is defined as $X\hat{\beta} + \frac{r}{\hat{y}}$, where **r** refers to the model residuals, and $\hat{y}$ refers to the fitted values from the model (Hilbe 2011: 52). To transform 3.3 into a variables-by-cases matrix whose rows sum to the overall Poisson regression coefficients, we again postmultiply by **Z** instead of **z**, where **Z** is a diagonal matrix with z_i as entries.

The Poisson distribution assumes that the mean and the variance are the same. In practice, the variance often exceeds the mean, making the distribution "overdispersed." One solution to this problem is to estimate a dispersion term. The negative binomial distribution assumes that the mean and the

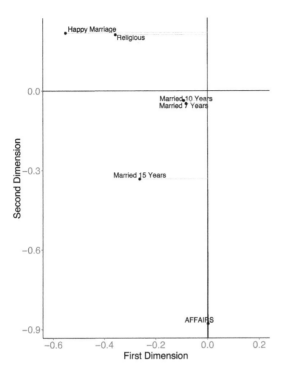

Figure 3.2   Visual representation of the Poisson regression model in Table 3.2

variance are related, but not equal. Specifically, the negative binomial model assumes that the mean response is equal to the variance, multiplied by 1 + an unknown parameter that is estimated from the data. This unknown parameter allows the variance of the negative binomial distribution to exceed the mean. So, in addition to the regression coefficients themselves, a negative binomial regression model necessitates estimating one additional unknown parameter – the overdispersion term.

Results from a negative binomial regression model are presented in Table 3.3. Again, appending the linear predictors (i.e., the log of the fitted values) to the design matrix and taking the SVD, the corresponding distances in the column space matrix $\mathbf{V}$ from the predictors to the fitted values are presented in Table 3.3. As above, the estimated coefficients are perfectly associated with these distances ($r = 1.00$). Figure 3.3 plots the two leading dimensions or vectors in $\mathbf{V}$. The similarities in the model parameter estimates between the Poisson and Negative Binomial specifications are also shown in Figures 3.2 and 3.3, as they show quite similar patterns.

The linear solution to the negative binomial regression coefficients also requires modifying $\mathbf{W}$ and $\mathbf{z}$ in Equation 3.3. The overdispersion term is

Table 3.3 Summary of a negative binomial regression predicting the count of extramarital affairs

	Full rank regression coefficients	Products in **V** (full rank)
Happy marriage[1]	−0.759**	−0.108
	(0.259)	
Religious[2]	−1.235***	−0.176
	(0.250)	
Married at least 7 years[3]	1.139**	0.162
	(0.372)	
Married at least 10 years[3]	0.869*	0.124
	(0.396)	
Married at least 15 years[3]	1.299***	0.185
	(0.289)	
Constant	0.435	0.062
	(0.282)	

Note: $^*p < 0.05$, $^{**}p < 0.01$, $^{***}p < 0.001$. $N = 601$.
[1] Reference category is Unhappy marriage.
[2] Reference category is Not Religious.
[3] Reference category is less than 7 years.

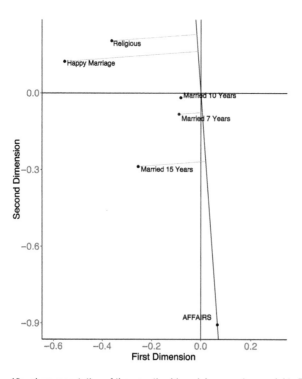

Figure 3.3 Visual representation of the negative binomial regression model in Table 3.3

included in the weight matrix, as follows: $\mathbf{W}$ is defined as a diagonal matrix

with $\dfrac{\hat{y}}{\left(1+\left(\dfrac{1}{\alpha}\right)\hat{y}\right)}$ as entries, and $\mathbf{z}$ is defined as $X\hat{\beta}+\dfrac{r}{\hat{y}}$, where $\mathbf{r}$ refers to

the model residuals, and $\hat{y}$ refers to the fitted values from the model (Hilbe 2011: 217).

3.4   Random Intercept Mixed Model

Before discussing fixed effects models, we want to introduce another extension. RIO also works in the context of mixed models that include both fixed and random coefficients. Below we describe this for a simple random intercept model, but do not provide a parallel illustration (see Chapter 5 for an application of turning a random intercept mixed model inside out).

In the context of mixed models, we begin by discussing derivation of the variables-by-cases matrix whose rows sum to the estimated fixed effects. In the context of mixed models, at least one iterative procedure is required to obtain the unknown parameters. First, the fixed effects are estimated using a (possibly weighted) regression, and then these values are included in a regression to estimate the variance components. This then iterates until convergence (Littell et al. 2006). The variance components are defined in Equation 3.4, where $\mathbf{Z}$ is an indicator matrix denoting units of nesting (an $n \times t$ matrix, or "number of cases" by "number of level two units"), $\mathbf{G}$ is a matrix of variance components ($t \times t$), and $\mathbf{R}$ is the residual matrix representing the error variance (diagonal) and possible serial correlation structure (off-diagonal).

$$\mathbf{V} = \mathbf{Z}\mathbf{G}\mathbf{Z}^{\mathrm{T}} + \mathbf{R} \tag{3.4}$$

Given the variance components, the fixed effects parameters are defined in Equation 3.5. In 3.5, the Moore-Penrose generalized inverse of $\mathbf{V}$ is taken (Littell et al. 2006). Now that we have defined the linear solution to the fixed effects, if we postmultiply by $\mathbf{Y}$ (a diagonal matrix with y_i as entries) instead of $\mathbf{y}$, we arrive at the variables-by-cases matrix whose rows sum to the estimated fixed effects. The R script corresponding to this chapter includes an example of decomposing a random intercept model.

$$\mathbf{b} = \left(\mathbf{X}^{\mathrm{T}}\mathbf{V}^{-1}\mathbf{X}\right)^{-1}\mathbf{X}^{\mathrm{T}}\mathbf{V}^{-1}\mathbf{Y} \tag{3.5}$$

There are many other models in the GLM aside from those we have covered here. Generally, appending the linear predictors to a function of the design matrix and taking the SVD will allow one to visualize the GLM. This approach works with the four versions of the GLM we review here, and we expect it to work with other instances of GLMs. However, we have not explicitly evaluated the entire GLM and encourage interested readers to push this line of work forward by doing so.

3.5   Fixed Effects Models with a Continuous Outcome

In addition to adjusting for data with noncontinuous outcomes, relatively minor modifications of the OLS model allow us to adapt RIO to models designed to account for continuous outcomes in longitudinal data. With longitudinal data structures, variation occurs both within groups over time as well as between groups. One common approach to isolating the level one variation, or the variation associated with changes through time, is to include cluster-level fixed effects. The model isolates within variation by removing between variation through a norming of the data or inclusion of cluster-specific intercepts (Allison 2009). Fixed effect estimates therefore reflect only the within-group variability. Isolating the within-group variability can also be achieved by group-centering the data (i.e., subtracting the cluster-specific mean from each predictor variable; Allison 2009; Raudenbush and Bryk 2002). In this way, OLS can reproduce the coefficients from a fixed effects model (Allison 2009). That is, OLS estimation of group-centered data yields the same coefficients/slopes as a fixed effects model that is estimated on noncentered data. The standard errors differ, but the slopes are the same. As such, we can group-center the data to turn fixed effects models inside out. In this context, working with the coefficients is fine, but do not use the standard error decomposition (see Chapter 4).[5] Furthermore, this norming of the data to include fixed effects can be used in conjunction with the other generalizations described in this chapter. That is, group-centered data can be used to include fixed effects in a RIO version of a logistic or negative binomial model. We illustrate applying RIO to a fixed effects model in of Chapter 5.

---

[5] Further development is required to decompose standard errors in the context of fixed effects models.

3.6 Summary

Taken together, this chapter provides a framework for extending RIO to the Generalized Linear Model and some of its extensions. All that is required is that the solution to the fixed effects can be written down in linear terms. In Chapter 2, we demonstrated how to turn an OLS regression model inside out. This entails two key components: a matrix of cases' contributions to the overall regression coefficients and a visualization of the regression model that illustrates key model properties, including the direction and magnitude of the effects of the predictors. Deriving the cases' contributions to the regression coefficients requires an algebraic expression of the model in linear terms. When the outcome is not assumed to be continuous, there is no closed-form solution to the model fixed effects. However, upon model convergence, the fixed effects of a GLM have a linear form, and they are defined in Equation 3.3. Generating the cases' contributions to the GLM fixed effect parameters simply requires postmultiplying by Y (a diagonal matrix with y_i as entries) instead of y. In this chapter, we illustrated how to do this in the context of logistic regression, Poisson regression, negative binomial regression, and random intercept mixed models.

The second aspect of regression inside out is the model visualization. In the context of GLMs that require a link function aside from an identity link, we found that using the linear predictors rather than the fitted values from the model maintains the linear relationship between the design matrix and the outcome. As such, appending the linear predictors to the (weighted) design matrix and taking the SVD results in coordinates that maintain the visualization properties of OLS models. Examples above include visualizations of logistic regression, Poisson regression, and negative binomial regression.

We have not explored the full range of available extensions but believe that further extensions are worth pursuing. Here, we have focused attention on some of the most commonly used models in the GLM. Additional work is required to investigate ordinal and multinomial logistic regression, as well as other specialized instances of the GLM. In the context of mixed models, random coefficient models, cross-classification, and models with serial correlation are also worth attention. These additions require adjustments to the variance components. However, these are part of the linear solution to the regression coefficients, which we present in Equation 3.5.

4   Turning Variance Inside Out (Coauthor: Eunsung Yoon)

In the two preceding chapters, we have shown how to turn a regression model inside out, computing cases' contributions to the overall regression coefficients. In Chapter 2, we illustrated this in the context of continuous outcomes (i.e., OLS regression) and in Chapter 3, we described how to generalize our methods to other outcomes in the generalized linear model. But regression relies on more than just coefficients. The coefficients tell us how independent variables are related to the mean of the outcome. But the variability of those coefficients is also important. Consequently, a full treatment of RIO needs to consider variability and how cases contribute to the variance of the regression model.

Just as regression coefficients can be decomposed by cases or subsets of cases, the variances and standard errors of those coefficients can be as well.[1] In this chapter, we detail how to calculate case-wise contributions to the standard error. We begin with a brief discussion of inference in the context of RIO and the utility of decomposing variance. We then elaborate key challenges in calculating individual case contributions to variances and standard errors of regression coefficients and suggest two methods to tackle those challenges in decomposing standard errors. We conclude by discussing the relative merits of these two approaches, ultimately advocating for one over the other under most circumstances.

4.1   Inference and Uncertainty

Coefficient standard errors are used in regression analyses to aid in statistical inference. If the probability of the coefficient is small (i.e., <0.05), assuming a normal functional form and that the ratio of the coefficient to the standard

---

[1] Ter Braak and Looman (1994) developed a biplot approach to multiple regression that enables t-ratios to be depicted in the same space as the coefficients. In principle, these methods could be coupled with the methods developed in this chapter.

error tells us about the underlying probabilities on that functional form, we say that the predictor has a "significant effect." This inference is designed to infer the properties of a larger population based on a representative sample, but is routinely used to distinguish between signal (i.e., meaningful relationships) versus random noise. Much has been written about the problems of using inferential statistics to draw general conclusions, especially when using data that are not a random sample of a larger population (for more detailed discussions, see, e.g., Berk 2004; Greenland et al. 2016; Tong 2019). As Greenland and colleagues (2016: 338) write, "Every method of statistical inference depends on a complex web of assumptions about how the data were collected and analyzed, and how the analysis results were selected for presentation." They go on to note that, while these assumptions seem deceptively simple, they are extremely challenging to satisfy, even under the best of circumstances.

We emphasize these challenges at the outset of this chapter to clarify that it is not possible to draw conclusions about the statistical significance of individual cases or sets of cases. When we identify cases' contributions to the regression model by turning the model inside out, those contributions are defined in relation to the regression model itself, and consequently, their relation to any observations outside the model is mediated by the model itself. To say that one observation's contribution to a regression coefficient is statistically significant implies a set of relationships between that case and a larger population of data that are not supported theoretically or mathematically.

What turning model variance inside out allows us to do is descriptively assess cases' contribution to the uncertainty in the model. Such descriptive analyses can direct our attention to cases of particular interest for more detailed substantive consideration. It can also help us to understand what cases are primarily driving the effects that are observed in the overall regression model, comparing across cases or sets of cases' contributions to the variance. For researchers interested in computing and interpreting inferential statistics, this should be done in the context of the full model, not on subsets of the data within the model. Turning the variance inside out can then be used to better make sense of the results of the overall model.

To again quote Greenland and colleagues (2016: 337), "correct use and interpretation of [statistical tests, confidence intervals, and statistical power] requires an attention to detail which seems to tax the patience of working scientists." McShane and Gelman (2017) similarly observe that null hypothesis significance testing "was supposed to protect researchers from over-interpreting data. Now it has the opposite effect." RIO is designed to help us better understand our regression models, and misusing inferential statistics is fundamentally counter to this goal. Consequently, treatments of case-level contributions to variance are limited to purely descriptive assessments. With this in mind, we turn to our discussion of the challenges of calculating case-level contributions to standard errors.

4.2   Challenges in Calculating Case Contributions to Standard Errors

On its face, calculating cases' contributions to the variance appears straightforward, but it is actually far from it. The original equation for variances of coefficients is Equation 4.1. Given this, the *assumed* equations for a single case contribution to variances of coefficients would be Equations 4.2 and 4.3.

$$var\left(\mathbf{b}_i\right) = \sigma^2 \left(\mathbf{X}^T\mathbf{X}\right)^{-1}_{ii} \tag{4.1}$$

$$var_j(\hat{\mathbf{b}}_i) = MSE(\mathbf{X}_j^T\mathbf{X}_j)^{-1} \tag{4.2}$$

$$MSE = \frac{1}{n-p}\mathbf{e}^T\mathbf{e}, \text{where } \mathbf{e} = \mathbf{y} - \hat{\mathbf{y}} \tag{4.3}$$

In Equation 4.1, $var\left(\mathbf{b}_i\right)$ refers to the variance of coefficient $\mathbf{b}_i$, σ^2 to the error variance, and $\left(\mathbf{X}^T\mathbf{X}\right)^{-1}_{ii}$ to the ith diagonal element of the variance-covariance matrix. The square root of $var\left(\mathbf{b}_i\right)$ is the standard error for coefficient $\mathbf{b}_i$.

In Equation 4.2, $var_j\left(\mathbf{b}_i\right)$ refers to case j's contribution to the variance of coefficient $\mathbf{b}_i$, MSE refers to the mean squared error, and $\mathbf{x}_j$ refers to the data matrix for case j. Note that Equation 4.3 uses only the data for an individual case, $\mathbf{x}_j$, instead of all cases, $\mathbf{X}$, to measure case contributions. Also, in Equation 4.2, σ^2 is replaced with MSE since the variance of errors, σ^2, is an unknown parameter and MSE is the unbiased estimator of σ^2 (Wackerly, Mendenhall, and Scheaffer 2014). The case contribution to standard errors would be the square root of $var_j\left(\mathbf{b}_i\right)$. The calculation of MSE is presented in Equation 4.4, where $\mathbf{e}^T\mathbf{e}$ represents the sum of squared residuals, n refers to the total number of cases, and p refers to the number of parameters in the model.

The intuition of variance decomposition is simple, but there are three reasons why case contributions to variances or standard errors cannot be calculated through linear operations involving matrices $\mathbf{X}$ and $\mathbf{y}$. First, one of the limitations of this approach is that it cannot be applied to single cases because we cannot calculate the inverse of the matrix $\mathbf{X}$ when we have only one case (i.e., when the rank of the matrix is one). Further, even when we can circumvent this problem by using subsets instead of single cases, it still has the problem that case contributions or subset contributions do not sum to the total variances[2] or standard errors.

Second, cases' contributions to the variance are not additive because the sum of inverse matrices is not equal to the inverse of the summed matrix (e.g., $\mathbf{X}^{-1} + \mathbf{Y}^{-1} + \mathbf{Z}^{-1} \neq \left[\mathbf{X} + \mathbf{Y} + \mathbf{Z}\right]^{-1}$). Equation 4.4 illustrates this point: suppose our data set is composed of three subsets and we would like to decompose the total variance of regression coefficients into the contributions from each subset to the total variance, using Equation 4.3. For convenience of calculation, we will focus only on the inverse matrix, the variance-covariance matrix.

$$(\mathbf{x_1}^T\mathbf{x_1})^{-1} + (\mathbf{x_2}^T\mathbf{x_2})^{-1} + (\mathbf{x_3}^T\mathbf{x_3})^{-1} \neq [(\mathbf{x_1}^T\mathbf{x_1}) + (\mathbf{x_2}^T\mathbf{x_2}) + (\mathbf{x_3}^T\mathbf{x_3})]^{-1} \qquad (4.4)$$

The sum of the variance-covariance matrices for subsets 1, 2, and 3 is not equal to the inverse of the squared sum of the three subsets. Given that the latter is equivalent to the total variance,[3] we can say that the sum of subset variances is not equal to the total variance. In most cases, the subset variances tend to be greater than the total variance because the greater number of cases you have, the smaller variances you obtain. According to the central limit theorem, variance decreases with more information (the inverse of the variance-covariance matrix is called the Fisher information matrix). They will be equal only when all subset variances and the total variance are zero.

Third, standard deviation decomposition is also not additive because the sum of square roots of case variances (or subset variances) is not equal to the square root of the sum (e.g., $\sqrt{2} + \sqrt{2} + \sqrt{2} \neq \sqrt{2+2+2}$). To obtain standard errors by case (or subset) using Equation 4.2, we need to take the square root of the diagonal elements in the variance-covariance matrix. Equation 4.5 shows the example using our three-subset scenario. As proven by Titu's lemma (see Nelsen 2020), the sum of the square root of each subset variance is equal to or greater than the square root of the sum of subset variances. They are equal only when the individual elements vanish.

$$\sqrt{var\left(\mathbf{b_1}\right)} + \sqrt{var\left(\mathbf{b_2}\right)} + \sqrt{var\left(\mathbf{b_3}\right)} \geq \sqrt{var\left(\mathbf{b_1}\right) + var\left(\mathbf{b_2}\right) + var\left(\mathbf{b_3}\right)} \qquad (4.5)$$

---

[2] The *total variance* refers to the variance of regression coefficients estimated from all cases. In contrast, we use *case variance* to refer to the variance of regression coefficients estimated from only one case, and *subset variance* to refer to the variance of regression coefficients estimated from only a subset of all cases. Given the number of cases in a subset is s, and the number of parameters is p, $\mathbf{x_j}$ can be either a $1 \times p$ dimensional vector when it comes to calculating case variances or an $s \times p$ dimensional matrix when it comes to calculating subset variances.

[3] We say that it is "equivalent to" because MSE was omitted.

Consequently, the contributions from individual cases or subsets to variances or standard errors cannot be decomposed such that they sum to the corresponding total variances or standard errors.

The net result is that there is no way to linearly derive case contributions to the standard errors. In the sections that follow, we describe two approaches to variance decomposition that circumvent these problems: (1) the squared residual approach, and (2) the leave-one-out approach. As we detail below, despite distinct limitations, we favor the squared residual approach for several reasons. The most important reason is that it is mathematically and conceptually consistent with the overarching logic of RIO because it focuses on the model at hand, whereas the leave-one-out approach relies on comparison across alternate models based on subsets of the data.

4.3   The Squared Residual Approach

One solution for decomposing variances of regression coefficients into case contributions is partitioning the *MSE* proportional to the squared residual of each case while not altering the variance-covariance matrix. Doing this enables us to use information about the estimated model to understand how cases contribute to the uncertainty in parameter estimates. In this regard, we do not wish to prove the asymptotic properties of our squared residual approach in order to make inferences about the contribution of an individual case or subsets of them. Instead, conditional on the model we have, our approach illustrates how cases contribute to the uncertainty of the fitted model. As is true with understanding how cases contribute to the regression coefficients, understanding how cases contribute to the uncertainty of the fitted model may imply a different model specification. However, our primary goal is to learn more from the model at hand.

The variance of regression coefficients is the product of the error variance and the variance/covariance matrix of the predictors (Equation 4.1). Rather than alter the variance/covariance matrix, the squared residual approach relies on decomposing the error variance. In particular, the squared residual approach decomposes the *MSE*, leaving the variance-covariance matrix untouched. For convenience of calculation, we present this approach only for the variances of regression coefficients. Results for standard errors can be readily obtained by taking the square root of the variance results. Equations 4.6 and 4.7 show how to calculate case variances using the squared residuals of individual cases.

$$var_j\left(\mathbf{b}_i\right) = MSE_j \cdot \left(\mathbf{X}^\mathsf{T}\mathbf{X}\right)^{-1}_{ii} \tag{4.6}$$

$$MSE_j = \frac{1}{n-p}\mathbf{e}_j{}^\mathsf{T}\mathbf{e}_j \tag{4.7}$$

Here, $var_j\left(\mathbf{b}_i\right)$ refers to case j's contribution to the variance of regression coefficient $\mathbf{b}_i$, $\left(\mathbf{X}^\mathsf{T}\mathbf{X}\right)^{-1}_{ii}$ to the ith diagonal element of the variance-covariance matrix, MSE_j to case j's contribution to the full MSE, $\mathbf{e}_j{}^\mathsf{T}\mathbf{e}_j$ to the squared residual of case j, n to the total number of cases in the data set, and p to the number of parameters in the model. Equation 4.6 suggests that we can calculate case variances by using MSE_j instead of the original MSE provided earlier in Equation 4.3. Equation 4.7 shows we can calculate MSE_j by using the squared residual of an individual case instead of using the sum of the squared residuals of all cases.

With this approach, we can obtain case variances, $var_j\left(\mathbf{b}_i\right)$, that sum to the total variance. Now we have additive case variances that reflect the share of each case to the MSE obtained from all cases. Considering that the MSE reflects the assumed disturbance of the regression coefficient under the assumption that the regression coefficient is unbiased, the squared residual of each case is a good estimate of the case contribution to the variance of the regression coefficient.

To provide an example for calculating case contributions to the coefficient variance using this approach, we revisit Kenworthy's (1999) analysis of the effects of welfare policy extensiveness on poverty, which we introduced in Chapter 2.[4] Before we compute case-wise contributions, we first need to run an OLS regression analysis to obtain the total variance for each regression coefficient. Here we compute a bivariate regression for simplicity. The posttax/posttransfer poverty rate is the dependent variable $(\mathbf{y})$ and the rate of government transfers is the regressor $(\mathbf{x})$. Table 4.1 shows the results of

Table 4.1 The results of OLS regression

	$\hat{\beta}$	$se\left(\hat{\beta}\right)$	$var\left(\hat{\beta}\right)$	p-value
Intercept	14.6810	6.2048	38.4990	0.0342*
x	−0.4161	0.4553	0.2073	0.3774

Note: *$p < 0.05$

---

[4] For a detailed discussion of the original analysis, see Chapter 2.

Table 4.2 Raw data (Kenworthy 1999) with squared residuals, MSE_j, and case variances

Country	y	x	$e_j^T e_j$	MSE_j	$var_j(b_i)$
Australia	11.9	7.3	0.06598041	0.00507542	0.0000211
Belgium	6.0	19.3	0.42168529	0.03243733	0.0001350
Canada	6.5	9.5	17.87269238	1.37482249	0.0057239
Denmark	5.9	13.5	10.00472014	0.76959386	0.0032041
Finland	3.7	10.4	44.26345595	3.40488123	0.0141758
France	9.8	17.8	6.38273205	0.49097939	0.0020441
Germany	4.3	14.8	17.82556412	1.37119724	0.0057088
Ireland	29.4	10.5	364.3722062	28.02863124	0.1166939
Italy	14.3	14.5	31.95779755	2.45829212	0.0102348
Netherlands	7.3	21.5	2.45282507	0.18867885	0.0007855
Norway	1.7	13.4	54.82867225	4.21759017	0.0175594
Sweden	5.8	14.6	7.86949778	0.60534598	0.0025203
Switzerland	3.8	9.4	48.57010252	3.73616173	0.0155551
United Kingdom	16.8	10.1	39.96866146	3.07451242	0.0128004
USA	11.7	8.8	0.46387894	0.03568300	0.0001486

OLS regression analysis. In addition to the usual regression results, we added a column for the variances of the regression coefficients. According to the resulting Table, the regression coefficient of **x** is −0.416, the standard error is 0.455, and the variance of the regression coefficient is 0.207.

Using this analysis as our point of departure, we demonstrate step-by-step how to decompose the variance of the regression coefficient of **x**, 0.2073, using the squared residual approach. Table 4.2 presents the raw data for **y** and **x** as well as the values we obtain at each step of the calculation, the squared residuals MSE_j, and the case contributions to the coefficient variance $var_j(b_i)$. The numbers are presented to eight decimal places for the convenience of readers to replicate the calculation with less error. The steps are as follows:

1. We begin by calculating the squared residuals for each case.
2. Once we obtain the squared residuals for each case, we divide them by $n-p$ to obtain MSE_j. In this example, we have 15 cases and 2 parameters, so $n-p$ will be 13. Note that their sum equals the total MSE, which is 49.793882.

$$MSE_j = \left(y_j - \hat{y}_j\right)^2 / 13$$

3. Finally, to obtain case variances $var_j(b_i)$, we multiply MSE_j by the ith diagonal element of the variance-covariance matrix corresponding to b_i. Below is the variance-covariance matrix without MSE. In the matrix, the

first diagonal element is for the intercept and the second diagonal element is for $\mathbf{x}$. Thus, we need to multiply MSE_j by 0.00416338. Note that the sum of all case variances is equal to the total variance, 0.2073.

$$\left(\mathbf{X}^\mathrm{T}\mathbf{X}\right)^{-1} = \begin{bmatrix} 0.77316783 & -0.05423499 \\ -0.05423499 & 0.00416338 \end{bmatrix}$$

$$var_j\left(\mathbf{b}_i\right) = MSE_j \times 0.00416338$$

One strength of the squared residual approach is that it can be readily calculated regardless of the size of the dataset. Also, the interpretation of case contributions is intuitive because summing over all individual contributions yields the total variance of a regression coefficient and thus users can take the value as the share of an individual case in the total variance of a coefficient $\mathbf{b}_i$.

However, there is a caveat to this approach. The weighted MSE is the same for all variables in the model. In our example, this did not matter because we had only one predictor. But in multiple regressions, the squared residual approach assumes that each case contributes equally to each variable. Although it is more reasonable to assume that a case will have different contributions to the variances of different coefficients, the ratio of case variance to the total variance under this approach will always be equal to the ratio of squared residual to the sum of squared residuals regardless of variable, that is, $var_j\left(\mathbf{b}_i\right)/var\left(\mathbf{b}_i\right) = e_j^\mathrm{T}e_j/e^\mathrm{T}e$.

Despite this limitation, the squared residual approach offers valuable descriptive insights into how cases contribute to the variance of regression model. That is, given the regression model, the squared residual approach enables us to estimate the contribution of each case to the overall variance of the predictors based solely on the estimated model. In Section 4.4, we will introduce an approach that relaxes the uniform contribution assumption of the squared residual approach but relies on fitting additional models (using subsets of the data).

4.4   The Leave-One-Out Approach

Another approach to variance decomposition is the leave-one-out approach or Jackknife (Efron and Stein 1981), which can be successfully applied for multivariate regression analyses. Leave-one-out is a quick and handy method for gauging the contribution of a case to the estimated value of a parameter, commonly used for many estimation strategies such as leave-one-out cross validation (LOOCV).

The leave-one-out approach for variance decomposition operates by dropping one case, observing the change in the estimated quantity (in this case, the variance of regression coefficients), and repeating the process for all cases.[5] Below, we show the equations for the leave-one-out approach in variance decomposition.

$$var\left(\mathbf{b}_i\right) = MSE \times \left(\mathbf{X}^T\mathbf{X}\right)^{-1}_{ii} \tag{4.8}$$

$$var_{-j}\left(\mathbf{b}_i\right) = MSE_{-j} \times \left(\mathbf{X}_{-j}^T\mathbf{X}_{-j}\right)^{-1}_{ii} \tag{4.9}$$

$$var_j\left(\mathbf{b}_i\right) = var\left(\mathbf{b}_i\right) - var_{-j}\left(\mathbf{b}_i\right) \tag{4.10}$$

Equation 4.8 shows the total variance for a regression coefficient, as presented earlier in Equation 4.1. As before, we define $var\left(\mathbf{b}_i\right)$, the variance of a regression coefficient estimated from all cases, as the total variance. The total variance of coefficient β_i is obtained by multiplying mean squared error and the ith diagonal element of $\left(\mathbf{X}^T\mathbf{X}\right)^{-1}$.

Equation 4.9 describes the leave-one-out variance. Here, $var_{-j}\left(\mathbf{b}_i\right)$ denotes the variance of a regression coefficient estimated from $n-1$ remaining cases after dropping case j, MSE_{-j} denotes the MSE calculated after omitting case j (which can be written out as $MSE_{-j} = \dfrac{1}{\left(n-p-1\right)}\mathbf{e}_{-j}^T\mathbf{e}_{-j}$, and $\left(\mathbf{X}_{-j}^T\mathbf{X}_{-j}\right)^{-1}_{ii}$ denotes the ith diagonal element of $\left(\mathbf{X}^T\mathbf{X}\right)^{-1}$ calculated also without case j. The leave-one-out variance is obtained by multiplying MSE_{-j} and $\left(\mathbf{X}_{-j}^T\mathbf{X}_{-j}\right)^{-1}_{ii}$. Note that MSE_{-j} has $n-p-1$ degrees of freedom whereas MSE has $n-p$ degrees of freedom. Equation 4.10 calculates the case contribution to the variance of a regression coefficient, which we will define as the case variance. The case variance of case j for coefficient $\mathbf{b}_i$, $var_j\left(\mathbf{b}_i\right)$, is computed by subtracting the leave-one-out variance from the total variance. This represents the actual amount of change in the variance of coefficient $\mathbf{b}_i$ caused by case j. Note, however, that the sum of these case variances over all cases is not equal to the total variance, as opposed to the case variances from the previously discussed squared residual approach.

The amount of change itself may be difficult to interpret without comparison. For example, it is hard to tell if $var_j\left(\mathbf{b}_i\right)$ of 74.28 is meaningful or not.

---

[5] We can also apply the leave-one-out approach at the level of subsets. In that case, we omit subset j when calculating the variance of coefficient i.

Thus, we suggest defining and using contribution ratios, as given by Equation 4.11. The contribution ratio can be understood as the case contribution normalized by the total variance. C_j^i refers to case j's contribution ratio for coefficient b_i as measured by the ratio of j's case variance to the total variance.

$$C_j^i = -\frac{var_j(b_i)}{var(b_i)} = \frac{var_{-j}(b_i)}{var(b_i)} - 1 \qquad (4.11)$$

For a more efficient computation of the ratio, we can skip computing case variances and directly obtain the ratio by subtracting 1 from the ratio of the leave-one-out variance to the total variance. The reason for multiplying the ratio by -1 is to make its interpretation more intuitive. Without flipping the sign, we will need to interpret the contribution ratio as the contributed "increase" in total variance when the contribution ratio is negative, and "decrease" in total variance when the contribution ratio is positive, which could be counterintuitive. By flipping the sign, we make negative ratios imply contributed decreases in the variance of a coefficient and positive ratios imply contributed increases in the variance of a coefficient.

The contribution ratio represents the fractional change in the total variance of a coefficient when we drop a case. For example, if the contribution ratio of a case is 0.16, we can interpret this by saying that omitting the case will increase the variance of the coefficient by 16%. Likewise, if the contribution ratio of a case is -0.32, we can infer that omitting the case will decrease the variance of the coefficient by 32%.

Another option is to construct contribution ratios by instead having case variances as numerators and leave-one-out variances as denominators, that is, $C_j^i = var_j(b_i) / var_{-j}(b_i)$. In that case, we can interpret the ratio as the fractional *increase* in the variance of coefficient b_i when *adding* case j. However, it becomes more difficult to compare contribution ratios for different cases this way, as all ratios have different denominators. This contrasts with the squared residuals approach, which makes it possible to directly compare contribution ratios across cases because all cases share the same denominator.

Case contributions to standard errors can also be obtained using the same leave-one-out process but substituting variances of coefficients with standard errors, as shown below.

$$se(b_i) = \sqrt{MSE \times (X^T X)^{-1}}_{ii} \qquad (4.12)$$

$$se_{-j}(b_i) = \sqrt{MSE_{-j} \times (X_{-j}^T X_{-j})^{-1}}_{ii} \qquad (4.13)$$

$$se_j(\mathbf{b}_i) = se(\mathbf{b}_i) - se_{-j}(\mathbf{b}_i) \tag{4.14}$$

$$C_j^i = -\frac{se_j(\mathbf{b}_i)}{se(\mathbf{b}_i)} = \frac{se_{-j}(\mathbf{b}_i)}{se(\mathbf{b}_i)} - 1 \tag{4.15}$$

As before, we define the standard error of a regression coefficient estimated from all cases as the total standard error $se(\mathbf{b}_i)$, the standard error of a regression coefficient estimated from the $n-1$ remaining cases after dropping a case as the leave-one-out standard error $se_{-j}(\mathbf{b}_i)$, and the case contribution to the total standard error as the case standard error $se_j(\mathbf{b}_i)$. Equation 4.12 shows that the total standard error is the square root of the total variance. Equation 4.13 shows that the leave-one-out standard error is also the square root of the leave-one-out variance. Equation 4.14 shows that the case standard error is the difference in the estimated standard error before versus after omitting a case. Finally, Equation 4.15 defines the contribution ratio of the standard error as the negative of the ratio of the case standard error to the total standard error. The contribution ratio can also be obtained by subtracting one from the ratio of the leave-one-out standard error to the total standard error. Again, we can interpret the contribution ratios as the fractional changes in the standard error of a coefficient when dropping a case.

Note that the contribution ratio for variances of coefficients is always greater than the contribution ratio for standard errors by a factor of $(se(\mathbf{b}_i) + se_{-j}(\mathbf{b}_i)) / se(\mathbf{b}_i)$. The relationship between the two is given by Equation 4.16. Because the total standard error and the leave-one-out standard error are the square roots of the total variance and the leave-one-out variance, the ratio of the square-rooted elements also shrinks accordingly.

$$
\begin{aligned}
C_j^i(variance) &= \frac{var(\mathbf{b}_i) - var_{-j}(\mathbf{b}_i)}{var(\mathbf{b}_i)} \\
&= \frac{\sqrt{var(\mathbf{b}_i)} + \sqrt{var_{-j}(\mathbf{b}_i)}}{\sqrt{var(\mathbf{b}_i)}} \times \frac{\sqrt{var(\mathbf{b}_i)} - \sqrt{var_{-j}(\mathbf{b}_i)}}{\sqrt{var(\mathbf{b}_i)}} \\
&= \frac{se(\mathbf{b}_i) + se_{-j}(\mathbf{b}_i)}{se(\mathbf{b}_i)} \times C_j^i(standard\ error) \tag{4.16}
\end{aligned}
$$

To illustrate the leave-one-out approach for variance decomposition, we will again use data from Kenworthy's (1999) analysis. However, this time we use a multivariate regression analysis. We regress the posttax/posttransfer relative poverty rate $(\mathbf{y})$ on the rate of government transfers $(\mathbf{X}_{[,1]})$, GDP per capita $(\mathbf{X}_{[,2]})$, and relative pretax poverty rate $(\mathbf{X}_{[,3]})$. Raw data

Table 4.3 The 15-country data set (Kenworthy 1999)

Country-Year	Posttax/Posttransfer Relative Poverty y	Transfer Rate $X_{[,1]}$	GDP Per Capita $X_{[,2]}$	Relative Poverty $X_{[,3]}$
Australia	11.9	7.3	7734.418	23.3
Belgium	6.0	19.3	6258.508	26.8
Canada	6.5	9.5	7894.777	22.5
Denmark	5.9	13.5	7450.465	26.4
Finland	3.7	10.4	5712.950	11.9
France	9.8	17.8	6938.063	36.1
Germany	4.3	14.8	6746.054	15.2
Ireland	29.4	10.5	3905.857	39.2
Italy	14.3	14.5	5507.270	30.7
Netherlands	7.3	21.5	7390.348	22.1
Norway	1.7	13.4	6507.316	9.2
Sweden	5.8	14.6	7965.854	23.7
Switzerland	3.8	9.4	11419.350	12.5
United Kingdom	16.8	10.1	7982.377	29.6
USA	11.7	8.8	11871.490	21.0

Table 4.4 The results of the OLS regression

	b	$se(\mathbf{b})$	$var(\mathbf{b})$	p-value
Intercept	8.9050	7.2283	52.2479	0.2436
$X_{[,1]}$	−0.7517	0.2575	0.0663	0.0140*
$X_{[,2]}$	−0.0006	0.0006	0.0000	0.2820
$X_{[,3]}$	0.6335	0.1255	0.0157	0.0004***

Note: $*p < 0.05$; $**p < 0.01$; $***p < 0.001$

are presented in Table 4.3 and the results of the OLS regression are provided in Table 4.4.

We now show the step-by-step process for variance decomposition, followed by Table 4.2 showing the case variances and contribution ratios for each variable. The numbers in the table are again presented to eight decimal places for convenience of readers to replicate the calculation with less error.

1. To begin the process, we need the variances of the regression coefficients. We can compute them using Equation 4.9, or simply by taking the square of the standard errors of the regression coefficients. The total variances are presented in Table 4.4.

$$var(\mathbf{b}_0) = 52.24786873$$

$$var(\mathbf{b}_1) = 0.066328673$$

$$var(\mathbf{b}_2) = 0.000000306$$

$$var(\mathbf{b}_3) = 0.015746709$$

Next, to obtain leave-one-out variances, we compute $MSE_{-j} \times (\mathbf{X}_{-j}{}^T\mathbf{X}_{-j})^{-1}_{ii}$. For example, let us consider $j = 15$ (United States) and observe the corresponding leave-one-out variances for different coefficients. Note that $var_{-15}(\mathbf{b})$ is not a scalar, but a vector in this example

$$var_{-15}(\mathbf{b}) = MSE_{-15} \times (\mathbf{X}_{-15}{}^T\mathbf{X}_{-15})^{-1}_{ii}$$

For MSE_{-15}, we compute the MSE after omitting the case of the United States. We have $15 - 1$ cases and 4 parameters including the intercept, that is, 10 total degrees of freedom. Note that $\hat{y}_j$ here is obtained from an OLS regression without the United States. If we divide the sum of squared residuals without the United States by 10 degrees of freedom, we obtain 13.39097.

$$MSE_{-15} = \sum_{j=1}^{14} (y_j - \hat{y}_j)^2 / 10 = 13.39097$$

Then, we omit the 15th row of X and compute the matrix $(\mathbf{X}_{-15}{}^T\mathbf{X}_{-15})^{-1}$. The values of its diagonal elements are as below.

$$\begin{matrix} & Intercept & trans & GDP & pov \end{matrix}$$
$$diag(\mathbf{X}_{-15}{}^T\mathbf{X}_{-15})^{-1} = [4.248160, 0.004753142, 0.00000003, \text{ and } 0.00116056]$$

Finally, if we multiply the above two, we get a vector of leave-one-out variances. We can see that the United States has greater leave-one-out variances than total variances for all parameters.

$$\begin{matrix} & Intercept & trans & GDP & pov \end{matrix}$$
$$var_{-15}(\mathbf{b}) = [56.88698, \quad 0.06364917, \quad 0.00000044, \quad 0.01554106]$$

2. To obtain the case variances of $\mathbf{U}$ for the United States, we subtract its leave-one-out variances from the total variances. Case variances represent the exact amount of change in the variances of coefficients caused by United States. At face value, it is difficult to tell whether these seemingly small numbers (e.g., 0.00000013 for GDP) are meaningful contributions to the total variances or not. Hence, we need to look at the contribution ratios.

$$var_{15}(\mathbf{b}) = var(\mathbf{b}) - var_{-15}(\mathbf{b})$$

$$var_{15}(\mathbf{b}) = \begin{matrix} Intercept & trans & GDP & pov \\ [-4.639109, & 0.00267951, & -0.00000013, & \text{and } 0.00020565] \end{matrix}$$

Also, it is worth noting that a case has different case variances for different coefficients. For example, Finland makes large contributions to the variances of all coefficients, while Australia or the United States contributes significantly only to the variances of certain coefficients.

3. To compute the contribution ratios of the United States, we divide its case variances by the total variances, then multiply them by -1. The resulting contribution ratios show that omitting the United States from the data set will decrease $var(\mathbf{b_1})$ (transfer rate) by 4% and $var(\mathbf{b_3})$ (relative poverty) by 1.3%, while it will increase $var(\mathbf{b_2})$ (GDP) by 44.4%. This implies that the United States contributes significantly to $var(\mathbf{b_2})$ while having marginal influences on the other parameters. With the contribution ratio, we can tell that the seemingly small value of $var_{15}(\mathbf{b_2})$, being -0.00000013, is in fact a significant contribution to $var(\mathbf{b_2})$, amounting to more than 40% of the total variance.

$$C_{15}^i = \frac{var_{15}(\mathbf{b})}{var(\mathbf{b})}$$

$$C_{15} = \begin{matrix} Intercept & trans & GDP & pov \\ [0.0887904 & -0.04039738 & 0.44380565 & -0.01305966] \end{matrix}$$

As these steps show, the case variances from the leave-one-out approach represent absolute changes in the variances of coefficients caused by each case. Readers familiar with conventional approaches to regression diagnostics will recognize a striking similarity between diagnostic techniques such as DFBETA, DFFIT, and COVRATIO and the leave-one-out approach. Indeed, leaving out individual cases and computing changes in model statistics is the basis for these common diagnostic tools (Belsley, Kuh, and Welsch 2004). In our case, we are computing how the variance of a regression coefficient changes by dropping a single case (Equations 4.9–12). DFBETA computes how the coefficients change, DFFIT computes how the fitted values from the model change, and COVRATIO computes the ratio of determinants of matrices with and without each case (Belsley, Kuh, and Welsch 2004: 13–22). While related to existing regression diagnostic techniques, the leave-one-out approach defined above sheds light on changes in the variance or second moment of the regression coefficient, whereas existing methods focus on changes in the means or implications of them (i.e., the fitted values).

4.5   Choosing between the Squared Residuals and Leave-One-Out

The squared residuals and leave-one-out approaches each offer unique ways to assess cases' contributions to the model variance but differ in important ways. The squared residuals approach is fully consistent with the logic of RIO: assuming that we have appropriately estimated our regression model, it allows us to understand how cases and sets of cases are contributing to *that* model. That is, the squared residual approach allows us to get more out of the regression model we have in hand, which is thematic of RIO's logic. The squared residual approach is more parsimonious than the leave-one-out approach and provides us a descriptive measure that is based on how each case contributes to the overall inferential statistics of the regression model. Because the denominator is the same for all cases using the squared residuals approach, contributions can be more intuitively and directly compared. However, the squared residuals approach allows us to account for each case's contribution to the overall variance and cannot be parsed at the level of individual variables. Moreover, it does not allow us to account for the direction of the contributions, as all contributions are positive.

In contrast, the leave-one-out approach offers a more complex assessment that is consistent with the logic of conventional regression diagnostics, focusing on the change observed when observations are dropped from the model estimation. In this context, separate models are estimated after systematically removing each case. The key benefit of this approach is that it allows us to account for each case's contribution to the variance for each individual variable and accounts for the direction (positive or negative) of the contributions. However, because the denominator for every contribution differs, comparisons are only possible by calculating contribution ratios, which have no concrete relationship to the regression model as it was estimated. In other words, the leave-one-out approach highlights case contributions to variability *as it is derived from different model specifications.*

We favor the squared residual approach, and throughout the remainder of the book, this is what we use. This preference is rooted primarily in the fact that it relies only on the model at hand and allows us to speak concretely in terms of that model at hand rather than comparing it to alternate models based on subsets of the data. Researchers with a particular interest in how cases contribute to a particular variable will find the leave-one-out approach useful. However, as emphasized earlier in this chapter, the ability to single out individual cases' contributions to the variance of a particular coefficient does not mean that we can calculate the statistical significance of a case's contribution to the overall regression coefficient of a particular variable in the conventional sense. Rather, both approaches provide a purely descriptive assessment of variance.

4.6 Summary

In this chapter, we discussed the role of inference in RIO and emphasized that our interest is in the descriptive analysis of cases' contributions to variance. We discussed the challenges of estimating case contributions to the variances/standard errors of OLS coefficients and introduced two approaches to overcoming those challenges: the squared residual approach and the leave-one-out approach.

The squared residual approach obtains case variances by partitioning the variance of OLS coefficients as proportional to the ratio of the squared residual of each case to the sum of squared residuals. This method is intuitive in the sense that the case contributions sum to the total variance of a coefficient, but is limited in that it assumes uniform contributions across all variables from a single case. This approach, however, requires only the estimated model and offers insights into variability therefrom. This is our preferred approach.

The leave-one-out approach produces case variances by computing the difference in the variance/standard error of OLS coefficients estimated from the whole dataset and after leaving one case out from the dataset. This approach is useful in that it provides the amount of change in variances/standard errors so that we can gauge the impact of the changes. It captures the different sizes and directions of case contributions to different coefficients, but case variances do not sum to the total variance. As with other nonparametric approaches, leave-one-out requires estimating several additional regression models.

Part II

Action and Interaction

5   Action Detection

The preceding chapters provide a conceptual and technical introduction to turning regression inside out. They highlight some of the possibilities that emerge when we turn attention to the observations that constitute our data, which are typically rendered invisible by regression analysis. We show how to turn OLS regression coefficients inside out in Chapter 2, how RIO can be generalized to other forms of the GLM in Chapter 3, and we offer two distinct approaches for determining each observation's contribution to the variance and standard errors in Chapter 4.

In this chapter, we bring these technical capabilities together to show how turning regression inside out can be used to gain novel substantive and theoretical insights. We focus specifically on showing how RIO can be used to identify cases and sets of cases that have unique or outsized effects on regression coefficients and standard errors. In his book *Regression Analysis: A Constructive Critique*, Berk (2004: 18) writes that,

Although the data used in regression analysis can provide only conditional distributions, researchers routinely draw inferences that go far beyond the information contained in those distributions. The inferences are the basis of a subject matter 'story' the researchers tell.

Building on this aphorism, the standard approach to interpreting regression coefficients and standard errors is to assume that these summary statistics represent the "action" – that is, the relationships among variables as constituted by patterns among observations – of the "stories" we tell. When a regression model meets all formal assumptions and data are generated using probability sampling, it is fair to assume that the coefficients and standard errors adequately represent these relationships and patterns (Cook and Weisberg 1999). However, when these conditions are not met, individual cases or sets of cases can have an outsized effect on the coefficients and standard errors, such that conventional summaries of the conditional distribution fail to reflect the underlying relationships in the data (i.e., the "action").

RIO provides an intuitive way for researchers to examine whether the single story implied by coefficients and standard errors is a reasonable representation of the data, or if they are imposing an overly simply storyline onto a more complex reality. Moreover, RIO does this in a way that fosters dialogue with theory and substantive knowledge. Because each observation's contributions to the overall coefficients and variance can sum to the overall regression coefficients and variance (see Chapters 2–4), it is easy to explore how subsets of cases within the data contribute to the overall regression coefficient. This is particularly important when, for instance, existing scholarship indicates that effects will differ across subpopulations within the data, or when there is a mismatch between cases and observations, as there often is with panel data where the case (i.e., the unit of inference) is constituted by multiple observations (i.e., the unit of analysis).

The bulk of this chapter centers on three examples that illustrate how RIO can be applied for the purposes of "action" detection. These examples are specifically selected to demonstrate how technical procedures that were introduced in earlier chapters can be used and combined in substantive analyses. As summarized in Table 5.1, these examples turn multiple forms of the GLM inside out using both cross-sectional and panel data with units of analysis ranging from individuals to countries. In doing so, we highlight some of the diverse ways that RIO can be applied.

Our first example turns fixed effects and random effects regression models inside out and applies the relational and geometric approach to data representation that was introduced in Chapter 2. For this illustration, we reanalyze data from Beckfield's (2006) study of the relationship between European integration and income inequality, which uses an unbalanced panel of 48

Table 5.1 Summary of examples

	Example 1	Example 2	Example 3
Method	Fixed Effects (FE); Random Effects (RE)	OLS	Logistic
Data type	Unbalanced panel	Cross-sectional	Cross-sectional
Unit of analysis	Country-years	Countries	Individuals
Substantive focus	Inequality and regional integration	Social determinants of health	Correlates of dog ownership
Reanalysis of …	Beckfield (2006)	Rambotti (2015)	NA

country-years. This data structure allows us to demonstrate RIO's utility for exploring the impact of cases on regression coefficients when those cases are constituted by multiple observations.

In our second example, we turn OLS models inside out to reanalyze a published cross-sectional country-level analysis of the relationship between income inequality and life expectancy (Rambotti 2015). This reanalysis demonstrates how RIO can help us make sense of contradictory findings in existing scholarship.

With the first two examples, we demonstrate RIO's capacity to inform and advance established scholarship by revealing substantive findings that could not be obtained using conventional regression analysis, and we show how these findings add depth to the stories implied by the overall regression models. Our final example takes a different approach, illustrating how RIO can be used for exploratory data analysis through a simple (previously unpublished) analysis of the correlates of dog ownership using data from the 2018 General Social Survey (GSS) (Smith et al. 1970–2018). In this example, we use logistic regression applied to large-N data. Before turning to substantive examples, however, we briefly discuss how using RIO for action detection differs from common approaches to identifying "unusual" (Habshah, Norazan, and Rahmatullah Imon 2009; Rambotti and Breiger 2020) observations.

5.1   Regression as Storytelling

Much as stories routinely reduce the complexities of lived experience to capture the essence of particular events, processes, or relationships, regression reduces the complexities in our data for the purpose of summarizing relationships within the data. When we use regression to tell a story about how religious habitus affects educational stratification (Horwitz et al. 2022), or how young peoples' substance abuse varies across policy contexts (Vuolo 2013), we rely on the coefficients and standard errors to establish the "who," "what," "where," "when," "why," or "how" (Burke 1969) of the story we are telling. In their book, *Regression and Other Stories*, Gelman and colleagues (2020: 93) emphasize this idea in their discussion of a relatively simple analysis forecasting elections. They observe that the findings "tell a story … based on the 'bread and peace' model created by political scientist Douglas Hibbs" (p. 93). However, as Gelman and colleagues elaborate throughout their book, far from being a straightforward representation of underlying realities, this process of data reduction and synthesis is both subtle and complex (Gelman et al. 2020).

While a regression equation can provide a reasonable and entirely appropriate anchor for the stories we tell about our data, anyone who has completed an introductory statistics course should know that there are a variety of factors that can affect the accuracy of these stories. Even when our data and chosen models meet the basic assumptions of regression analysis, there is still some risk that our results are being unduly shaped by one or more observations in the data. For this reason, we learn to check for "unusual" observations.

There are three types of unusual observations that researchers are commonly trained to look for when conducting statistical analyses: *outliers*, high *leverage* observations, or *influential* observations. Outliers are observations that differ significantly from the distribution of other observations. In a regression context, they can be defined as observations that are poorly predicted by the regression model, as indicated by unusually large residuals. Outliers attenuate model fit, and their removal should improve the model R^2 (although improvement in measured fit is, by itself, never a sufficient reason for ignoring an observation).

Leverage is a measure of how far an observation's values on the independent variables are from other observations in the dataset. When an observation's values on the independent variable are far from those of the other observations, the high-leverage observations will alter the fitted regression line. Leverage is assessed via diagonal values on the Hat matrix $(\mathbf{H})$. The presence of high leverage observations can increase (unduly) the model R^2.

Finally, *influence* can be thought of as a product of both outlierness and leverage. Influential observations are those whose removal from the data noticeably change the model coefficients. Common measures of influence are Cook's distance and DFBETA. Both measure the effect of removing each observation in the data, with Cook's distance measuring the effect net of the whole model and DFBETA assessing the impact on each predictor in the model.

Each of these constructs (*outliers, leverage,* and *influence*) and the methods used to detect them assume that certain observations or sets of observations are "unusual" (Habshah et al. 2009; Rambotti and Breiger 2020), necessarily implying that the rest of the data can be considered "usual." Yet, this assumption that most of the data are "usual" can be substantively, theoretically, and analytically problematic. As Belsley, Kuh, and Welsch (2004: 31) put it, "Unusual observations can only be recognized relative to the bulk of the remaining data that are considered to be typical, and we must select an initial base subset of observations to serve this purpose. But how is this subset to be found?" Moreover, sometimes differences between subsets of cases are not easily quantifiable, and thus may not be evident in the data. For example, in the context of the comparative study of welfare states, qualitative distinctions between observations – such as the difference between Christian-Democratic welfare states and Social-Democratic welfare states – are not easily operationalized quantitatively but may imply different explanations for key outcomes (Esping-Andersen 1990; Kersbergen 2003; Korpi and Shalev 1980). Consequently, far from there being "usual" and "unusual" observations, what we would reasonably consider substantively "usual" can differ a great deal between seemingly comparable sets of observations, as well as between different models. Similarly, intersectionality scholarship emphasizes critical differences in the experiences of people at the intersection of multiple forms of oppression, such that "usual" experiences and perceptions differ markedly based on the intersection of multiple social positions (Sewell 2015).

Accounting for these forms of heterogeneity is critical to ensuring that the stories we tell with regression represent the phenomena we are telling stories about. RIO facilitates the identification and elaboration of more complex stories than are usually told using regression. Rather than imposing a single linear ("usual") narrative, it allows for the possibility that there are multiple narratives that can emerge from the data. It provides a means for exploring and interrogating the results of the regression model that goes beyond stress-testing certain findings to ensure that no single observation or set of observations will undermine the story that the researcher has developed, as is the goal of conventional diagnostic techniques. When using RIO to look at how individual cases contribute to the overall regression model, it may be that cases with particularly large contributions are also outliers, high leverage points, or influential observations. However, it is also possible that clusters of seemingly typical observations represent major sources of action in the model and reveal distinct stories that are not captured by the overall coefficients or standard errors. It would be easy for this structuring of the data to go undetected, and easier still to miss out on other possible stories that might emerge from the data. In the examples that follow, we illustrate how RIO can be used to explore these possibilities.

5.2 Example 1: Inequality and Regional Integration

In 2006, Jason Beckfield published analyses exploring the links between regional integration and inequality. Observing that a robust collection of scholarship shows that globalization has increased income inequality in advanced capitalist economies, Beckfield contends that the construction of international economies and polities in negotiated regions – such as the European Union – should similarly contribute to increases in inequality. As he summarizes in the abstract,

Regional economic integration should raise income inequality, as workers are exposed to international competition and labor unions are weakened... political integration should drive welfare state retrenchment in market-oriented regional polities as states adopt liberal policies in a context of fiscal austerity.

Using both fixed effects (FE) and random effects (RE) models to analyze unbalanced panel data on 12 Western European countries, Beckfield explores this relationship and finds that regional integration explains nearly half of the increase in income inequality in countries analyzed in the article.

Beckfield's analyses are sophisticated, thorough, and thoughtful, and his findings are compelling. The analyses nevertheless reflect a key tension in comparative political economic research that uses multiple regression. As Shalev (2007: 263–64) summarizes,

[Multiple regression] works by rendering the cases invisible, treating them simply as the source of a set of empirical observations on dependent and independent variables. However, even when scholars embrace the analytical purpose of generalizing about relationships between variables, as opposed to dwelling on specific differences between entities with proper names, the cases of interest in comparative political economy are limited in number and occupy a bounded universe. They are thus both knowable and manageable. Consequently, retaining named cases in the analysis is an efficient way of conveying information and letting readers evaluate it. Moreover, in practice, most producers and consumers of comparative political economy are intrinsically interested in specific cases. Why not cater to this interest by keeping our cases visible?

While it should be evident that, as authors of a book on regression analysis, we are enthusiastic users of multiple regression, we also agree with Shalev's assertion that it is in everyone's interest to keep the cases visible, particularly in contexts where a key goal is to use variables to draw conclusions about those cases. Yet, this is not easily accomplished using conventional regression analysis, and becomes all the more challenging when cases (e.g., countries) are constituted by multiple observations (e.g., country-years). Here, we show how this can be accomplished by turning Beckfield's analyses inside out.

We start by turning the FE models inside out. We do this for two reasons. First, FE models can be estimated with OLS regression, making the math and corresponding code easier to follow. Second, as Beckfeld (2006: 971) notes, "The FEM provides a stringent test of the hypothesis that regional integration affects income inequality, given that the associations between the regional integration covariates and income inequality are estimated net of all unmeasured between-country effects." That is, Beckfield had methodological reasons to prioritize the FE model, and we have mathematical ones. After we have presented the results of the FE model, we turn the RE model inside out.

Before delving into these results, we note that FE models do not present any problems for RIO (see Section 3.5). FE models remove between cluster variation, either by including cluster-specific dummies or by simply norming the data within each cluster before the analysis (group mean centering). In the latter case, the FE model is estimated using OLS on normed data. This is the approach we take here – by removing the cluster mean from each cluster, between variability is removed and we estimate only the within effect. Because these data are longitudinal, we can easily compute – using the tools described in Chapter 2 – how clusters contribute to the overall model coefficients. That is, while the between-cluster variability is removed in an FE model, we can still compute the cluster's contribution to the within or FE. The between-cluster effect is removed before the analysis via norming the data, but RIO can tell us how each cluster contributes to the overall estimated within effect.

The first two columns of Table 5.2 reproduce the results of Beckfield's FE analyses, as presented in Table 2, p. 977 of the original article. Our Model 1 is identical to Beckfield's Model 4 (his full model). For our reanalysis, we standardize the variables. The results with standardized variables are presented in Model 2 of table 5.2. To turn the FE regression model inside out, we start by constructing a biplot of Model 2. This is presented in Figure 5.1. As detailed in earlier chapters, to construct this plot, we append $\hat{y}$ to the data matrix X, then take the SVD of the matrix.[1] The biplot represents only the first two dimensions of the model.

Figure 5.1 is difficult to interpret, as the cases largely cluster around the origin and overlap a great deal. Consequently, to better visualize how each country (case) contributes to the overall regression coefficient, we plotted

---

[1] As we discussed in Chapter 2 and Appendix B, SVD is a factorization of a matrix that yields three distinct matrices: an $n \times p$ matrix (U) of orthogonal row scores (where n is the number of rows and p is the number of columns in the original matrix), a $p \times p$ matrix of orthogonal column scores (V), and a $p \times p$ diagonal matrix of weights (S).

Table 5.2 Replication of Beckfield's (2006) results

	Fixed Effects Models		Random Effects Models	
	Model 1	Model 2	Model 3	Model 4
Year	0.018	0.030	0.354**	0.602**
	(0.181)	(0.308)	(0.116)	(0.198)
Political	0.068*	0.272*	0.057	0.231
Integration	(0.033)	(0.131)	(0.029)	(0.119)
Economic	1.602*	3.905*	1.232*	3.003*
Integration	(0.624)	(1.522)	(0.578)	(1.409)
Economic	−0.013*	−4.257*	−0.010**	−3.300**
Integration^2	(0.005)	(1.640)	(0.004)	(1.467)
GDP/cap	0.303	0.221	−0.594	−0.432
	(0.481)	(0.349)	(0.316)	(0.230)
Social Security	0.026	0.027	−0.210	−0.213
Transfers	(0.203)	(0.206)	(0.140)	(0.143)
FDI Outflow	−0.453	−0.140	−0.246	−0.076
	(0.412)	(0.127)	(0.403)	(0.124)

Note: $N = 48$. Following Beckfield (2006), *$p < 0.05$ using a one-tailed *t*-test (*$p < 0.10$ two-tailed test). FE analysis replicate Model 4, Table 2 (p. 977). RE analysis replicates Model 4, Table 1 (p. 975).

each country individually. We present plots for four countries in Figure 5.2: Denmark, Great Britain, Spain, and Italy. As detailed in Chapter 2, we can take the coordinates for the position of each observation and the coordinates for the origin ($x = 0$, $y = 0$) as opposite corners of a rectangle and calculate the area of the rectangle to identify each observation's contribution (in two dimensions).

To briefly revisit what these contributions tell us, they represent the intensities of association for each cluster with each variable, with the contributions summing to the (respective) overall regression coefficients for the full model. These intensities define the relationship among variables and cases in the field defined by the overall model space.

Examining each country's contributions, we see that for most countries, observations cluster around the origin. This is illustrated well by both Denmark (DNK) and Spain (ESP). There are two countries, however, that stand out as having particularly strong contributions to the overall model: Great Britain (GBR) and Italy (ITA). Both cases have observations farther from the origin, and those observations are aligned with the projection of

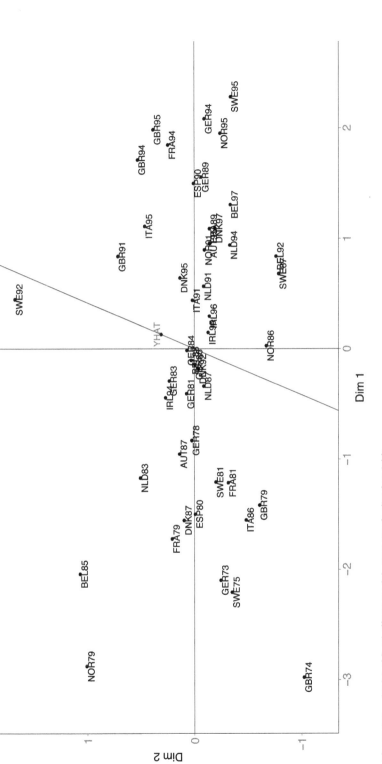

Figure 5.1 Biplot of fixed effects model using standardized variable

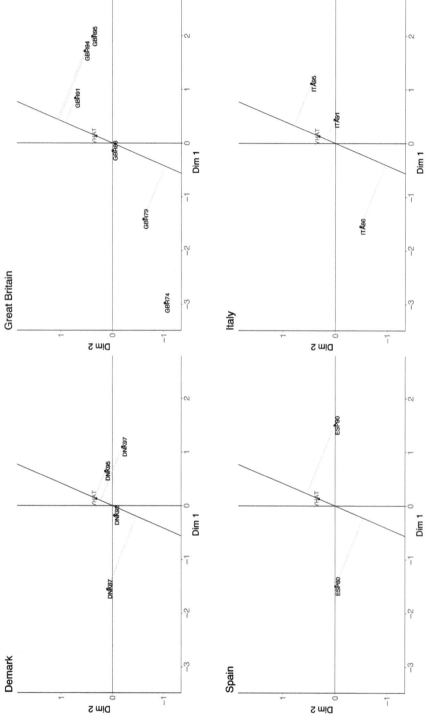

Figure 5.2 Biplots of Model 2, Table 5.2 for Denmark, Spain, Great Britain, and Italy

Table 5.3 Contributions of Great Britain and Italy versus other countries

	Great Britain	Italy	All Others	Unstandardized Coefficients (Model 1)
Year	0.046	0.085	−0.113	0.018
Political Integration	0.024	0.045	−0.001	0.068
Economic Integration	1.559	−0.17	0.213	1.602
Economic Integration^2	−0.012	0.001	−0.002	−0.013
GDP/cap	−0.005	−0.153	0.461	0.303
Social Security Transfers	0.001	−0.055	0.081	0.027
FDI Outflows	−0.171	−0.126	−0.156	−0.453

the fitted values. Given that the plot is illustrating the leading dimensions underlying the regression model, this suggests that these two countries are doing much of the heavy lifting for the coefficients in the model.

We can assess this more directly by comparing the contributions of Great Britain's six observations and Italy's three observations with the contributions of all other observations combined. These results are presented in Table 5.3. Focusing first on Beckfield's measure of Political Integration, our results show that Great Britain's six observations account for 35.3% of the FE of Political Integration (0.024/0.068), Italy's three observations account for 66.2% of the FE (0.045/0.068), while the remaining 10 countries (39 observations) attenuate the overall effect by 1.4% (−0.001/0.069). Turning to the coefficient for Economic Integration, we see again see that Italy and Great Britain have an outsized influence on the overall regression coefficient. Great Britain accounts for 97.3% of the overall regression coefficient (1.559/1.602), Italy attenuates the effect by 10.6% (−0.170/1.602), while the remaining 10 countries (39 observations) account for the 2.7% of the overall regression coefficient. Importantly, Italy's negative contribution still represents an outsized effect, as the countries other than Italy and Great Britain barely offset Italy's attenuation of the overall regression coefficient. Finally turning to Beckfield's measure of Economic Integration squared, consistent with the contributions to Economic Integration, Great Britain makes up 92.3% of the effect (−0.012/−0.013), while Italy again attenuates the effect, by 7.7% (0.001/−0.013), with the remaining countries accounting for 15.4% of the overall effect (−0.002/−0.013).

Table 5.4 FE with and without Great Britain (GBR) and Italy (ITA)

	Full Dataset	Without GBR and ITA
Year	0.018	−0.129
	(0.181)	(.156)
Political Integration	0.068[*]	0.048
	(0.033)	(.054)
Economic Integration	1.602[*]	0.722
	(0.624)	(.951)
Economic Integration^2	−0.013[*]	−0.006
	(0.005)	(0.007)
GDP/cap	0.303	0.546
	(0.481)	(.421)
Social Security Transfers	0.026	0.085
	(0.203)	(.170)
FDI Outflow	−0.453	−0.269
	(0.412)	(0.388)

Note: Following Beckfield (2006), [*]$p < 0.05$ using a one-tailed t-test
([*]$p < 0.10$ two-tailed test).

Looking inside the FE model thus indicates that the main results of the analysis are driven by variability internal to Great Britain and Italy. The effect of political integration is driven predominantly by Italy, whereas the effect of economic integration is driven by Great Britain. These outsized contributions suggest that the effects of integration may not generalize across all countries, but rather are more limited in scope. To assess whether these two countries in fact constitute the effects observed by Beckfield, we can rerun the FE model, omitting the nine observations for those two countries.

Table 5.4 replicates the FE model with and without Great Britain and Italy in the dataset. As the results show, none of the substantive variables are statistically significant when Great Britain and Italy are removed. These results suggest that the data do not, in fact, support the assertion that regional integration explains income inequality in Western European countries, net of a variety of control variables identified in the literature. Rather, they show that the effect of regional integration in Great Britain and Italy is so great that these two countries mask an otherwise null contribution across the remaining 10 cases (i.e., 39 observations).

It is important to emphasize that Beckfield could not reasonably have found what we do. Absent using RIO, as we have done, common methods for identifying influential observations that would have been available to

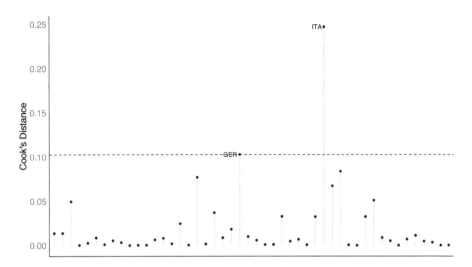

Figure 5.3   Cook's distance for Model 1, Table 5.2

Beckfield at the time these results were published do not clearly indicate that these two countries are driving the model. For the FE model, arguably the best diagnostic measure is Cook's distance. We compute Cook's distance for Model 1 of Table 5.2 and report results in Figure 5.3. We do this to evaluate whether it identifies Great Britain and Italy as problematic. The dashed line indicates the common threshold for high influence, where $D_i > 4/(n\text{-}k\text{-}1)$. Here, we see that one (out of three) observation from Italy and one from Germany is flagged. While this identifies Italy as a potentially problematic case, it also identifies Germany, which we found to be unproblematic. Moreover, it only identifies one observation from Italy and not the entire case.

Despite identifying Italy as potentially influential according to Cook's D, rerunning the analysis without Italy shows no meaningful difference in the results – the key variables remain statistically significant, and the direction of all significant variables is unchanged (see Table 5.5). The same is true if we drop *both* Italy and Germany (not shown).[2] In contrast, when we omit only Great Britain from the analysis, the effects disappear. This is particularly notable, as it shows that, of the two countries (i.e., cases) identified as driving the results using RIO, the one that is *not* identified as problematic using the

---

[2] Dropping the observations for these two cases attenuates the effect sizes of significant variables, but these variables remain significant and similarly conform with the published results.

Table 5.5 FE without Italy, without Great Britain

	Without Italy	Without Great Britain
Year	−0.113	−0.025
	(0.173)	(0.162)
Political Integration	0.100*	0.051
	(0.052)	(0.03)
Economic Integration	1.571*	0.239
	(0.587)	(1.011)
Economic Integration^2	−0.013*	−0.003
	(0.005)	(0.008)
GDP/cap	0.664	0.314
	(0.465)	(0.433)
Social Security Transfers	0.080	0.037
	(0.188)	(0.184)
FDI Outflow	−0.579	−0.295
	(0.403)	(0.388)
N	45	42

Note: Following Beckfield (2006), *$p < 0.05$ using a one-tailed *t*-test
(*$p < 0.10$ two-tailed test).

most common method for detecting influence that was available to Beckfield is driving the results of the model. This further reinforces (i) the value added of RIO, and (ii) that the author of the original analysis could not have reasonably been expected to identify this source of heterogeneity in the context of FE models.

Turning to Models 3 and 4 from Table 5.2, we now work with the RE results. Model 3 closely replicates[3] Beckfield's Model 4 from Table 1 (p. 975). Considering that both the FE and RE models are doing much of the same thing, at least in terms of the estimation of the FE, we will not reproduce all the results we estimated for the FE models. Rather, our aim is to illustrate that the inside out versions of the FE and RE models are very similar. Figure 5.4, based on Model 4, is the RE version of Figure 5.2 (based on Model 2) and shows the same patterns as Figure 5.2. Here again, we see that Italy and Great Britain drive the effects of political and economic integration, and subsequent results are similar in this context as well.[4]

---

[3] There are minor differences between our replication of the RE models and Beckfield's original analysis, but they are nearly identical.

[4] In online replication materials (see Chapter 1), we illustrate how to turn this random intercept model inside out. We discussed this in Chapter 3, but did not provide an example.

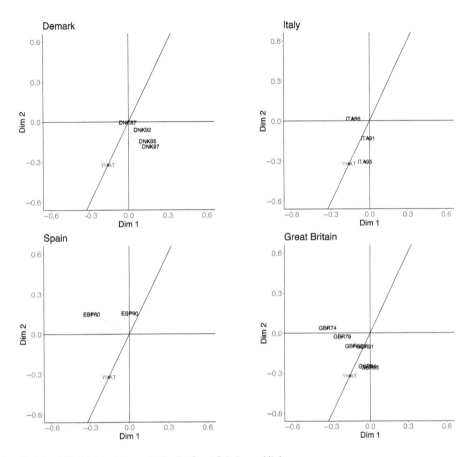

Figure 5.4   Biplots of Model 4 for Denmark, Spain, Great Britain, and Italy

For FE models, the best diagnostic tool available is Cook's distance. However, in the context of RE models, there are cluster-level diagnostics that are better suited to identifying influential *cases*. Specifically, in 2010, Cook's distance was generalized to the cluster level in the context of mixed models (Van der Meer, Te Grotenhuis, and Pelzer 2010). Figure 5.5 shows the case-level Cook's distance, and we see that this method does flag Great Britain as having an outsized effect on inequality, along with the Netherlands.

We want to highlight three important points with regard to the cluster-level Cook's distance. First, turning the model inside out does not indicate that the Netherlands is driving the results, and when we drop the Netherlands from the data and rerun the analyses, the only thing that changes is that the significance for Political Integration drops from $p < 0.05$ to $p < 0.10$, which is still within the threshold for statistical significance used by Beckfield. Thus again,

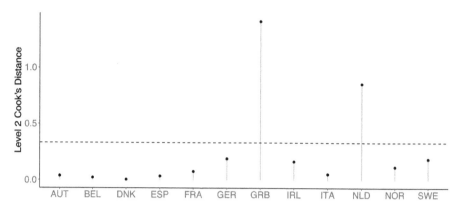

Figure 5.5   Cook's distance for clusters from Model 3, Table 5.2

just as we found when we calculated Cook's distance at the observation level for the FE results, Cook's distance flags one of the cases that we identify as driving the action of the regression model, but also identifies another that does not play an equivalent role. Second, while cluster-level Cook's distance allows us to identify influential sets of observations using RE models, we are aware of no similar methods other than RIO that would allow us to account for these contributions using FE models. Finally, this method for estimating cluster-level Cook's distance was developed after Beckfield's (2006) paper was published, meaning that the more conventional diagnostic tool capable of showing Italy and Great Britain's outsized contributions was not available to him. We emphasize this final point to again reinforce that there was no reasonable basis for Beckfield to have concluded that the results do not generalize across all observations in his original analysis.

Taken together, the results of our reanalysis indicate that what we find when we turn the regression model inside out is more complicated than the story implied by conventional regression analysis. Here, the "action" of our story is really taking place in two cases. While a conventional approach to regression generalizes the action to all observations in the model, turning the model inside out reveals a more complex reality underlying the data.

5.3   Example 2: Poverty, Inequality, and Life Expectancy

Over the past 40 years, an extensive multidisciplinary collection of scholarship on the economic determinants of health has emerged. While a great deal of scholarship has advanced this area of study, as Rambotti (2015: 123) notes, the publication of Richard Wilkinson and Kate Pickett's (2011) book *The Spirit Level* "marked a pivotal moment in the literature on health disparities." Wilkinson and Pickett make the case that a huge array of social ills – from poor health to violence to incarceration – are the product of economic inequalities. Specifically with regard to health, they posit that income inequality has a deleterious effect on health outcomes. They develop these claims empirically through a series of cross-sectional, bivariate regression analyses comparing across countries and across states within the USA.

Despite a great deal of praise, Wilkinson and Pickett's claims regarding the links between income inequality and life expectancy were not uncontroversial. Their work in this area contributed to an extensive collection of scholarship that has found, at best, mixed evidence for the links between income inequality and health. For example, through a meta-analysis of 28 studies that collectively included more than 60 million subjects, Kondo and colleagues (2009: 8) find evidence to suggest that income inequality is associated with only a "modest excess risk of premature mortality" (quoted in Rambotti 2015). Similarly, other cross-national studies find little evidence that income inequality has adverse health consequences (e.g., Beckfield 2004).

In a 2015 article, Rambotti (2015) revisited Wilkinson and Pickett's data and extended their analyses. Building on research showing that economic factors have a nonlinear effect on health outcomes, he argues that inequality should matter more for life expectancy at the high end of the income distribution, while poverty – which Wilkinson and Pickett did not directly measure in their analysis – should matter more at the bottom of the income distribution. Rambotti (2015) shows that inequality and poverty interact across countries, such that inequality matters little in countries with low levels of poverty, while the detrimental effects of inequality are strong in countries with high rates of poverty.

Following a rebuttal by Pickett and Wilkinson (2015), Rambotti and Breiger (2020) published a series of analyses that used RIO to explore how a focus on the cases underlying the regression coefficients can offer deeper insights into the mixed findings that characterize the literature on the relationship between income inequality and health. Their analysis provides an exemplary illustration of how RIO can be used to understand the multiple story lines that are embedded in the regression model. Here, we partially replicate their analysis and extend their work by decomposing the variance in the model.[5]

---

[5] In the original analysis, Rambotti and Breiger apply RIO only to assess cases' contributions to the coefficients.

Table 5.6 Replicating Rambotti and Breiger (2020)

	Model 1	Model 2	Model 3	Model 4
Inequality	−0.356		−0.732*	−0.675*
	(0.214)		(0.267)	(0.238)
Poverty		0.066	0.559	0.752**
		(0.229)	(0.267)	(0.250)
Inequality x Poverty				−0.488*
				(0.200)
N	20	20	20	20
R²	0.126	0.004	0.297	0.479

Rambotti and Breiger's analysis focuses on four OLS regression models, replicated here in Table 5.6. Models 1 and 2 show results for bivariate regression of life expectancy on inequality and poverty, with neither effect reaching $p < 0.05$. In Model 3, inequality reaches conventional levels of statistical significance with the inclusion of poverty, while Model 4 provides evidence that the two variables interact. The interaction effect supports Rambotti's (2015) hypothesis that the effects of inequality vary based on levels of poverty. Rambotti and Breiger turn these models inside out to see which cases are driving the observed statistical effects (or lack thereof). We focus our attention on the bivariate analyses, examining the effects of inequality (Model 1) and poverty (Model 2), which show null effects for each variable.

Turning first to the decomposition of model 1, Figure 5.6a[6] plots standardized measures of life expectancy against income inequality for the 20 countries included in the analysis. The size of the points in the plot is proportional to each country's contribution to the overall regression coefficient. Interpreting the meaning of each case's contribution to the overall regression coefficient, the authors write,

Those contributions with positive signs are produced by countries whose x and y values are on the same side of the origin (e.g., Switzerland and Denmark in [Figure 5.6a]). Conversely, contributions with negative signs result when countries are above average on one variable and below average on the other (e.g., Sweden and the United States in [Figure 5.6a]).

They proceed by detailing how the effect of income inequality on life expectancy is driven by the four countries with the largest individual contributions to the

---

[6] Figure 5.6a replicates Rambotti and Breiger's Figure 2, p. 6.

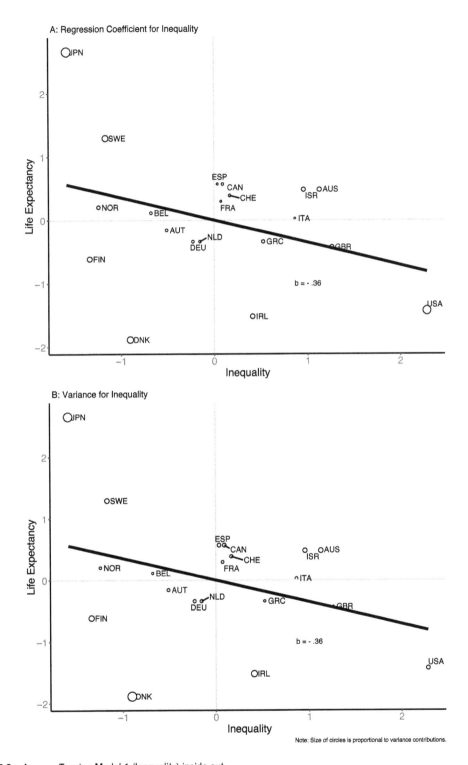

Figure 5.6a–b   Turning Model 1 (Inequality) inside out

regression coefficient: Denmark (0.0896), Japan (−0.2209), Sweden (−0.0795), and the United States (−0.1724). Summing across these four high-contributing countries shows that their aggregate contribution is −0.3832, which is almost exactly the overall regression coefficient (−0.3557). The remaining 16 countries contribute negligibly (0.0275) to the overall regression coefficient.

In Figure 5.6b, we replicate this plot, but the size of each point is proportional to each country's contribution to the variance. We calculate contributions using the squared residuals approach. Here we see that two countries are contributing the most to the overall variance: Japan and Denmark. Together, these two observations account for 55.8% of the overall model variance, with Denmark contributing 29.3% and Japan 26.5%. In contrast, the United States and Sweden together contribute only 7%.

In contexts where there are substantive or theoretical reasons to believe that the relationship will differ across subsets of the data, assessing the degree to which those subsets are contributing to the overall variance of the model allows us to descriptively assess the degree to which these differences represent a story line that is distinct from the overall regression model. We want to reemphasize the point made in Chapter 4 that this approach to decomposing the error term cannot be equated with traditional standard errors and used as a basis for inference; instead, it is a descriptive measure of a case's contribution to the coefficient error.

The fact that Denmark and Japan have outsized contributions to the model variance indicates that they may represent substantively meaningful anomalies to the overall trend, and therefore warrant deeper investigation. This interpretation of the variance contributions benefits from considering *how* each of the four high-contributing cases is shaping the model. Specifically, we look at the relative contributions of each case. Japan, Sweden, and the United States all have relatively large negative contributions to the overall (negative) regression coefficient. However, consistent with its position on the negative side of the origin on both the x and y axes, Denmark's contribution is positive. While Denmark's absolute contribution to the overall regression coefficient is not the largest (the largest is Japan's), the fact that its large effect attenuates the overall coefficient, in conjunction with it having the largest contribution to the overall variance, indicates that what Denmark is contributing to our understanding of the relationship between inequality and life expectancy is quite different than what the other countries are contributing.

At a case level, Rambotti and Breiger interrogate Denmark's contribution in greater detail. They first show that by omitting this one country from the

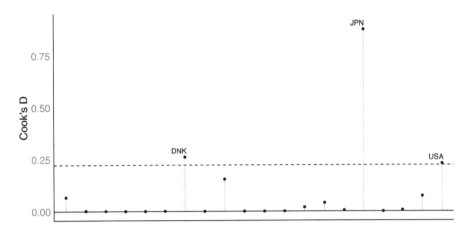

Figure 5.7   Cook's distance for Table 5.4, Model 1

data, the regression coefficient changes from −0.356 to −0.470 and becomes statistically significant ($p = 0.02$).[7] They then use qualitative data to explore why Denmark – with very low levels of economic inequality and poverty – nevertheless has the lowest life expectancy of any country in the data. Summarizing their case-based analysis of Denmark, they write,

Low longevity among Danes is well documented in the health literature. A possible explanation looks at the role of wealth inequality [as opposed to income inequality] … which is particularly high in Denmark. However, a number of analyses identify a more specific contribution to low longevity: the high risk of mortality for women born between the two world wars (pp. 8–9).

They proceed by citing research showing that interwar women in Denmark exhibited rates of smoking that exceed the rates for women in any other European country, resulting in higher rates of mortality among that cohort which, in turn, drives down overall life expectancy in the country. What is so striking about this assessment is that, if correct, the effects of this historically specific driver of low longevity will fade over time, thereby altering the statistical relationship between income inequality and longevity.

While RIO points us toward Denmark as the most *substantively* influential case, conventional measures of statistical influence (i.e., Cook's distance) point to Japan as the most *statistically* influential. Figure 5.7 plots the Cook's distance for Model 1. As in Figure 5.3, the dashed line marks $D_i > 4/(n\text{-}k\text{-}1)$

---

[7] Consistent with Rambotti and Breiger (2020), for this nonrandom sample of countries we report *p* values only for the purpose of descriptive assessment of model fit.

Table 5.7 Results for Model 1, Table 5.6 with countries omitted

	w/o Japan	w/o Denmark	w/o USA	w/o Japan, Denmark, and USA
Inequality	−0.155	−0.465*	−0.359	−0.094
	(0.197)	(0.187)	(0.218)	(0.193)
N	19	19	19	17
R²	0.033	0.255	0.131	0.015

as our threshold for identifying influential cases. While Denmark and the United States are both identified as being influential using this threshold, their influence is less than half that of Japan.

Table 5.7 presents a series of bivariate OLS models regressing life expectancy on inequality but omitting in turn each of the countries identified as highly influential using Cook's distance, and then omitting all of them at the same time. As expected, dropping Japan and rerunning the model results in a greater change in the coefficient; however, it does nothing to change the substantive story of the overall regression coefficient (i.e., the effect of inequality still fails to meet conventional standards for statistical significance, indicating that income inequality has no discernible effect on life expectancy). Similarly, dropping the United States or all three observations (Denmark, Japan, and the United States) together in no way alters the substantive story associated with a standard interpretation of the regression coefficient. In contrast, when we drop just Denmark, the effect of inequality reaches conventional thresholds for significance. The reason that we see this shift only when we drop Denmark (and not when we drop all the influential cases in conjunction) is because removing Japan and the United States along with Denmark omits the cases that are driving the negative relationship between inequality and life expectancy. Taken together, these results illustrate the difference between detecting the action in the regression model versus identifying statistically influential cases.

Turning now to Model 2, Figure 5.8a plots the standardized measure of life expectancy against poverty, with point sizes proportional to each case's contribution to the coefficient. Again, in Figure 5.8b, point sizes are proportional to contributions to the variance. As Rambotti and Breiger detail, the same countries – Denmark (0.1155), Japan (0.0566), Sweden (−0.0720), and the United States (−0.1594) – drive the results for Model 2, this time with Israel also making a substantial contribution (0.0617). However, in this analysis, the contributions of these five cases effectively cancel one another out,

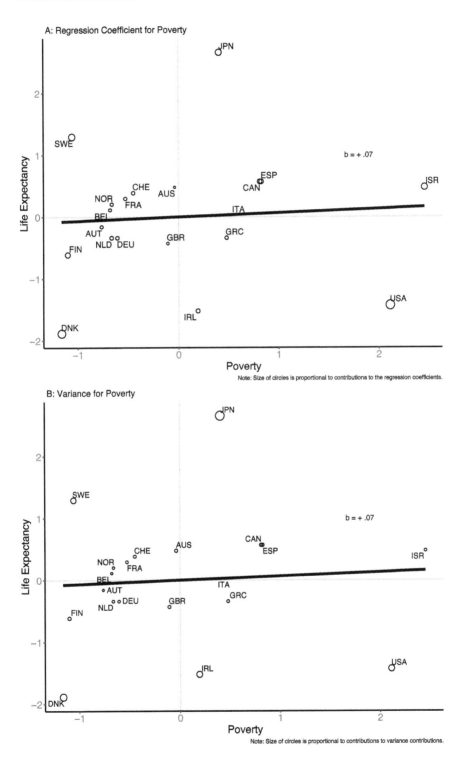

Figure 5.8a–b   Turning Model 2 (Poverty) inside out

summing to 0.0024. In contrast, the remaining 15 cases sum to 0.0633 (~95% of the overall regression coefficient).

Considering the five high-value countries, the fact that the contributions of Denmark, Israel, Japan, Sweden, and the United States cancel one another out suggests the possibility of multiple underlying stories within that set of cases. Sweden and the United States fully conform with the story that higher levels of poverty decrease life expectancy. In contrast, Denmark and Israel seem to suggest the inverse.

As Figure 5.8b shows, these five countries are also contributing the most to the overall variance, with Japan making by far the largest contribution. Together, these five countries account for 77.3% of the overall model variance, with Japan alone contributing 36.6%. Thus, in this model, this outsized contribution to the variance points to Japan in particular as complicating the larger story of the relationship between poverty and life expectancy, warranting further exploration.

Again, Rambotti and Breiger's case-level analyses support this conclusion. In their examination of Japan, they note that following World War II life expectancy in Japan was approximately 20 years lower than in most Western European nations, but by 1990, the life expectancy in Japan was higher than in any other country in the world. While they review several existing explanations for this turnaround, including culture and diet, they highlight one explanation in particular as being the most sociologically interesting. As they write,

… this shift toward healthier lifestyles and dietary habits is the result of a precise political agenda. In fact, as the Japanese economy started growing after World War II, the health and longevity of Japanese people prospered under 'the government's strong stewardship in investing in key interventions for public health' (Ikeda et al. 2011: 1094).

They proceed by detailing how Japan's high life expectancy was driven by explicit government programs intended to foster greater health and longevity. This suggests that policy priorities at the national level explain why Japan is such an outlier in the relationship between poverty and life expectancy.

While Rambotti and Breiger's own analyses further explore how a case-based approach can inform our understanding of Models 3 and 4 in Table 5.6, our replication and extension of their analyses illustrate how RIO can be used to detect the action that suggests multiple story lines and show how the decomposition of standard errors can be used to descriptively explore which contributions appear to represent signal versus noise.

5.4   Example 3: Dog Ownership in the United States

In our final example, we provide an illustration of one possible way that RIO can be used for exploratory data analysis. We do this through a simple analysis of the determinants of dog ownership using data from the 2018 GSS (Smith et al. 1970–2019). In this wave of the GSS, respondents who reported that their family had a pet were asked the question, "What kind of pet does your family have?" The survey offered 10 options for types of pet, one of which was "Dog." We use logistic regression to assess the correlates of dog ownership. For the sake of simplicity, we focus on the difference between respondents who report owning a dog versus those who do not own a dog but do report owning a pet ($N = 558$).

While we have no real theory of dog ownership, for the purposes of our illustration, it is useful to start with a basic explanatory framework (a naïve theory, of sorts) to guide our analysis, interpretation, and subsequent "story" about dog ownership. A researcher might reasonably assume that dogs (like many other pets) require a moderate amount of time, labor, and expense. They need to be exercised regularly and require daily feeding and routine visits to the veterinarian. For this reason, people who own dogs likely need to be at least moderately physically active and have sufficient resources to pay for food and medical care. We might therefore hypothesize that people with higher incomes will be more likely to own a dog, whereas the probability of dog ownership will decline with age due to reduced time and/or physical abilities. Because of these requirements, a common motivation for owning a dog is to gain practice in care work. For instance, a casual web search for "why get a dog?" returns a variety of websites that suggest dog ownership as a good way for both children and would-be parents to learn or cultivate responsibility. Therefore, we might hypothesize that people who are married will be more likely to own a dog than people who are not. Finally, it seems reasonable that kids might ask their parents for family dogs, so we would hypothesize that the more kids a family has, the more people there are asking for a dog, which increases the probability that the family will adopt.

Based on these expectations, we specify a model. We include as independent variables marital status (1 = married, 0 = not married), number of children, age, and income. We also control for respondent's sex (1 = classified as female, 0 = male) and race (1 = White, 0 = other). With this as our point of departure, Table 5.8 presents results of a logistic regression of dog ownership. Consistent with our expectations, we see that married respondents are more likely to own a dog, as are men. Moreover, the odds of dog ownership

Table 5.8 Correlates of dog ownership

Race	−0.392
	(0.281)
Sex	0.414*
	(0.200)
Children	0.144*
	(0.068)
Married	0.417*
	(0.21)
Age	−0.007
	(0.006)
Income	0.025
	(0.046)
Constant	0.806
	(0.612)
N	588

increase with each additional child. Race, age, and income have no significant effect on the probability of dog ownership.

In this context, the utility of a case-oriented approach to regression may not be immediately apparent. We are using survey data where individuals are the unit of analysis, and data were collected using a representative sample from a known population. With these kind of data, most reasonable analysts have little interest in the cases themselves. Unlike in analyses where the individual observations are of inherent interest in their own right, the fact that regression renders individuals "invisible" (Shalev 2007: 263) seems to be entirely unproblematic.

Yet, there may be instances where we want to know more about the cases than conventional regression can tell us. For example, while we have some basic expectations about factors that affect the likelihood of dog ownership, there are a variety of reasons to expect nonrandom variation within the population, which would point to more than one "story" for our data to tell. For example, we assume that dogs are family pets. However, some people may choose to own a dog for companionship in the absence of family. In their book, *Modern Romance*, comedian Aziz Ansari and sociologist Eric Klinenberg (2015) report that, when online dating, men who use a profile picture that includes a pet are more successful than those who do not. They find that the opposite is true for women. Thus, perhaps there is reason to expect a different story to emerge for unmarried men versus unmarried women versus married individuals. Each of these possibilities implies a case-oriented logic that emphasizes how the variables (and the relationships among them) are co-constituted by the cases (for a more detailed discussion, see Chapter 8) and allows for the possibility that the relationships among variables will differ across subsets of cases.

While researchers can use theory to guide exploratory analysis, lacking any real theory (and to serve illustrative purposes), we use an entirely inductive approach here and apply a clustering algorithm to partition the data. Importantly, the subsequent aggregation and interpretation of clusters' contributions to the overall regression coefficient are identical regardless of whether the clusters are defined inductively or deductively.

Our first step in this process is to identify subgroups within the data. We have proposed elsewhere (Breiger and Melamed 2014; Melamed, Breiger, and Schoon 2013) that a useful way to do this is by using a standard clustering algorithm on the matrix $\mathbf{U}$, which is the orthogonalized row space obtained using SVD on the matrix of independent variables ($\mathbf{X}$).[8] Clustering on $\mathbf{U}$ is more effective than clustering on $\mathbf{X}$ because the data have been clarified through the orthogonalization process (Skillicorn 2006: 371; van de Geer 1971: 256–57).

To identify sets of cases within the data, we use k-means clustering, which completely partitions the observations into a predetermined number of clusters such that the distance between each case and its corresponding cluster mean is minimized. K-means provisionally allocates each data point to each cluster and recomputes the cluster mean with the addition/subtraction of each data point, with the goal of minimizing the movement of each cluster's mean (Hothorn and Everitt 2006). When using k-means to cluster data, the analyst specifies the number of starting points (i.e., cluster means) and the number of iterations. With large data, a low number of starting points and iterations can produce inconsistencies such that the clustering solution cannot be replicated. Consequently, we use a high number of starting points and iterations (for our analyses, we use 10,000). Our use of k-means to cluster the data was not driven by substantive considerations or a belief that it is the best clustering algorithm. K-means' primary advantage is its low runtime.

To identify the most parsimonious clustering of data, we run 9 k-means cluster analyses with 2 through 10 clusters. Then, following Hothorn and Everitt (2006), we compute the total within sums of squared errors for each analysis. We then plot the within sums of squared errors by number of clusters. This plot can be interpreted like a scree plot, where we look for an inflection point or "knee" in the plot. This inflection point indicates the number of

---

[8] For more on clustering algorithms and potential issues associated with their use, see Chapter 6.

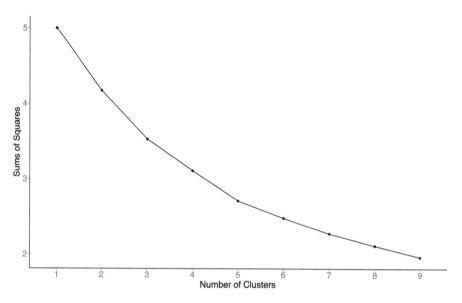

Figure 5.9   Sums of squared errors for *k*-means cluster solutions

clusters that best balance model fit (i.e., smaller sums of squared errors) and parsimony (the fewest clusters).

Figure 5.9 plots the within sums of squared errors for *k*-means with 2 through 10 clusters. Based on this plot, it seems that a 3-cluster or 5-cluster solution is best, but there is an ever-so-slightly clearer inflection point at 5 clusters. Moving forward with the 5-cluster solution, we can explore what substantively distinguishes the cases (i.e., individual respondents) that constitute each of these clusters from those in other clusters. While this can be done in a variety of ways, we focus our attention on descriptive patterns across clusters.

Table 5.9 reports within-cluster descriptive statistics for each of the five clusters. As these statistics show, all respondents in Cluster 1 are married White men, with an average of almost two children. Moreover, the GSS measures income in 12 categories, with 12 being the highest measured income level. Here, we see that the average income of respondents in Cluster 1 is 11.82. Finally, the average age is almost 46. The key distinguishing feature of Cluster 2 is that all respondents are White women. Just over half are married, and respondents average 1.665 children. Like Cluster 1, respondents in Cluster 2 have incomes higher than the overall average. In Cluster 3, all respondents are non-White. Nearly 60% are male, and just over one-third are married. They have, on average, lower income than the two clusters of

Table 5.9 Descriptive statistics by cluster

		Race	Sex	Children	Married	Age	Income	Distinguishing Characteristics of Cluster
Cluster 1	Mean	1.000	1.000	1.914	1.000	45.680	11.820	White, married men
(N = 105)	Min	1.000	1.000	0.000	1.000	20.000	8.000	
	Max	1.000	1.000	5.000	1.000	79.000	12.000	
Cluster 2	Mean	1.000	0.000	1.665	0.522	48.670	11.650	White women
(N = 209)	Min	1.000	0.000	0.000	0.000	18.000	8.000	
	Max	1.000	0.000	8.000	1.000	89.000	12.000	
Cluster 3	Mean	0.000	0.587	2.217	0.370	45.200	11.280	Non-White
(N = 92)	Min	0.000	0.000	0.000	0.000	19.000	7.000	
	Max	0.000	1.000	8.000	1.000	83.000	12.000	
Cluster 4	Mean	0.615	0.462	2.038	0.231	48.460	2.846	Low income
(N = 26)	Min	0.000	0.000	0.000	0.000	18.000	1.000	
	Max	1.000	1.000	7.000	1.000	89.000	6.000	
Cluster 5	Mean	1.000	1.000	1.817	0.000	50.470	11.230	White, unmarried men
(N = 126)	Min	1.000	1.000	0.000	0.000	19.000	7.000	
	Max	1.000	1.000	6.000	0.000	89.000	12.000	
All data	Mean	0.817	0.532	1.855	0.450	47.930	11.120	
(N = 558)	Min	0.000	0.000	0.000	0.000	18.000	1.000	
	Max	1.000	1.000	8.000	1.000	89.000	12.000	

entirely White respondents, are slightly younger, and have more children on average. Cluster 4 is comprised of low-income respondents. This cluster is just over 60% White, just less than half male, but on average has more children than the population average and all clusters except Cluster 3. Cluster 5 is demographically very similar to Cluster 1, except all respondents are *unmarried* and they are, on average slightly older, slightly less wealthy, and have slightly fewer children.

With these distinct clusters of cases identified, we can explore how each cluster is contributing to the overall effects reported in Table 5.8 and explore effect heterogeneity within our data. Table 5.10 reports the contributions of each cluster. Sums across any row of Table 5.10 are equal to the corresponding logistic regression coefficient in Table 5.8. What is immediately apparent is that there is, in fact, heterogeneity across clusters. The feature arguably distinguishing the five clusters the most is race, with three clusters composed entirely of White respondents, one composed entirely of non-White respondents, and only one that includes both White and non-White respondents.

Table 5.10 Logistic regression coefficients by cluster

	Cluster 1 (White married men)	Cluster 2 (White women)	Cluster 3 (Exclusively Non-White)	Cluster 4 (White & Non-White, Low income)	Cluster 5 (White unmarried men)
Race	0.287	0.368	−1.371	−0.029	0.353
Sex	0.582	−0.678	0.107	−0.003	0.405
# Children	−0.012	0.071	0.031	0.013	0.041
Married	0.641	0.158	0.053	0.037	−0.472
Age	−0.003	−0.002	−0.002	0.000	0.000
Income	0.008	0.023	0.041	−0.072	0.025
Intercept	−0.492	0.012	0.862	0.847	−0.423

For that reason (and despite being nonsignificant in the overall model), the relationship between race and dog ownership across clusters can help us make sense of what these contributions are telling us.

Clusters 1, 2, and 5 all have positive contributions (0.287, 0.368, and 0.353, respectively) for race, while Cluster 3 has a strong negative contribution (−1.371) and Cluster 4 has a small negative value (−0.029). The difference between positive and negative contributions follows an intuitive logic: the overall effect of race indicates that non-White people are more likely to own a dog, therefore the association between race and dog ownership is positive among clusters that have only White respondents (Clusters 1, 2, and 5) and negative in the cluster that includes only non-White respondents.

In this context, Cluster 4 tells the most novel story about the effect of race on dog ownership, as it is the only cluster that includes both White and non-White respondents. While still predominantly White (61.5%), Cluster 4 nevertheless slightly attenuates the effect of race. What this suggests is that, for this cluster, race – or, more specifically, being White – does not have the same effect on the probability of dog ownership among people who have substantially lower income as it does for respondents in other clusters.

Similarly, when we look at the effects of marriage (which does reach a conventional threshold for statistical significance), we see that all clusters contribute positively to the effect of marriage except for Cluster 5, where none of the respondents are married. The strongest contribution by far is in Cluster 1, where all respondents are married. Again, focusing on Clusters 2–4 where marital status is not a defining feature of the cluster itself, we see that regardless of race or income, marriage is positively associated with dog ownership.

We can similarly explore heterogeneity in clusters' contributions to variables that do not meaningfully distinguish the respondents in each cluster.

Turning our attention to the effect of age, while the average age for each cluster ranges from just under 46 years old to just over 50 years old, the average age for the overall population is approximately 48. Thus, while there are differences, they are not so stark that we would consider age a meaningful marker distinguishing the cases representing each cluster.

Despite the absence of substantively meaningful differences in the age of respondents across clusters, we do see meaningful differences in the effect of age. The coefficient for age in the overall model rounds to −0.008. This coefficient is effectively driven by the first three clusters. If we look at the contributions down to the fifth decimal place (not shown), we see that Cluster 4 has a slight negative contribution while Cluster 5 has a slight positive contribution. However, for all intents and purposes, respondents who are low-income (Cluster 4) and White, unmarried men (Cluster 5) make no distinguishable contribution to the effect of age. Again, the "story" implied by the coefficient for age in the overall model differs between Clusters 1–3 versus Clusters 4–5.

This is a simple illustration of one way that RIO can be used to explore where the action is in the regression model and identify multiple story lines underlying our data. Despite its simplicity, it allows us to illustrate a novel application using logistic regression. It is also suggestive of how a case-oriented approach to regression can yield novel insights, even when analyzing large-N data that meet the core assumptions driving conventional interpretations of regression models, a topic we explore further in Chapter 8.

5.5 Summary

In this chapter, we have illustrated a range of ways that RIO can be used to locate the "action" in a regression model. While regression is, by design, a variable-oriented method of analysis, we use those variables to tell stories about people, organizations, countries, and many other varieties of cases. When both the data and the model meet key assumptions, we can reasonably assume that the stories implied by regression coefficients apply to the cases in our data and beyond. However, there are often reasons to expect heterogeneity, and particularly when cases are of individual interest – such as when they are organizations or countries – it is important not only to allow for, but to explore the possibility that there is more than one story underlying our data. Whether simply partitioning our data (inductively or deductively) to evaluate distinct tendencies within the model coefficients, exploring which observations are contributing signal versus noise in our analysis, or identifying influential cases that are otherwise hidden inside the model and undetectable via standard approaches, turning a regression model inside out adds analytic depth and fosters greater dialogue between theory and method, getting more out of the standard regression model. We illustrated these points through three examples. Each of the examples uses a different form of the Generalized Linear Model, relies on different types of data with distinct units of analysis, and engages with different substantive areas.

6 Interaction Detection

As we have emphasized throughout the preceding chapters, unlike regression diagnostics where the goal is to improve our analysis by altering either the data or the model itself, the primary purpose of RIO is to learn more from the model at hand. However, sometimes learning more about what is happening inside our model suggests specific ways that the model can be improved. One thing that RIO allows us to do with particular ease is to identify discontinuities in statistical effects across subsets of cases. These discontinuities indicate nonlinear relationships, which conventional regression analysis accounts for by estimating interaction or polynomial terms.

In this chapter, we show how RIO's ability to reveal discontinuities in effects across subsets of cases can be used to detect statistical interaction effects (Melamed, Breiger, and Schoon 2013). As we show in Chapter 5 (and detail further in Chapter 8), discontinuities in the effects of certain variables can be productively explored without revising the model to include an interaction term. However, there will be instances where it is more desirable to retain a conventional approach to regression and revise the model by incorporating an interaction term. In such cases, RIO not only reveals nonlinearities, but also provides an inductive framework for consistently identifying statistically significant interaction effects. Of course, there are theoretical and historical reasons that social scientists might test or predict statistical interactions (Collins 2000; Crenshaw 1991), such as the one discovered in our first example below. But here we illustrate the intuition and logic of using RIO to infer statistical interactions.

In the sections that follow, we describe two different approaches to inductively identifying statistical interaction effects using RIO. First, we present an approach that relies on subsetting case contributions to coefficients by states of an important/theoretically motivated predictor, or by clusters of cases.[1] This approach builds squarely on the logic of examining variation in subsets

---

[1] This approach has been published previously. See Melamed, Breiger, and Schoon (2013).

of cases' contributions to the regression model, as illustrated in preceding chapters. In this context, by identifying systematic variation in the effects of predictors, we can infer likely candidates for statistical interactions. Consider a statistical interaction between a dummy variable and any other predictor. Using RIO, we can subset cases by the dummy variable and examine how the effect of the other predictor varies between subsets of the data. A statistical interaction effect means that the effect of one predictor variable is contingent on the value of another predictor variable. Finding large differences in estimated effects by subsets indicates an interaction effect that could be included in a subsequent model.

Our second approach to interaction detection identifies whether any particular predictor interacts with any of the other predictors in a model by regressing each case's contribution to that corresponding regression coefficient on the independent variable matrix. This approach relies on statistical benchmarks rather than case-level exploration. While descriptively less rich, it is exceptionally reliable in its identification of interactions that meet conventional thresholds for significance.

6.1   Decomposing by Predictor States or Clusters

Our first approach is particularly useful for the purposes of exploratory data analysis (see also Melamed, Breiger, and Schoon 2013). In order to use RIO for exploratory data analysis or to look at how patterns of effects vary by covariates, we need to decompose our baseline regression model to obtain each observation's additive contribution to the regression coefficients (see Chapters 2 and 3 for details on how this is accomplished). This decomposition gives us $\mathbf{P}$, the p by n matrix whose rows sum to the regression coefficients. When we sum over the columns by subsets of cases, we are able to use $\mathbf{P}$ to infer patterns or identify potential interaction effects. An interaction effect is implied by discontinuities in the contributions to the overall regression coefficient across clusters.

To illustrate, we use a simple multiple regression model predicting respondents' education in the General Social Survey from 2016 (Smith et al. 1972–2019). These data entail responses from 2,856 respondents. We predict education by whether the respondent identifies as "white" (=1), whether the respondent identifies as "female" (=1), and paternal occupational prestige. For simplicity, we standardize all variables (z-transform) and (thereby) suppress the intercept in the regression model.

Table 6.1 Summary of two OLS models predicting respondent education

	Model 1	Non-White	White	Model 2
Female = 1 (F)	0.021	0.024	−0.003	0.021
	(0.018)			(0.018)
White = 1 (W)	0.070***	0.071	−0.001	0.071***
	(0.019)			(0.019)
Paternal Occupational	0.215***	0.062	0.153	0.214***
Prestige	(0.019)			(0.019)
F × W				−0.037*
				(0.018)

Results from the multiple regression are presented in Model 1 of Table 6.1, and the decomposition of those regression coefficients by race is also presented in Table 6.1, with the contribution of non-White and White respondents labeled respectively. Note that, again, summing over Non-White and White subsets results in the full model coefficients (e.g., 0.024–0.003 = 0.021). We point out that the effect of gender varies by participant race. In particular, those racialized as White contribute a small negative amount to the effect of being female, while those racialized as non-White show a large contribution to the effect of being female. This implies an interaction between gender and race such that among Whites, there is a small difference between men and women (favoring men), and among non-Whites, there is a larger difference between men and women (favoring women). This can be verified by including the interaction in the regression. Model 2 in Table 6.1 summarizes this model, showing that there is indeed a significant interaction between gender and race on education. Figure 6.1 illustrates the interaction effect with marginal means drawn from the model, showing the exact same pattern that can be inferred from the regression decomposition.

Notably, the regression decomposition from the model without the interaction effect tracks with the marginal means from Model 2 (Figure 6.1). Considering that our predictors are binary, this is intuitive. Just as marginal means can be recovered by adding regression coefficients for models with binary predictors, the regression decomposition shows the marginal order of categories (even without the interaction specified in the model). Based on the regression decomposition, non-White males show the lowest predicted education (i.e., 0.062; their contribution to occ prestige when it is set to the average). Non-White females show the second lowest (i.e., 0.062 + 0.024 = 0.086), White females show the next lowest (i.e., 0.153 −0.001 −0.003 = 0.149), and White males

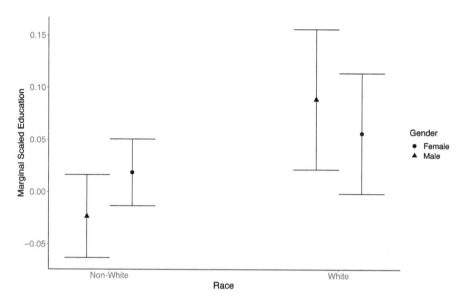

Figure 6.1   Marginal means from Model 2 in Table 6.1 illustrating the interaction between race and gender on education

show marginally higher education than White females (i.e., 0.153−0.001 = 0.152). The statistical interaction between race and gender shows up in a model with only main effects, you just need to know where to look.

We now illustrate with another example from the GSS, regressing occupational prestige on education, paternal occupational prestige, whether the respondent identifies as female (=1), and whether the respondent identifies as White (=1). In this example, we do not scale any of the variables, and the categorical variables are dummy coded. Model 1 in Table 6.2 summarizes the baseline OLS model. We find that education and paternal occupational prestige predict respondent occupational prestige, and that respondents who identify as White have a higher occupational prestige.

Suppose that we are interested in decomposing Model 1 of Table 6.2 by participant education, which was measured as the number of formal years of schooling completed. Figure 6.2 presents a histogram of education for the 2,856 respondents for whom we have complete data on the relevant variables. Given this distribution, we subset the cases by those 1,203 (42.1%) respondents with 12 or fewer years of schooling, those 738 (25.8%) respondents with some college (13–15), and those 915 (32%) respondents with a bachelor's or more. Table 6.2 shows the decomposition of Model 1 with these education-based subsets. This illustrates how the effects in Model 1 vary with states or levels

Table 6.2 Summary of three OLS models predicting occupational prestige

	Model 1	Educ < 13	Educ 13–15	Educ 16 +	Model 2	Model 3
Education (E)	2.269***	−4.486	0.215	6.540	1.859***	2.144***
	(0.092)				(0.176)	(0.135)
Paternal Occupational	0.059***	−0.001	−0.023	0.083	−0.104	0.058***
Prestige (P)	(0.013)				(0.061)	(0.013)
Female = 1 (F)	−0.952	−0.609	−0.429	0.086	−0.993	−4.014
	(0.527)				(0.526)	(2.519)
White = 1	1.635**	2.358	−0.552	−0.172	1.721**	1.669**
	(0.606)				(0.607)	(0.607)
E × P					0.012**	
					(0.004)	
E × F						0.223
						(0.179)
Constant	8.518***	75.479	9.076	−76.037	14.020***	10.213***
	(1.320)				(2.406)	(1.898)

Note: N = 2,856. $^{*}p < 0.05$, $^{**}p < 0.01$, and $^{***}p < 0.001$.

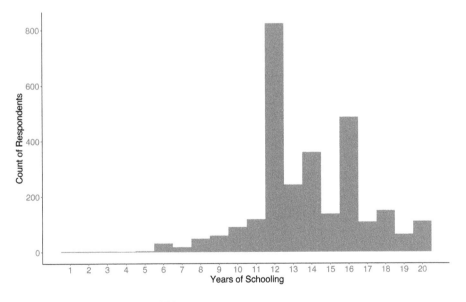

Figure 6.2   Histogram of education from the GSS

of education. It appears that the effects of both paternal occupational prestige and female differ based on levels of educational attainment, showing a negative association at lower levels of education but a positive association at higher levels. In contrast, the effect of White inverts from positive to negative as levels of education increase.

For paternal occupational prestige, the regression decomposition suggests that the effect is largely driven by those with more education; there is a significant main effect in Model 1, but only the effect for the most educated subset is positive in the decomposition. For female, the effect is monotonically larger for each level of education. The overall model coefficient is not significant. The decomposition implies that education may be suppressing the effect of female, with women gaining an increase in occupational prestige with more education, but a decrease to their occupational prestige with lower levels of education. The decomposition also suggests that the positive effect of being White on occupational prestige is largely observed among those with relatively little education.

Based on these descriptive patterns in the regression decomposition, it seems education plausibly interacts with paternal occupational prestige, female, and White. To assess this, we modeled each of these interactions separately. We find a significant interaction between education and paternal occupational prestige, but neither of the other two interactions reached the conventional level of significance ($p = 0.05$). Models 2 and 3 in Table 6.2 show the first two models with interaction effects. While the interactions are not consistently statistically significant, the interaction terms themselves enable the marginal means from the model to have differential effects. Figures 6.3 and 6.4 illustrate the interaction effects. We show these figures simply to point out that the marginal means from the models with the interactions *show the same patterns as the regression decomposition without the interaction*. In Figure 6.3, including the interaction shows that the effect of paternal occupational prestige increases as the respondent's education increases. Similarly, Figure 6.4 shows that at low levels of paternal occupational prestige, females are at a disadvantage, but at higher levels of paternal occupational prestige, females slightly outperform males. These are the same patterns we described above when interpreting the regression decomposition.

These two examples focus on summing across subsets of **P** based on variables that are already included in the model. However, using this approach, it is also possible to detect interactions more inductively through the use of clustering algorithms. This entails (i) clustering the cases, (ii) including cluster membership as a set of dummy variables in the regression model to assess whether cluster membership adds to the baseline statistical model, and (iii) identifying the interaction by searching for the largest absolute or squared differences in effects across clusters (see Melamed, Breiger, and Schoon 2013).

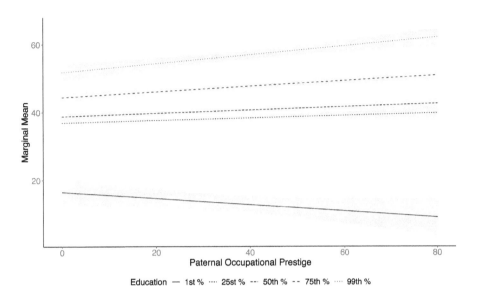

Figure 6.3   Marginal means from Model 2 in Table 6.2 illustrating the interaction between education and paternal occupational prestige on respondent occupational prestige

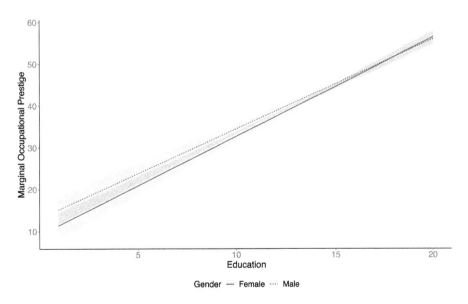

Figure 6.4   Marginal means from Model 3 in Table 6.2 illustrating the interaction between paternal occupational prestige and gender on respondent occupational prestige

However, clustering is a notoriously hard problem. We assume that the clustering we employ somehow provides an optimal data partition, but we have no basis to assess this assumption. In terms of point *ii,* assessing whether cluster membership adds to the model also assumes that cluster membership is picking up the same pattern as the interaction we are trying to detect. But cluster membership is driven by all variables or dimensions, so there will be ambiguities regarding identifying the two most likely variables for the interaction. Moreover, point *iii* is prone to researcher biases (e.g., confirmation bias) when looking for patterns in the data. Thus, to some extent, each of the steps in this approach leaves room for error.

Nevertheless, as we have just illustrated, regression decomposition by subsets of cases can shed light on meaningful interactions, even though the link between the decomposition of a regression model into subsets and another model that specifies a statistically significant interaction is not direct. Not all variation across subsets of cases implies a statistically significant interaction term, as our second example illustrates. And as noted above, it is also possible that the subsets may not be optimal (e.g., binning education differently would yield different results). Moreover, simulations reveal that compositional effects of qualitative predictors can drive whether it appears as if there is an interaction in a regression decomposition (code and results for these simulations are provided in Appendix D). For this reason, we recommend that analysts using this inductive approach to identify potential interaction effects rely on averages within subsets rather than sums. While the sums add up to the regression coefficients, they are a product of both the effect of the predictor and the composition of the variable across subsets. This is not an issue when the goal is to understand the model at hand, because compositional effects necessarily define the attribute space of the model. However, when it comes to using RIO as a basis for specifying an alternate model that includes interaction terms, simulation evidence suggests that using the mean as opposed to the sum avoids composition effects.[2]

6.2   Regressing on Rows of P

While the above approach provides a useful way to explore regression models and interrogate interrelationships between the effects of independent variables, it does not perfectly predict when a statistically significant

[2] We thank Adam Slez for suggesting that we consider compositional effects in this context.

interaction will occur. An alternative is to skip subsetting the cases alto-gether and predict $\mathbf{P}_i$ as a function of $\mathbf{X}_i$. In contrast to the former approach, this approach does less to push researchers to really look inside their mod-els, which we consider to be a key benefit and hallmark of RIO. However, it nevertheless provides a consistent way to identify statistically significant interactions.

Rows of $\mathbf{P}$ represent each case's contribution to that corresponding regres-sion coefficient. That is, the rows of $\mathbf{P}$ are effects of variables on the outcome, spread across all the cases. If one independent variable predicts the effect of another independent variable on $\mathbf{y}$ (i.e., its row in $\mathbf{P}$), this fits the definition of an interaction effect.[3]

To illustrate, consider again the first model above (Table 6.1), predicting education as a function of gender, race, and paternal occupational prestige. Once again scaling all the variables and suppressing the intercept, we then compute $\mathbf{P}$ such that the rows sum to the regression coefficients from the model. Table 6.3 presents the results of using OLS regression to predict the first row of $\mathbf{P}$, which corresponds to the effect of female on education. We predict this variable with the other variables in Model 1 of Table 6.1 (race and paternal occupational prestige). Note that we include an intercept in this model since the effect of gender on education has not been scaled, but the estimated intercept resembles zero since the effect of gender is not very strong.

As illustrated in Table 6.3, both race and paternal occupational prestige predict the effect of gender on education (i.e., the row in $\mathbf{P}$ corresponding to gender for Model 1 in Table 6.1). Note in particular that the effect of White is

Table 6.3 Summary of an OLS regression model predicting the effect of gender on education

White = 1 (W)	-0.00002^{**}
	(0.00000)
Paternal Occupational Prestige	0.00001^{*}
	(0.00000)
Intercept	0.0000
	(0.0000)

Note: $N = 2{,}856$. $^{*}p < 0.05$, $^{**}p < 0.01$, and $^{***}p < 0.001$.

[3] One might think that each predictor residualized from the others would better predict the interaction, but the variable itself contains the same information since the main effect of both variables is controlled when specifying an interaction effect.

the strongest predictor (in terms of effect and significance). While paternal occupational prestige predicts the effect of gender on education (Table 6.2; $b = 0.000014$, se $= 0.000007$, $p = 0.042$), the interaction between paternal occupational prestige and gender is not itself significant ($b = 0.033$, se $= 0.0182$, $p = 0.07$). This approach is not deterministic, as the degrees of freedom and corresponding standard errors will be slightly different when comparing main effects models to models with interaction effects specified.

To assess the extent to which this approach to identifying interactions works more generally, we use a Monte Carlo simulation (see Appendix E). The simulation is different from our empirical example. For exploratory data analysis, we asked whether we could find a meaningful interaction regardless of whether one existed in the data. In this simulation, we know that there is an interaction effect between two of eleven variables, and here we are asking whether we can find the right interaction effect when one is embedded in the data. To do so, we simulated a dataset with 5,000 cases and 11 predictor variables. Each simulated dataset ensured that the 11 predictors had an asymptotic effect of .1 on the outcome, and that there was an interaction effect of .1 between the 10th and 11th predictors. All other interaction effects were constrained to be asymptotically 0. We then applied our approach, focusing on whether any other predictor interacted with the 11th predictor. Specifically, we regressed predictors 1 to 10 on the effect of predictor 11 on the outcome (i.e., predictor 11's row in $\mathbf{P}$), determined which predictor had the largest t-value, whether it was predictor 10 (known to be the correct answer) and then determined whether that particular t-value was significant. We repeated this process 1,000 times. This enables us to assess whether our approach detects a significant interaction when there is one in the data. Indeed, we recovered the correct predictor (#10) in 1,000 out of 1,000 runs. As these results illustrate, regressing the rows of $\mathbf{P}$ on the other predictors is a powerful means of determining whether there is a signal in the data consistent with a statistical interaction.

6.3 Relation to Existing Approaches to Interaction Detection

RIO was not developed to identify statistical interactions. Rather, identifying interaction terms is merely a consequence of looking inside the regression model. If the effect of one variable is contingent on the states of another, that is the definition of a statistical interaction. It turns out this is remarkably easy to see when looking inside the model. As illustrated in this chapter, we can formalize this approach by predicting rows of $\mathbf{P}$. Rows of $\mathbf{P}$, as defined above, refer to the effect of a predictor on the outcome. If another variable predicts the effect of a focal variable, that implies a statistical interaction.

Of course, there are other approaches to discovering statistical interactions in a dataset. One of the most common approaches relies on regression trees, or recursive partitions of the data (Li, Dusseldorp, and Meulman 2019; Loh 2002; Morgan and Sonquist 1963). This is more computationally intensive than is our approach, as the combinatorics of partitioning the data is a much larger space than our search procedure entails. Other methods are similarly computationally expensive. Lasso regularization (Lim and Hastie 2015) and neural networks (Tsang, Cheng, and Liu 2018), for example, can each identify interaction effects, but require arbitrary terms to be specified or machine learning methods for optimization, respectively. Each of these methods, including our own, relies on adjusting the data and reestimating regression models. In our case, however, the regression model is predicting the effect of another variable, rather than predicting the original outcome as a multiplicative function.

6.4　Summary

RIO entails thinking about how the cases in a regression model are related to one another, and how those relationships sum to the quantities in the regression model. Throughout this book, we focus on how understanding the role of the cases in the regression model can help us learn more from that model, not how it can lead us to an entirely different model. However, sometimes understanding what is going on inside our regression model indicates a need for respecification. In this chapter, we illustrated this through a discussion of interaction terms.

As we show, understanding how main effects vary within regions of the sample space can identify higher-order processes or signals in the data. Turning our regression inside out allows us to explore the variability in regression coefficients that implies statistical interaction terms. We illustrated this with two examples from the General Social Survey showing how systematic effects in the regression decomposition translate into substantive interaction effects.

We also described how to use regression decomposition inductively. Specifically, predicting the effect of a particular predictor on an outcome (i.e., rows of $\mathbf{P}$) identifies the most likely interaction effect with that particular predictor. While not deterministic, Monte Carlo simulations show that, when a statistically significant interaction is present, this method identifies the interaction term 100% of the time. In these ways, looking at a regression model inside out can leverage insights into model specification via statistical interactions.

Part III

RIO as a Gateway

7   RIO as a Gateway to Case Selection

As discussed in Chapter 1, the final section of this book (Part III) explores how RIO can serve as a bridge between regression and other methodological approaches. We begin this exploration by focusing on algorithmic (also commonly referred to as quantitative) case selection, showing how turning regression inside out can advance efforts to use regression models to select cases for intensive analysis. As Seawright and Gerring (2008: 294) observe, "Case selection is the primordial task of case study research, for in choosing cases, one also sets out an agenda for studying those cases." For case study research, case selection represents the step in the research process where the relationship between a particular case (or a small set of cases) and a larger population of cases is determined. Given its importance for case study research, scholarship on case selection is vast and identifies an array of strategies, each of which serves different theoretical and substantive ends (Elman, Gerring, and Mahoney 2016). Most case study research in the social sciences relies on substantive knowledge of the topic and the potential population of cases to select a case or cases based on qualitative criteria associated with one or more selection strategies (Gerring 2017). However, case study research that uses algorithms to assist with selecting cases that fit the theoretical criteria associated with different strategies is becoming more common (Dafoe and Kelsey 2014; Fearon and Laitin 2011; Goertz 2017; Lieberman 2005; Nielsen 2016; Schneider and Rohlfing 2016; Seawright 2016a, 2016b; Seawright and Gerring 2008). Algorithmic case selection is particularly useful for mixed-method research that aims to integrate quantitative and qualitative evidence (Seawright 2016b), and while it has distinct limits, it also offers nontrivial benefits including greater replicability, easier management of complexity, and an ability to directly assess representativeness (see Gerring 2017: Chapter 6).

The benefits of using RIO as a gateway to case selection are grounded in what we contend is a basic misalignment between the goals of case studies and the goals of conventional regression analyses. Namely, case studies are designed to shed light on a larger population of cases, whereas regression is designed to shed light on the relationships among variables. While these goals are often complementary, there are nevertheless theoretically consequential differences. Common approaches to algorithmic case selection rely on a summary of the relationships among variables (e.g., the residuals from the regression model; see Seawright 2016b). However, by design, indicators that summarize the relationship among variables render the cases invisible (Breiger and Melamed 2014; Rambotti and Breiger 2020; Shalev 2007). Consequently, when cases are selected based on quantitative summaries of relationships among variables, the case in question can only reliably shed light on the relationships among variables. To be clear, this is extremely valuable and often desirable. It is common for mixed-method research to use regression to identify relationships among variables across cases, then to use case studies to explore the relationships among variables within specific cases. However, despite the fact that cases and variables are co-constituted (see Breiger 2009), when regression is used to select the case(s) for in-depth analysis, any broader claim about the relationships among cases necessarily takes as an article of faith that the relationships among cases are adequately represented by the relationships among variables.

By turning regression inside out, we bring the relationships between cases into direct dialogue with the relationships among variables. Building on the techniques introduced in Chapters 2 and 3, we show how RIO can inform and augment conventional approaches to algorithmic case selection that rely on regression. We begin by reviewing common case selection strategies and providing a brief overview of their logic and uses. This is not a comprehensive review of scholarship on case selection. Rather, it is intended to orient readers for the discussion that follows. After reviewing common case selection strategies, we discuss conventional algorithmic approaches for pursuing these strategies for case selection. While the term *algorithmic* can be used to describe approaches to case selection ranging from random sampling to the use of qualitative comparative analysis (QCA) (see Fearon and Laitin 2011; Schneider and Rohlfing 2016), we focus our attention on case selection strategies that are grounded in the logic of regression.

Armed with this foundation, the remainder of this chapter centers on two didactic examples. First, we revisit Kenworthy's (1999) analysis of the effects of welfare policy extensiveness on poverty, which we explored in detail in Chapter 2. This example includes only a small number of cases ($N = 15$) and thus facilitates an intuitive and accessible discussion of the relationships among cases and variables. We then explore Wimmer, Cederman, and Min's (2009) analysis of the determinants of ethnic armed conflict. This second example is more consistent with the kind of large-N analyses where algorithmic case selection is most likely to be applied. Together, these examples allow us to demonstrate how turning regression models inside out can inform and advance efforts to use regression models as a foundation for case selection.

7.1   Case Studies and Case Selection

A case study is "an intensive study of a single case or small number cases which draws on observational data and promises to shed light on a larger population of cases" (Gerring 2017: 28). Case studies play an essential role in progressive scientific development, allowing scholars to extend existing theories, develop subtheories, specify scope conditions, or identify mechanisms (Burawoy 1989; Emigh 1997; Ermakoff 2014; Pacewicz 2020). They can be used for diagnostic purposes – such as assessing theories, mechanisms, or statistical models – and to identify omitted variables or sources of measurement error (Gerring and Cojocaru 2016; Seawright 2016a, 2016b). They facilitate descriptive analysis, are instrumental to the development of constitutive arguments (i.e., analytic descriptions about the makeup and categorization of a phenomenon), and can be used to identify necessary and sufficient conditions (Elman et al. 2016; Pacewicz 2020).

Despite their many functions, case studies share the common goal of gaining deeper insights into a larger population of cases, and proper case selection is pivotal to achieving this goal. This is reflected in the fact that many well-known methods for case study research center primarily on the process of selecting appropriate cases. For example, in Emigh's (1997) influential work in negative case methodology, the core of the methodology is the identification of cases where "some theoretically predicted outcome did not occur" (Emigh 1997: 656). Thus, while case selection is not the only consideration when conducting case study research (George and Bennett 2005), it is widely recognized as foundational.

7.1.1   Case Selection Strategies

Existing scholarship elaborates a variety of case selection strategies, each of which is associated with distinct theoretical goals and logics. Consequently, scholars have developed typologies of case selection strategies that vary in terms of how many strategies are identified and goals that are accounted for.

For instance, in one influential treatment, Lieberman (2005) argues that strategies for case selection differ depending on whether a researcher's goal is model testing versus model building. When testing a model, Lieberman writes, "scholars should only select cases for further investigation that are *well predicted* by the best fitting statistical model" (Lieberman 2005: 444; emphasis in original). This is because the statistical analysis treats deviant cases as unexplained noise. In contrast (and consistent with the logic of Emigh's negative case methodology),

a very different set of strategies for case selection should be adopted in the case of [model building]. First, *at least one case* that has not been well predicted by the best-fitting statistical model should be selected... the central goal is to try to account for important patterns of variation on the outcome (Lieberman 2005: 445; emphasis in original).

This distinction between model testing versus model building is a useful one, but accounts for only a fraction of the goals associated with case study research. Gerring and Cojocaru (2016) offer a typology that distinguishes between two broad goals for case study research – descriptive versus causal analysis – each of which is further subdivided into distinct categories. Gerring (2017) subsequently elaborated this typology, adding an omnibus category that includes a variety of common case selection strategies ranging from logistical case selection (i.e., selection based on the accessibility of evidence) to the intrinsic importance of the case, resulting in a total of 18 distinct strategies.

It is beyond the scope of this chapter to review the full range of possible case selection strategies existing in the literature today. We, therefore, instead briefly review a subset of seven case selection strategies: *typical, deviant, influential, extreme, most-similar, most-different,* and *diverse.* We focus on these strategies because they are commonly used and widely recognized. Table 7.1 lists the case selection strategies we focus on and commonly recommended algorithmic approaches to each.

Typical cases represent features that are common in a larger population. Some scholars advocate using typical cases for confirming or disconfirming theories (Seawright and Gerring 2008) or exploring causal mechanisms (George and Bennett 2005; Weller and Barnes 2016). However, more recent scholarship contends that they are best suited for purely descriptive purposes (i.e., to describe a common phenomenon rather than to engage with some broader theory; see Gerring 2017). The difference between research using typical cases for causal versus descriptive analysis is the referent for typicality.

Table 7.1 Case selection methods

Strategy	N of cases	Method for Algorithmic Selection
Typical	1 or more	Minimize $\left\|Y_i - \hat{Y}_i\right\|$
Deviant	1 or more	Maximize $\left\|Y_i - \hat{Y}_i\right\|$
Influential	1 or more	Cook's distance; DFBETA; Hat matrix
Extreme	1 or more	$\left\|\dfrac{X_i - \overline{X}}{sd}\right\|$
Most-similar	2 or more	Mahalanobis matching
Most-different	2 or more	NA
Diverse	2 or more	NA

Notes: Selection criteria for *typical* and *deviant* drawn from Seawright (2016), selection criteria for *influential* and *extreme* drawn from Seawright and Gerring (2008), and selection criteria for most-similar drawn from Nielsen (2016). We did not identify algorithmic approaches to most-different and diverse cases that clearly satisfy the theoretical parameters of these methods.

For causal analyses, typicality is defined in reference to a representation of the social phenomenon. Researchers develop a causal framework or explanation (i.e., a regression model), then identify a case that is typical of that representation. For purely descriptive analyses, typicality is defined in reference to a broader population of cases. Building from a regression model, Seawright and Gerring (2008) recommend identifying typical cases by identifying observations with low residuals.

In contrast, *Deviant* cases are those which depart from theoretical or substantive expectations (i.e., cases that are in some way anomalous). Deviant cases are used to amend, extend, or disconfirm existing theories, and identify additional causal pathways. In mixed-methods research involving regression, deviant cases are also well suited to identifying measurement error (Seawright 2016a, 2016b). Deviant case selection is particularly common in qualitative research, as reflected in methods such as negative case analysis which center cases that exhibit theorized causes but not the expected outcome (Emigh 1997). In a regression context, deviant case selection is the analytic inverse of typical case selection: observations with particularly large residuals are considered deviant cases (Seawright and Gerring 2008; Seawright 2016b).

Influential cases are those "whose status has a profound effect on the probability of a hypothesis being true" (Gerring and Cojocaru 2016: 403). Influential cases are valuable for assessing assumptions underlying a causal process or statistical model, or for identifying measurement error, faulty scope conditions, causal heterogeneity, confounders, or errors in causal mechanisms. In a regression context, there are a variety of ways that influential cases can be identified. One common measure of influence in a regression context is leverage, a measure of how extreme an observation's values are on $\mathbf{X}$, where $\mathbf{X}$ is an $n \times p$ matrix of n observations and p predictor variables. Leverage is measured using the Hat matrix, which is the matrix that, when postmultiplied by the outcome vector, yields the predicted values from the model (also commonly called the projection matrix; see Belsley, Kuh, and Welsch 2004). The diagonal entries of the Hat matrix represent the distance between the values on $\mathbf{X}$ for the ith observation and the mean of the values on $\mathbf{X}$ for all observations. Observations with extreme or unusually large values on the diagonal of the Hat matrix have high leverage. However, leverage is a measure of influence that is based solely on the independent variable matrix, and thus does not account for influence in terms of the outcome ($\mathbf{y}$). Consequently, this can be understood as a measure of *potential* influence (Seawright and Gerring 2008). Other common regression-based measures of influence include Cook's distance (Cook 1977), which is used to detect observations' influence on the fitted values of a regression model, and DFBETA. Seawright (2016a) notes that Cook's distance accounts for influence net of the full regression model, and consequently might identify cases that are influential but largely affect control variables. Consequently, he recommends using DFBETA as a measure of influence (see Belsley, Kuh, and Welsch 2004) because it measures the difference in each parameter estimate with and without each observation. DFBETA allows researchers to focus on cases that are influential for the parameter estimates of variables that are determined to be theoretically or substantively salient.

Extreme case selection focuses on one or more cases that exhibit extreme tendencies on one or more indicators. Extreme case selection is common in qualitative research, as extreme cases can be used to identify limits of standard classifications or categories, highlight new classes of objects, or magnify relational patterns (Ermakoff 2014). In a quantitative context, extreme cases are valuable for exploratory purposes, providing "a way of probing possible causes of Y or effects of X, in an open-ended fashion" (Seawright and Gerring 2008: 302). As such, they are also valuable for identifying omitted variables, pathway variables, or measurement error (Seawright 2016b). One of the challenges of identifying extreme cases is that the parameters for extremity vary widely. An extreme case might be defined in theoretical terms, or in terms of a single independent variable or a dependent variable. Thus, there are a variety of algorithmic approaches to selection. Here, we follow Seawright and Gerring (2008: 301) and look for cases that lie "far away from the mean of a given distribution," measured as

$$\text{extremeness} = \left| \frac{X_i - \overline{X}}{sd} \right|$$

where X is a single predictor variable.

There are a variety of approaches to specifying *most-similar* cases, several of which integrate other case selection strategies not covered here (e.g., incorporating a control case with a *pathway* case for a most-similar case analysis; see Gerring 2017: 114). However, the basic logic of most-similar case selection is that cases are selected because they share similar characteristics. We identified two variants of most-similar case analysis. The first focuses on cases that share similar background characteristics but differ in the outcome of interest (Gerring 2017). In this basic form, most-similar cases are well-suited to exploratory analysis because this design facilitates the identification of previously unknown causes of **y**, and thereby the development of novel hypotheses. The second does not condition case selection on different outcomes, and rather only demands that the outcome of interest be exhibited in at least one of the cases (Nielsen 2016). In this form, most-similar case selection is best suited for process tracing (George and Bennett 2005), using thought experiments (rather than data) to inform counterfactual statements (Nielsen 2016). Existing scholarship identifies a variety of statistical approaches to identifying most-similar cases, including exact matching, coarsened exact matching, Mahalanobis matching, propensity score matching, and genetic matching (for a more comprehensive discussion of these procedures and resources on how to use them, see Nielsen 2016).

Most-different case selection is the inverse of most-similar, with the two cases sharing a common outcome but exhibiting substantial differences in background conditions. Also commonly referred to as the method of agreement (Mill 1869), most-different case designs are uncommon because it imposes strong assumptions, namely that the same outcome will emerge from the same causes across disparate conditions (Gerring 2017). This is also an assumption of regression analysis (Abbott 1988). Methodologically, Seawright (2016a) proposes identifying most-different cases by maximizing the overall difference in background characteristics between two cases. However, Gerring (2017) contends that most-different case design requires that all variables be dichotomized because "differences across cases must generally be sizable enough to be interpretable in an essentially binary fashion" (p. 87).

Moreover, if the differences between cases are not sufficiently great as to be interpretable in a binary fashion, "the results are uninterpretable" (Gerring 2017: 87). For this reason, most scholars recommend against most-different case selection because it is particularly prone to the possibility that unmeasured conditions account for similarities in outcomes. Here, we engage with the method for illustrative purposes. However, we were unable to find conventional protocols for identifying most-different cases.

Finally, *diverse* case selection focuses on two or more cases that represent a range of values for either the causal conditions/independent variables, or the outcome/dependent variable. Diverse case selection can be confirmatory or exploratory. It is particularly suited to identifying multiple causal pathways, exploring the causes-of-effects (as opposed to the effects-of-causes), wherein researchers identify an outcome (effect) and work to identify its various causes (Gerring 2017: 89). Here again, we were unable to identify conventional protocols for algorithmically identifying diverse cases.

7.2   Regression Inside Out as a Gateway to Case Selection

Each of these selection strategies provides unique theoretical and substantive leverage. However, as noted above, when using quantitative indicators (and, in particular, when using a regression model) to select cases, the relationships among cases are obscured by the variables. In the earlier chapters, we show how turning regression inside out allows us to unmask the relationships among cases and variables. In what follows, we show how this ability to bring cases to the fore in our regression models can both complement and augment existing approaches to algorithmic case selection.

To be clear, our goal is not to develop a novel algorithm or set of criteria for identifying cases. This work has already been done quite well by others, who have leveraged regression and various quantitative indicators to identify cases that match the theoretical criteria associated with each case selection strategy (e.g., Dafoe and Kelsey 2014; Fearon and Laitin 2011; Goertz 2017; Lieberman 2005; Nielsen 2016; Schneider and Rohlfing 2016; Seawright 2016a, 2016b; Seawright and Gerring 2008). Instead, we show how using RIO extends these efforts to offer novel insights into how the relationships among variables speak to the relationships among cases. Thus, as case studies are, by definition, intended to "shed light on a larger population of cases" (Gerring 2017: 28), turning regression models inside out helps us to make sense of where those cases fit within that larger population and how the population (and various subpopulations) relate to one another. Thus, RIO offers a way to explore and interpret the results of existing approaches to algorithmic case selection. In the remainder of this chapter, we apply RIO in tandem with existing approaches to algorithmic case selection. We use these applications to show how turning regression inside out allows us to gain more leverage when using algorithms to select cases for in-depth analysis.

7.3   The Effects of Welfare Policies on Poverty

Our first example comes from Lane Kenworthy's (1999) multinational analysis of the effect of social welfare policies on poverty. In Chapter 2, we presented a detailed reimagining of Kenworthy's analysis by turning the published regression models inside out, and we revisited this example again in Chapter 4 in our discussion of variance. Readers will recall from Chapter 2 that Kenworthy's analysis centers on 15 of the most affluent industrialized nations, with one observation per nation. Using multiple ordinary least squared (OLS) regression models, Kenworthy examines the effects of government tax and transfer programs on rates of poverty to answer the question: do social welfare policies reduce poverty? In addition to providing a useful touchstone and an easily digestible example, Kenworthy's analyses are particularly productive for the purposes of this chapter. Kenworthy does *not* include case studies (as defined by Gerring 2017) as a part of his analysis. However, the small number of observations in the data and the fact that each observation represents an industrialized nation on which data are widely available facilitate our own exploration.

As detailed in Chapter 2, Kenworthy (1999) presents three regression models in his original analyses. These three models differ based on which measures of social welfare policy extensiveness are used. We focus our attention on the model that uses government transfers as a measure of social welfare policy extensiveness.[1] Table 7.2 replicates Kenworthy's analysis where government transfers are the measure of social welfare policy extensiveness. All variables are standardized.

The results of this regression show that the largest predictor of posttax/transfer poverty is the poverty rate before government transfers were implemented. However, the results also show that government transfers do, on average, reduce levels of poverty.

---

[1]   The other two measures of social welfare policy extensiveness are decommodification and "social wage" (i.e., the percentage of a worker's income that they will receive if they stop working).

Table 7.2 Kenworthy's (1999: 1131) Table 4, government transfers

Variable	Coefficient (SE)
Government transfers	−0.444*
	(0.146)
GDP per capita 1960	−0.182
	(0.154)
Pretax/pretransfer absolute poverty	0.783***
	(0.148)

Notes: All coefficients are standardized. Standard errors are in parentheses. Replication data for this analysis are presented in Chapter 9, Table 9.1.***$p < 0.001$, **$p < 0.01$, *$p < 0.05$

7.3.1 Algorithmic Case Selection

Building from this model, we can apply common algorithmic approaches to case selection. We will move through each case selection strategy listed in Table 7.1 before turning the regression model inside out. We do this with the goal of identifying cases that fit the theoretical and algorithmic criteria for each type of case selection so that we can then examine the cases in relation to one another using RIO.

Beginning with recommendations for identifying typical and deviant cases, we calculate the model residuals, which are presented in Figure 7.1. Using the criterion that the typical case is the observation with the smallest absolute residual, we find that the most representative case in the data is Italy. Conversely, using the criterion that the deviant case represents the observation with the largest absolute residual, we find that the most deviant case in the data is Ireland. These two countries are indicated by lighter shading in the plot.

Turning next to the identification of influential cases, we use all three approaches for selection: Cook's distance, DFBETA, and the diagonal entries of the Hat matrix. Figure 7.2 plots the Cook's distance scores for Kenworthy's analysis. There are a number of approaches to interpreting influence using Cook's distance. As noted in Chapter 5, one common cutoff is $D_i > 4/(n − k − 1)$, where n is the number of observations and k is the number of parameters (Chatterjee and Hadi 1988). Others recommend an absolute cutoff of $D_i > 1$, while still others prefer relying on graphical representations to assess relative differences in influence (see Fox 2019). In Figure 7.2, we include visual representations for both numerical cutoffs.

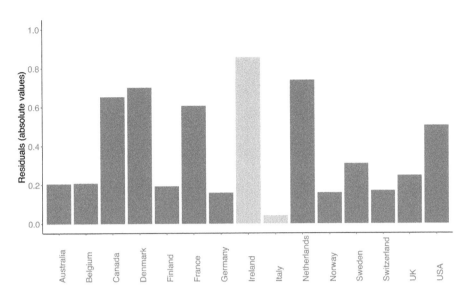

Figure 7.1   Residuals plot for Table 7.2

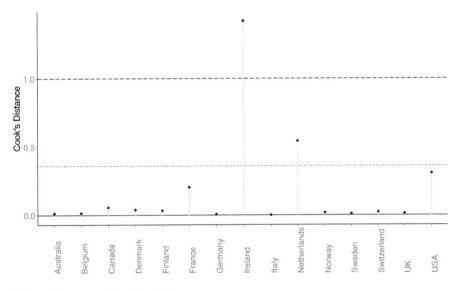

Figure 7.2   Cook's distance results for Table 7.2

Using any of these approaches to interpreting Cook's distance, it is clear that Ireland is an influential case. Using the more inclusive measure, the Netherlands is also identified as an influential case. Visually, both the USA and (to a lesser extent) France appear to have some influence, but neither pass conventional thresholds.

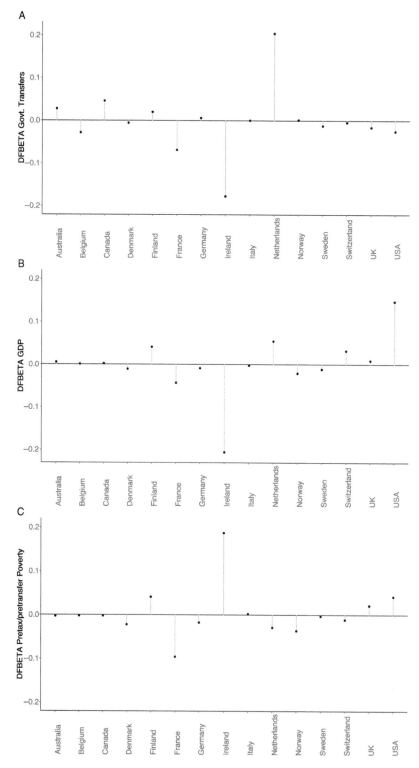

Figure 7.3 DFBETA for (A) Government transfers, (B) GDP, and (C) Pretax/pretransfer poverty from Table 7.2

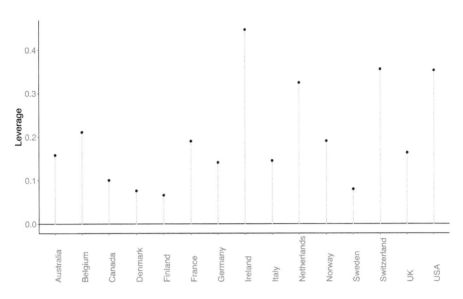

Figure 7.4   Diagonal values on the Hat matrix for Table 7.2

Figure 7.3 presents DFBETA for each variable in Kenworthy's model. A common threshold for high influence using DFBETA is $\dfrac{2}{\sqrt{n}}$, which for our analysis is ±0.516. These results give us a roughly similar understanding of influence in the model. While no case exceeds the standard threshold for influence on any indicator, visually we see that Ireland, the Netherlands, France, and the USA have outsized influence relative to other cases across all three variables, with Ireland being the most consistently influential. Finally, Figure 7.4 shows the values for each country on the diagonal of the Hat matrix. Here, the clearest candidate for an influential case is Ireland.

Turning to selecting extreme cases, we focus now on identifying cases with extreme values on the key variable of interest in Kenworthy's analysis: government transfers. As discussed earlier, recommendations for identifying extreme cases are fairly straightforward. Here, we focus on the absolute value of deviations from the mean of government transfers. Figure 7.5 shows these values, with the Netherlands identified as being the most extreme on this measure.

To select most-similar cases, we use Nielsen's (2016) R package *case-Match*, a useful tool that facilitates matching based on Euclidean distance or Mahalanobis distance. In our own analysis, we use yet another approach to measuring similarity (the cosine between two points), because it has a

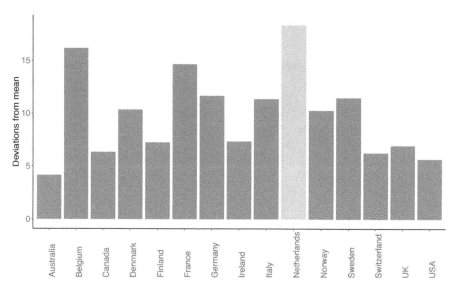

Figure 7.5   Deviations from the mean value on government transfers

straightforward and intuitive interpretation that pairs well with our approach to visualizing the regression model. Each of these approaches to measuring the similarity (or distance) between two points has different features, and it is beyond the scope of this chapter to provide a full review of these features. In brief, Mahalanobis matching is a generalization of Euclidean distance where the identity matrix (used to calculate Euclidean distance) is replaced by the covariance matrix. Whereas Euclidean and Mahalanobis distance measure the direct distance between two points, the cosine is a measure of similarity based on the angle connecting the two points to the origin (each point is represented by the vector of its coordinates). While qualitative approaches to case selection typically work to identify most similar cases that are exactly matched on key dimensions, within a regression context where there are multiple continuous covariates, Euclidean distance, Mahalanobis distance, and cosine similarity all allow researchers to identify cases that are as similar as possible, if not matched exactly. Because Nielsen (2016) recommends Mahalanobis over Euclidean matching in most instances, that is what we use here.

Table 7.3 presents the best matched pairs among cases based on the matrix of independent variables using Mahalanobis distances, along with their raw values on each of the three independent variables. In this context, the most-similar pair is Australia and Canada.

Table 7.3 Best matched pairs of countries based on Mahalanobis distance calculated on independent variable matrix for Table 7.2

			Transfers as		Pretax/transfer
Pair	Countries	Distance	% of GDP	GDP/capita	Absolute Poverty
1	Australia	0.535	7.3	7,734	23.3
	Canada		9.5	7,895	22.5
2	Germany	0.831	14.8	6,746	15.2
	Norway		13.4	6,507	9.2
3	Denmark	1.074	13.5	7,450	26.4
	UK		10.1	7,982	29.6
4	Finland	1.103	10.4	5,713	11.9
	Norway		13.4	6,507	9.2
5	Denmark	2.142	13.5	7,450	26.4
	Sweden		14.6	7.966	23.7

Because there is no standard method for selecting most-different or diverse cases algorithmically, we do not attempt to do so here. However, we do speak to possibilities of using RIO to assist with both case selection strategies when we turn Kenworthy's regression model inside out.

7.3.2   Turning the Regression Model Inside Out

Table 7.4 lists the cases that were algorithmically identified for each case selection strategy. Using these as a point of departure, we can illustrate how turning regression inside out offers novel insights for researchers interested in using regression models to select cases for in-depth analysis.

We begin by visually representing the relationships among cases and variables, following the procedures detailed in Chapters 2 and 3. Figure 7.6 represents the regression model, with relationships among cases and variables plotted in a two-dimensional space. The cases we are interested in (listed in Table 7.4) are represented with circles, the remaining cases are represented with solid squares, while the variables are represented with dots. A line is projected from the predicted outcome (labeled *YHAT*) to the origin of the plot, with points projected from each variable to intersect this central line at a 90-degree angle. The coordinates for each point in Figure 7.6 are presented in Table 7.5. These coordinates can be used to calculate the associations and similarities between points in the regression space (in two dimensions). As detailed in Chapter 2, the direction and magnitude of each variables' effect

Table 7.4 Cases representing each selection strategy for Kenworthy (1999)

Strategy	Candidate Case(s) Identified via Algorithm
Typical	Italy
Deviant	Ireland
Influential	Ireland, Netherlands, USA, France
Extreme	Netherlands
Most-similar	Australia and Canada

Notes: Cases identified as influential are listed in order of their relative influence across measures, as determined by (a) the number of indicators (i.e., Cook's distance, DFBETA, Hat matrix) of influence, and (b) the relative strength of their influence on those indicators.

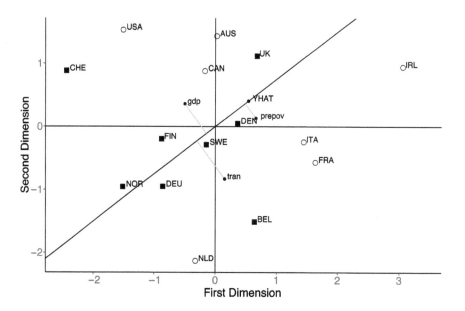

Figure 7.6   OLS of effects of social welfare policies on poverty

can be derived from its distance to the origin along this line and its position relative to YHAT.

Analogously to the interpretation of coefficients given in Chapter 2 for a portion of Kennworthy's data, a simple descriptive interpretation of Figure 7.6 shows that pretax/pretransfer poverty (labeled *pre-pov*) has a positive effect on the outcome (as indicated by the fact that it intersects the line in the same quadrant as YHAT) while GDP/capita (labeled *gdp*) and government

Table 7.5 Coordinates for points in Figure 7.7

		X	Y
Variables			
	TRAN	0.153	−0.828
	GDP	−0.498	0.362
	POV	0.661	0.133
	YHAT	0.540	0.406
Cases			
	AUT	0.022	1.436
	BEL	0.639	−1.511
	CAN	−0.171	0.882
	DEN	0.363	0.048
	FIN	−0.879	−0.197
	FRA	1.635	−0.566
	DEU	−0.859	−0.951
	IRL	3.060	0.945
	ITA	1.446	−0.246
	NLD	−0.324	−2.132
	NOR	−1.511	−0.956
	SWE	−0.148	−0.288
	CHE	−2.447	0.883
	UK	0.679	1.117
	USA	−1.504	1.535

transfers (labeled *tran*) have negative effects on the outcome. Moreover, the absolute distance between where *prepov* intersects the line and the origin of the plot (i.e., where the X and Y axis intersect) is greater than the distance from where *gdp* or *tran* intersect, indicating a larger effect size. These relationships are entirely consistent with the results that are presented in Table 7.2.

In addition to showing the relationships among variables, the contributions of individual cases to the regression are mapped onto this figure and we can derive the relationships among cases based on their relative position in this figure. The ability to account for each observation's unique contribution to the overall regression coefficients and to explore the relationships among cases vis-a-vis the regression model is central to RIO's capacity to inform and advance algorithmic approaches to case selection.

Our discussion of typical, deviant, influential, and extreme cases (the first four of the seven selection strategies we discuss) centers on the cases identified via conventional algorithmic case selection strategies rather than focusing on the selection strategies themselves. We do this because some cases are associated with multiple strategies, and focusing on the cases allows us to bring these strategies into clearer dialogue and explore the implications of a single case representing multiple theoretical logics. After discussing the cases associated with these first four case selection strategies, we turn our attention to the overall model space to explore the relationships among cases associated with selection strategies that require the identification of two or more cases. We begin our discussion of comparative case selection strategies with the cases we identified as most similar using a conventional algorithmic approach and use this as a point of departure for discussing how RIO can contribute to identifying most-different and diverse cases for comparative analysis.

7.3.3 Italy

The first case we turn our attention to is Italy, which we identified as the typical case in the model based on having the lowest residual. As noted above, a typical case exemplifies some broader cross-case tendency and can thus be thought of as a *representative case* (Seawright and Gerring 2008). However, typical cases are not representative in the sense of a representative sample of a larger population. Rather, they are representative in the sense that a measure of central tendency represents the overall distribution of data (Gerring 2017).

Much as the information provided by a measure of central tendency is most useful when paired with additional parameters, such as the range and standard deviation, a typical case's capacity to shed light on a broader population of cases is enhanced by understanding the relationships among cases in the broader population. When we select a case based on the residuals of a regression model, we use the regression model to represent the broader population of cases. Thus, the case that is typical of the population is defined as the case that is best represented by the regression model. However, even when the regression model is well-specified, the degree to which the model itself represents any given case will vary. Turning the model inside out allows us to shift focus back to the relationships among cases (as defined by the model), as opposed to the relationship between cases and the model.

To explore Italy's relationship to other cases vis-a-vis the model, we can begin by looking at its similarity to other cases within the overall model space of the regression. Building from Figure 7.6, using cosine similarity to calculate the degree of similarity between cases allows for both precise mathematical analysis and an intuitive assessment. As noted briefly above, cosine similarity assesses the association between two points based on the angle

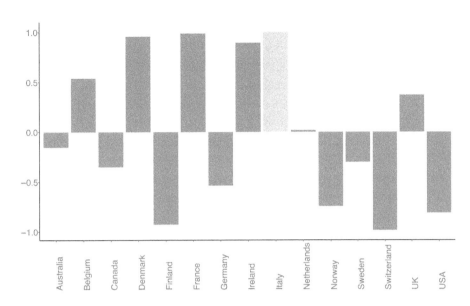

Figure 7.7   Cosine similarity between Italy and all other cases

formed when the two points are projected on the origin (i.e., where the X and Y axes intersect). An acute angle indicates similarity, while a right angle (90 degrees) indicates an orthogonal relationship, and an obtuse angle indicates dissimilarity. For example, the cosine relating Italy and France (which are located quite close together in the lower right quadrant of Figure 7.6) is 0.986, indicating an extremely high degree of similarity, whereas Italy and the USA (which are located in opposite quadrants of Figure 7.6) have a cosine of −0.809, indicating a high degree of *dis*similarity.

Figure 7.7 presents the cosines between Italy and all other cases represented in Figure 7.6, which are calculated using the coordinates presented in Table 7.5. Italy is included in this figure for reference, with a cosine of 1. Because we can calculate the association between all observations and variables vis-a-vis the model specification, we can begin to make sense of the degree to which the typical case offers insights into some broader set of cross-case relations, as is the purpose of a case study.

For example, some researchers might aim to "find a typical case of some phenomenon so that he or she can better explore the causal mechanisms at work in general, cross-case relationships" (Seawright and Gerring 2008: 299). If a researcher's goal was to understand the effects of government transfers on overall rates of poverty, then they might conclude that insights gained via an in-depth analysis of Italy can inform a deeper understanding of the relationship between transfers and poverty in France (cosine = 0.986), Denmark (cosine = 0.955), Ireland (cosine = 0.896), or perhaps even Belgium (cosine = 0.538), but that the dynamics exhibited in Italy might be unrelated to those in the Netherlands, which has an effectively orthogonal relationship (cosine = 0.017), or extremely dissimilar to those found in Switzerland (cosine = −0.984) or the United States (cosine = −0.809).[2]

The fact that Italy is dissimilar or effectively orthogonal to the majority of the cases in our dataset (9 out of 14) reinforces the assertion that typical cases are poorly suited for identifying mechanisms (see Seawright 2016a, 2016b), and are instead best suited for descriptively exploring "features that are common within a larger population" (Gerring 2017: 56). In this context, results presented in Figure 7.6 can also help us to make sense of what an in-depth analysis of Italy might tell us if our goal is to produce a general portrait of an average case.

In his discussion of how typical cases are used to elaborate features of an average case, Gerring (2017) identifies several exemplars in existing research, including William Foote Whyte's (1943) classic study of street corner society where he conducts a detailed ethnography of a street gang, Le Roy Ladurie's (1978) study of a small village in France, and Lynd and Lynd's (1957) study of "Middletown" (the pseudonym they used for Muncie, Indiana). In each study, the authors selected cases they thought were typical (and thus in some way representative) of street gangs in urban America, small villages, or midsized U.S. cities, respectively. Considering the criteria for case selection of these exemplar studies, what makes the cases typical is not the *presence* of particular features, but rather the *absence* of any standout characteristics. This is reflected in Lynd and Lynd's (1957) justification for selecting Muncie, Indiana for their study. In explaining their selection, they list a variety of characteristics that made the city suitable, including its temperate climate, typical growth, and some degree of economic diversity. They conclude by saying that Muncie exhibited an "absence of any outstanding peculiarities or acute local problems which would the city off from the midchannel sort of American community" (quoted in Gerring 2017: 57).

Defining typicality in terms of the absence of any notable distinguishing characteristics (which is admittedly not how it is generally defined), Italy's

---

[2] Similarity is necessarily conditioned only on the variables in the model. Thus, two countries can appear quite similar but exhibit dramatically different characteristics that are otherwise unaccounted for. For instance, Kenworthy (1999) compares the USA and Canada, noting their high degree of similarity in the predictors but stark differences in the success of transfer programs.

algorithmic identification makes a great deal of sense. In Kenworthy's analysis, Italy is barely mentioned, coming up only in a discussion that lists countries with absolute levels of poverty that exceed the United States (a country that receives far more attention). However, the data on Italy fully conform with Kenworthy's conclusion that pretax/pretransfer absolute poverty levels are substantially higher than posttax/posttransfer absolute poverty levels. On a purely descriptive level, the difference in pretax/pretransfer and posttax/posttransfer absolute poverty levels ranges from 7.5% to 26.3%, with an average difference of 14.01%. Italy's pre/post difference is quite close to the average, at 16.4%. In fact, on most indicators, Italy also falls close to the mean. Substantively, Italy exhibits no policy characteristics that stand out as unique. Thus, looking both in Kenworthy's original analysis and at the overall data, Italy's identification as typical does not seem to suggest that it is representative of all other cases, but rather that it does not stand out on any particular measure and is thus close to the central tendencies of most variables. In these terms, Italy represents the overall model very well.

Revisiting Figure 7.6, what RIO helps us to see is that Italy's lack of distinguishing characteristics actually makes it somewhat *atypical* in the context of these 15 nations. As Mahoney (2021) observes, social categories (such as the category *affluent industrialized nations,* which is how Kenworthy characterizes the cases that make up this dataset) are based on mental models rather than any naturally occurring similarities among the cases. Looking at the overall model space, we see this observation playing out as all countries fit the same mental model, but arguably exhibit substantively meaningful differences. Thus, despite the fact that Kenworthy's original regression model is robust, his analyses are carefully constructed, and his interpretations considered and appropriately qualified, turning the model inside out reveals heterogeneity among the cases. Quantitatively, this heterogeneity is not so great as to undermine the regression model, but when it comes to the identification of typical cases in dialogue with the regression model, it highlights the limits of drawing conclusions about relationships among cases based on relationships among variables (Shalev 2007).

In light of these findings, researchers might reasonably want to incorporate qualitative characteristics of Italy (and other cases) into the case selection process in dialogue with the results of the regression model. As Gerring (2017: 126) observes, however, a key limitation of algorithmic approaches to case selection is that "some criteria are hard to measure, ex ante, across a large sample of cases and therefore are not features that an algorithmic case-selection method can condition on." While RIO cannot address these measurement issues, it does allow researchers to apply substantive and theoretical insights that are exogenous to the regression model when interpreting what a typical case can tell us. For example, in Esping-Andersen's (1990) hugely influential book, *Three Worlds of Welfare Capitalism,* the author argues that welfare state regimes consist of qualitatively different arrangements between state, market, and family, resulting in three distinct types of welfare states: *liberal* welfare states, which use means testing, provide only modest assistance, and have market-differentiated welfare programs; *corporatist* welfare states, which are nonmarket, have negligible redistribution, and include social insurance programs that benefit those who pay in; and *social democratic* welfare states, which have universal benefits, are characterized by decommodification, and workers have full participation in the quality of rights enjoyed by the privileged. Based on Esping-Anderson's (1990, 1999) typology, the nations included in Kenworthy's dataset can be divided among these three worlds, with Australia, Canada, Switzerland, the UK, and the USA characterized as liberal welfare states; Belgium, France, Germany, Ireland, Italy, and the Netherlands characterized as corporatist welfare states; and Denmark, Finland, Norway, and Sweden characterized as social democratic welfare states.

By looking at the relationships among cases, we can use this classification scheme to inform our assessment of Italy's identification as the typical case. Figure 7.8 reproduces Figure 7.6, but countries are distinguished by regime type. What should be immediately clear from this plot is that there is a high degree of clustering among liberal welfare regimes and social democratic welfare regimes. While countries with liberal welfare regimes vary in their level of posttransfer poverty (with the UK being the highest and Switzerland being the lowest), they all have high GDPs and low rates of transfers. Similarly, among the social democratic regimes, all have lower levels of both pre- and posttransfer poverty, but middling GDPs and transfers. While the clustering is less clear among corporatist welfare states (due in no small part to Ireland which, as we discuss in Section 7.3.4, is identified as both a deviant and an influential case), we nevertheless again see commonalities.

Looking at our representation of the regression model through the lens of Esping-Andersen's three worlds of welfare capitalism, Italy in fact appears to be fairly representative of the corporatist states. While it is orthogonal to the Netherlands and dissimilar to Germany, Italy has a high degree of similarity to the other corporatist welfare states and might make a good candidate for

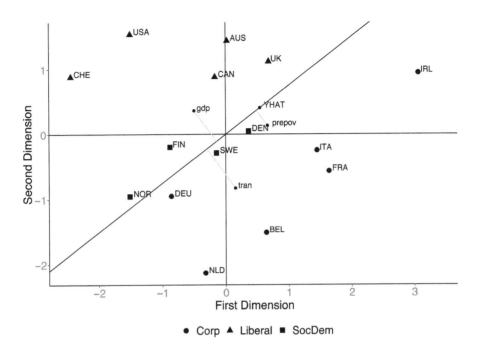

Figure 7.8   OLS of effects of social welfare policies on poverty by welfare regime type

either identifying mechanisms or developing a more general portrait of the average case among this substantive subset of countries. In contrast, Italy is quite atypical of both liberal and social democratic welfare regimes. Again, by looking beyond the cases' relationships to the variables and accounting for the relationships among cases alongside the qualitative characteristics of the cases, we are able to better understand the scope of Italy's utility as a "typical" case.[3]

Taking our exploration of Italy one final step further, Italy's identification as a typical case makes sense from the perspective of the regression model, yet turning the regression model inside out and layering on substantive insights suggests it is more typical of corporatist welfare states rather than all affluent industrialized nations in the data. Consequently, we may want to investigate the role that corporatist welfare states, more generally, are playing in the overall model. As detailed in Chapter 2, by turning the regression model inside out, we can identify each observation's contribution to the regression coefficients. Because these contributions are additive (i.e., they sum to the

---

[3] As shown in Chapter 2, we can also look for patterns among cases inductively.

Table 7.6 Contributions to regression model by welfare regime type

	Liberal	Corporatist	Social Democratic	Coefficient
Government transfers	−0.071	−0.396	0.023	−0.444
GDP per capita 1960	−0.010	−0.343	0.171	−0.182
Pretax/pretransfer absolute poverty	0.129	0.407	0.246	0.783

overall regression coefficient), we can similarly look at the contributions of sets of cases. In Table 7.6, we present the combined contributions of nations represented by each type of welfare regime. The final column reports the coefficients presented in Table 7.2, which are also the sums of the contributions presented in the first three columns.

As this decomposition shows, the corporatist countries (of which Italy is at the center in Figure 7.8) account for 89.2% of the effect of government transfers on poverty (−0.396/−0.444). Similarly, it is the driving force behind the effect of GDP (Social Democratic regimes substantially attenuate the overall effect, while Corporatist states contribute 97.17% of the negative effect) and represents more than half of the overall effect of (52%) pretax/pretransfer poverty. All of this, even though corporatist nations constitute only 40% of the cases in the data.

These results shed a great deal of light on the relationship between Italy, the other cases, and the regression model. The fact that Italy is most similar to the majority of other corporatist states *and* most typical of the overall regression model makes a great deal of sense, insofar as the effects we are observing in the overall regression model are largely due to the contributions of cases that are characterized as corporatist welfare regimes.

Taken together, our investigation of Italy illustrates how turning the regression inside out can help us better understand how and in what ways the typical case sheds light on a broader population of cases. It allows us to observe its relationship to other cases vis-a-vis the model specification and clarify the theoretical nature of its typicality as a case that is lacking in distinguishing characteristics that make it stand out significantly in the context of the overall data. Moreover, by shifting focus to the cases, we are better able to apply qualitative insights that are not included in the regression model and use those insights to not only further make sense of the algorithmic selection, but of the model itself.

7.3.4   Ireland

Ireland is identified as both a deviant case and an influential case using conventional algorithmic approaches to case selection. As detailed above, deviant case selection orients researchers toward one or more cases that depart from established theoretical or substantive expectations (i.e., cases that are in some way anomalous). In a context where the number of cases is small and identifying measurement error is not a major concern, deviant cases are best suited to amending, extending, or disconfirming existing theories, or identifying unaccounted for causal pathways. *Influential* cases are those "whose status has a profound effect on the probability of a hypothesis being true" (Gerring and Cojocaru 2016: 403). They are used to assess the assumptions underlying a causal process or statistical model.

Looking at Ireland's relationship to the other cases and its unique contributions to the regression coefficients helps us make sense of why conventional approaches to algorithmic case selection identify Ireland as both deviant and influential, and how an in-depth analysis of Ireland might shed light on a broader population of cases. We can start by looking at Ireland's contributions to the overall regression coefficients. Table 7.7 shows each case's individual contributions to each of the three coefficients. Looking across all variables, we see that Ireland's contribution to the overall regression

Table 7.7 Case contributions to regression coefficients from Table 7.2

	Transfers	GDP	Poverty
AUS	−0.040	−0.007	0.004
BEL	−0.049	0.001	−0.004
CAN	0.024	0.001	−0.001
DEN	−0.004	−0.007	−0.014
FIN	0.051	0.102	0.104
FRA	0.006	0.004	0.008
DEU	−0.022	0.033	0.064
IRL	−0.286	−0.333	0.302
ITA	0.001	−0.037	0.030
NLD	−0.046	−0.012	0.006
NOR	−0.006	0.092	0.161
SWE	−0.018	−0.017	−0.005
CHE	0.013	−0.092	0.033
UK	−0.058	0.031	0.077
USA	−0.010	0.057	0.016
Coefficient	−0.444	−0.184	0.781

coefficients far outstrips any other case. Looking first at the effect of government transfers, we see that Ireland's contribution alone accounts for 64.4% of the overall regression coefficient, and in absolute terms, it is nearly five times larger than the next largest contribution (United Kingdom). For the effect of GDP, Ireland's contribution is equivalent to 181% of the overall regression coefficient (for the effect of GDP, there are strong countervailing contributions that attenuate the overall negative effect, making Ireland's contribution greater than the overall coefficient and helping to explain the nonsignificance of GDP), and in absolute terms, Ireland's contribution is three times that of the next most influential country (Finland). In terms of the effects of pre-tax/pretransfer poverty, Ireland is contributing 38.7% of the overall regression coefficient, and in absolute terms, its contribution is nearly twice that of the next most influential country (Norway). These results clearly align with Ireland's identification as an influential case, and with the fact that it was flagged by all methods for assessing influence that we apply above (unlike other cases, which were flagged by one or two, but not all three).[4]

To make sense of Ireland's identification as a deviant case considering its influence, it helps to visualize Ireland's position vis-a-vis the other cases. While we can see Ireland is positioned at the periphery of the OLS space in Figure 7.8, rather than focusing on the entire space at once, it is useful to look at each variable in turn. Figure 7.9 plots posttax/posttransfer poverty by residualized government transfers,[5] with the slope for transfers (−0.444) imposed on the figure (for more detail on these plots, see Chapters 2 and 5). The size of the points in each figure is proportional to each country's absolute contribution to the coefficient for government transfers. By visualizing the case contributions in this way, we can see why Ireland is both influential and deviant. Ireland falls far from the regression slope because its values on the outcome and the key variable of interest deviate so considerably from the other cases. Moreover, seeing that values from the other cases cluster within a much smaller range helps to explain Ireland's high degree of influence relative to other cases. In the absence of any strong countervailing observations in the opposite quadrant of the plot (which would come either from more cases with high government transfers and low posttransfer poverty or a single case that was similarly extreme but with inverse values to Ireland), Ireland has an outsized influence on the overall regression coefficient.

---

[4] This information also informs our understanding of Italy, as Ireland is one of the corporatist nations that is driving the overall model, and it has a high degree of similarity to Italy.
[5] Residualizing the variable shows us each nation's values net of the other variables in the model.

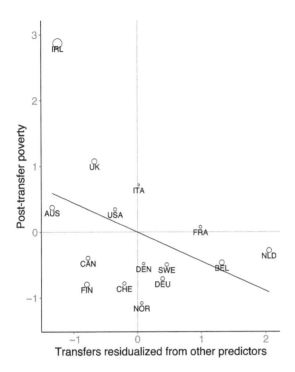

Figure 7.9   Poverty by residualized government transfers

We see similar patterns when we examine the other two variables. While Ireland's position is less extreme relative to other cases in terms of its values on pretransfer poverty (Figure 7.10b), for both the effects of GDP and pretransfer poverty, Ireland is positioned far from the regression slope and has a high degree of influence. Looking across variables helps us to contextualize why Ireland was identified as deviant based on the overall model residuals.

Understanding Ireland's position relative to other cases in this way helps us make sense of how this one case can shed light on a broad population of cases. As we see in Figures 7.9 and 7.10, what makes Ireland deviant is not that it departs from theoretical or substantive expectations. Rather, Ireland is an extreme illustration of the theorized relationship between transfers, GDP, and pretax/pretransfer poverty and posttax/posttransfer poverty, exemplifying the assertion that low levels of government transfers, low GDP, and high pretransfer poverty are all associated with higher rates of posttransfer poverty. In Ireland, these associations are magnified relative to all other cases. Thus, while we cannot rule out the possibility that an in-depth analysis of Ireland could be used to amend, extend, or disconfirm assumptions about

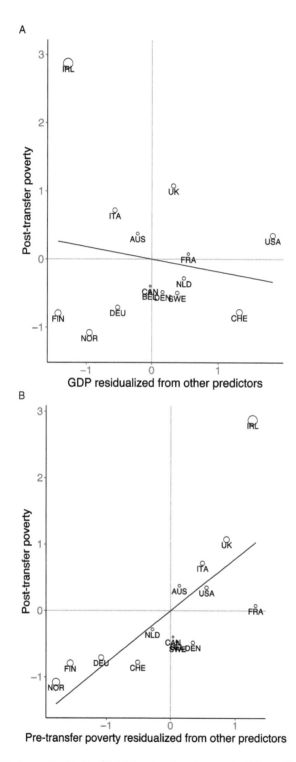

Figure 7.10a–b Residualized GDP (a) and pretransfer poverty (b) by posttransfer poverty

the relationship between welfare extensiveness and poverty, turning the regression model inside out raises questions about the utility of treating it as a deviant case. The relationships among cases instead suggest that Ireland is more usefully treated as an influential case, which corroborates Kenworthy's hypothesis.

7.3.5 Netherlands

The Netherlands is identified as one of the potentially influential cases and an extreme case, based on the extent to which its value on government transfers deviates from the mean. As noted above, influential cases are those that have an outsized influence in the probability of a hypothesis being true and thus are useful for assessing causal processes and assumptions, while extreme cases are those with extreme values on a particular variable and are useful for probing possible effects of a predictor. Thus, influential and extreme cases serve similar ends, each representing a different sort of unusualness that is algorithmically captured in distinct ways.

Regarding the Netherlands' identification as an influential case, looking back at Figures 7.2–7.4, where we use Cook's distance, DFBETA, and the Hat matrix to identify influential cases, we see that the Netherlands exceeds the lower of two thresholds for influence based on Cook's distance, and its influence exceeds that of other cases on some variables using DFBETA. Moreover, it is one of four cases that stand out in terms of its value on the Hat matrix. Its identification as an extreme case is based on its deviation from the mean on government transfers. In absolute terms, the Netherlands' level of government transfers is the highest in the data and is more than two standard deviations above the mean.

Given the preceding discussions of Italy and Ireland and the accompanying analyses, the Netherlands's identification as influential and extreme may seem somewhat incongruous, as it does not particularly stand out in any of these analyses (see Figures 7.6, and 7.9–7.10). While the Netherlands is at the margins of the OLS space, it is not the most marginal (the most marginal is Ireland), nor is it the furthest point from the origin along the line transecting the outcome and the origin (see Figure 7.6). Thinking in terms of Esping-Andersen's three worlds of welfare capitalism (discussed above and represented in Figure 7.8), the Netherlands stands out in part for being somewhat dissimilar to the majority of other corporatist welfare states, but it has a reasonably high degree of similarity to Germany, which is the most dissimilar to Italy (our typical case). Its contributions to the regression coefficients are modest, and across the three substantive variables, it fits the slopes quite well (see Figures 7.9 and 7.10). While the case is extreme on our key independent variable, when we control for the other variables in the model, it does not particularly stand out, and it is not driving the results of the coefficient for government transfers.

So, how does the Netherlands shed light on the broader population of cases? Looking at it in relation to other cases, the Netherlands reflects the fundamental relationality of the regression model and consequently, the fundamental relationality of how we define both influential and extreme cases. Focusing on Figure 7.8, we see that the Netherlands is positioned opposite Ireland, the most influential case in the data. It is also positioned opposite the USA and Switzerland, both of which were similarly identified as potentially influential cases and are similarly positioned at the margins of the model space. This suggests that the Netherlands is functioning as a counterbalance to other influential cases in the model. Its utility as an influential case is thus best understood in relation to other influential cases in the model: it is influential in part because it differs substantially from other influential cases, thus shifting the weight (and the regression slope) in ways that other cases are not positioned to do.

The Netherlands remains an excellent candidate for exploring other possible outcomes of having high levels of government transfers, as we would expect from an extreme case. What we can tell from turning the regression model inside out is that, when controlling for other variables, the effect of extreme values on government transfers for the Netherlands is mitigated by slightly lower levels of GDP and pretransfer poverty (based on the distributions of those two variables). But this is only when we consider government transfers in relation to our outcome and control for GDP and pretransfer poverty. Thus, it is entirely possible that there are other outcomes that government transfers might influence, ranging from employment rates to various indicators of population health. In these instances, the unusually high levels of government transfers exhibited by the Netherlands may yield valuable insights that could inform subsequent analyses.

7.3.6 France and the United States

Along with Ireland and the Netherlands, we also flagged France and the USA as potentially influential cases based on the DFBETAs for pretax/pretransfer poverty and GDP, respectively. In both cases, these two countries were not the most influential. However, they did stand apart from the other countries in their values. For these two nations, turning the regression model inside out does not yield significant new insights. Neither case has markedly high contributions to the respective regression coefficients. Figure 7.10a–b shows that the USA departs from the trend for GDP, with high posttax/posttransfer poverty relative to its GDP, while France has relatively low posttax/posttransfer poverty relative to its pretax/pretransfer poverty. While these two cases deviate from the overarching pattern, their contributions indicate that they are not driving the regression model. This is consistent with the finding of Kenworthy's sensitivity tests, which show that excluding each of these two cases from the data does not alter the substantive results of the regression model. Thus, a closer look at these cases and their relationship to the other cases confirms that they are at the margins of the OLS space based on unusual values on specific variables, but neither is a particularly strong candidate for more detailed analysis as an influential case.

7.3.7   Australia and Canada

The two cases identified as most similar using case Match's Mahalanobis matching are Australia and Canada. In Figure 7.11, we again plot the model space for our regression model, but this time we insert dashed lines from the origin to each of the points representing our cases. Again, the solid line transects the origin and the outcome. In examining Figure 7.11, as we would expect, the points representing Australia and Canada form a highly acute angle with the origin, indicating a high cosine similarity (cosine = 0.979). As noted above, these two measures of similarity have meaningful differences. For this reason, the similarity between Australia and Canada is not, for example, as great as what we observed with France in our discussion of Italy (cosine between Italy and France = 0.986). We highlight this to emphasize that we are comparing the results *only* because the Mahalanobis matching allows us to identify two focal cases for comparison using an established method for identifying most-similar cases.

The benefit of turning the model inside out to explore the relationships among variables is that it allows for a high degree of flexibility in identifying paired cases. As Gerring (2017) emphasizes, researchers often start with one case that they are interested in and aim to identify a case that exhibits similar characteristics in some context. Thus, if a researcher has already collected data on one case (e.g., they might have identified an influential case and want to match that case with another), they can quickly and intuitively explore the relationship between that case and all other cases in the model. Moreover,

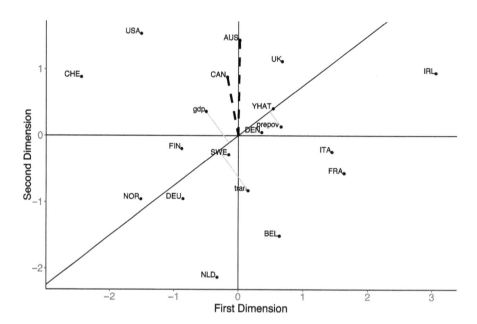

Figure 7.11   OLS of effects of social welfare policies on poverty, most-similar

in doing so, they can simultaneously account for cases' relationships to variables as well. Thus, if we are interested in identifying a case that is most similar to the United Kingdom, we can easily see that Australia, Canada, and Denmark form acute angles with the UK, thus indicating a high degree of similarity. However, in doing so, we can also see that Denmark is more similar to the UK in terms of its pretax/pretransfer poverty level (as indicated by their greater proximity to that variable in the OLS space; UK pretrax/pretranfer poverty = 29.6, Australia = 23.3, Canada = 22.2, Denmark = 26.4), whereas Australia and Canada are more similar to the UK with regards to transfers, as indicated by Denmark's greater proximity to that variable relative to the other three (UK transfers = 8.1, Australia = 7.3, Canada = 9.5, Denmark = 13.5). In this way, we can easily identify cases that share an overall degree of similarity, and simultaneously account for the nature of those similarities.

This ability to simultaneously explore relationships among cases and variables yields even greater dividends when we analyze datasets with a larger number of observations (which we do with our next example). As the N increases, so does the number of possible combinations. In this dataset of 15 observations, there are 105 possible pairs of cases that we could account for. However, increasing from 15 to 50 cases results in a dramatic increase to 1,225 possible pairs of cases. As noted at the outset, we began with Kenworthy's analysis for our illustration of how RIO can serve as a gateway to case selection because it is small and because we have already analysed it in some detail in earlier chapters, making it a useful example for exploring the possibilities that RIO offers as a gateway to case selection. When accounting for datasets where cases account for hundreds of organizations, social movements, geographical areas, or other phenomena, this intuitive visualization of relationships among cases becomes significantly more valuable and can meaningfully assist with the selection of matched cases.

7.3.8   Beyond Most-Similar: Differences and Diversity

Before concluding our exploration of Kenworthy's data and moving on to a second example that uses more complex data, we want to briefly build on our discussion of most-similar case selection and discuss how turning our regression model inside out can help facilitate the identification of most-different and diverse cases. For each strategy, the same principles that we apply for facilitating most-similar case selection can be used for most-different and diverse.

We want to reiterate that most-different case selection should be reserved for instances where the variables can be interpreted dichotomously (Gerring 2017). However, following Seawright's (2016a) assertion that most-different cases should maximize differences in background characteristics, we illustrate how turning the regression model inside out allows us to explore a variety of possible dissimilar pairs via Figure 7.11. The cases that maximize differences in background characteristics will be those where the angle connecting two points is as close to 180 degrees as possible. For example, the angle formed by Switzerland, France and the origin is nearly 180 degrees, and we see nearly perfect dissimilarity (cosine = −0.999). Likewise, the angle formed by Sweden and the UK indicates extreme dissimilarity (cosine = −0.998), as does the angle formed by the Netherlands and Australia (cosine = −0.991). While we could conceivably calculate the cosines for all possible matched pairs and identify the least similar countries, this visual representation readily facilitates such assessment and allows for the incorporation of substantive, theoretical, or logistical considerations (e.g., if a researcher already has one case selected, and is simply looking to identify a second).

In some instances, identifying orthogonal (rather than dissimilar) cases might also yield valuable insights. Again, we can identify orthogonal cases simply by looking for those that form a right angle. Readily evident candidates include the United States and Germany (cosine = −0.060), France and the Netherlands (cosine = 0.017), and Ireland and Belgium (cosine = 0.100).

Finally, the same basic logic applies to the identification of diverse cases. One simple way to identify diverse cases is to select cases from different quadrants of the model space. Alternately, to identify multiple pathways to the same outcome, we might select cases with a similar relationship to the outcome but relatively distinct background characteristics, such as the Netherlands and Switzerland, which appear in opposite quadrants but intersect the line that transects the origin and the outcome at nearly the same distance to the origin. This orientation signals dissimilar background characteristics, but similarly predicted posttransfer poverty, indicating equifinality (i.e., distinct pathways to the same outcome). For Switzerland, the data indicate that low poverty rates are the result of low pretransfer poverty and high GDP, which is reflected in its high similarity to GDP and dissimilarity to pretransfer poverty. For the Netherlands, the data indicate that low poverty rates are the result of extreme levels of government transfers and are nearly orthogonal to pretransfer poverty.

Taken together, these possibilities illustrate how turning the regression model inside out can assist with and advance algorithmic approaches to case selection that build on regression analysis. In Section 7.4, we apply the same procedures in an example with more complex data.

7.4   Determinants of Rebellion by Excluded Groups

For our second application, we use the Ethnic Power Relations (EPR) dataset, and estimate a modified version of an analysis by Wimmer, Cederman, and Min (2009) as our baseline model. Developed by Wimmer and colleagues (2009), the EPR provides data on ethnic groups' access to state power, identifying 733 politically relevant ethnic groups in 157 sovereign states from 1946 through 2005. In their analysis, the authors use multinomial logistic regression to assess the correlates of different types of armed conflict onset. For ease of discussion, we present a logistic regression of one of the three outcomes they consider in their multinomial model: rebellion fought in the name of an excluded ethnic group. For this outcome, Wimmer and colleagues theorize that the key predictor for rebellion by an excluded ethnic group is the size of the excluded population. Our model replicates the specification used by Wimmer and colleagues (see Wimmer et al. 2009: Table 3, Model 1, p. 332), and results are presented in Table 7.8. The significance and magnitude of all effects are fully consistent with results presented by Wimmer and colleagues for this outcome.

Table 7.8 Logistic regression of rebellion by excluded

Coefficient (SE)	
Excluded population	0.546***
	(0.109)
Center segmentation	0.041
	(0.056)
Imperial past	0.061
	(0.376)
Linguistic fractionalization	1.536**
	(0.523)
GDP per capita	−0.081*
	(0.035)
Population size	0.393***
	(0.082)
Ongoing war	0.111
	(0.621)
Constant	−13.650
	(13.180)
N Observations	7,725

Note: Following Wimmer, Cederman and Min (2009), time controls – including year, number of peace years, and a cubic spline function – are not shown.
$*p < 0.05; **p < 0.01, ***p < 0.001$.

We selected these data for two reasons. First, the EPR represents the kind of large-N data where algorithmic case selection is arguably most warranted. As Seawright (2016b: 76) observes, algorithmic case selection is designed to reduce scholars' reliance on individual judgment, instead relying on the algorithm itself to take "a certain kind of information as an input, and then follows logical or mathematical rules to convert that input into a case." With smaller datasets, such as Kenworthy's, it is easier (and sometimes preferable) to select cases based on substantive or theoretical knowledge rather than quantitative indicators. However, using substantive knowledge is far more prone to bias as the number of cases increases.

Second, this dataset exemplifies a key challenge for multimethod research, namely that there is a mismatch between observations and cases. While this is a large-N dataset ($N = 7{,}725$), *cases* are defined as countries (country-$N = 157$). Thus, each case is represented by an average of 50 observations. From the perspective of a time-series cross-sectional regression model, this is unproblematic. However, the criteria for algorithmically selecting cases listed in Table 7.1 are designed to identify observations. This raises important questions: if a single observation is algorithmically identified as typical/deviant/influential/extreme, or two observations are identified as most-similar, do we assume that the case as a whole meets those selection criteria? Or, do we revise our definition of a case to align with the unit of analysis (e.g., cases as country-years rather than countries)? RIO allows us to circumvent this question by moving seamlessly between cases and observations.

Thus, with this example, we apply RIO for case selection with more complex data that reflects a distinct challenge in mixed-method social science (i.e., how to deal with repeat observations for an individual case). As we illustrate below, our solution to this particular challenge is to aggregate the contributions of the observations after the model has been fitted. We do this by focusing on the average position of each case in relation to all other cases (i.e., by taking the mean of the coordinates for each case). The choice to focus on the mean is one of convenience. Using the same procedures, we could just as easily use another measure of the central tendency. Moreover, we are not limited to aggregating. We could, for example, examine the relationships among observations that are coded "1" on the outcome, and see how the country-years with an onset of rebellion by an excluded group relate to one another and to the variables. As Collier and Sambanis (2005) note in their own discussion of case selection, selecting the dependent variable in this way is often necessary when using algorithmic approaches because otherwise there is a high probability of selecting cases where the outcome of interest is absent. With RIO, it is possible to condition our case selection on the outcome while still accounting for the relationships among all cases (for further discussion of this point, see Chapter 8).

Exploring all of these possible goals and the means of pursuing them by turning regression inside out is beyond the scope of this chapter. Instead, we provide a framework for exploring the relationship among cases and variables that researchers can adapt to their needs. We nevertheless highlight these possibilities because case selection should be driven by researchers' substantive and theoretical goals, and the techniques we discuss can be used to serve multiple purposes.

Because the purpose of our reanalysis of Wimmer, Cederman, and Min (2009) is to demonstrate how the analytic techniques illustrated in our reanalysis of Kenworthy (1999) transfer to larger, more complex data, here we attempt to more closely model how researchers might apply RIO in practice. Therefore, instead of beginning with existing approaches to case selection, we begin with RIO and then discuss how our findings correspond with other approaches. Because we have shown above how the same basic architecture can be used to explore multiple approaches to case selection, here we focus on a more limited set of goals: identifying deviant cases and most-similar cases.

7.4.1   Turning the Regression Model Inside Out

Figure 7.12a–c offers three distinct representations of the regression space. First, Figure 7.12a presents the relationships among variables in the model. Figure 7.12b shows the relationships among variables and the *observations,* but without aggregating observations (Figure 7.12b–c has been truncated so that two outlying observations are not shown). As this figure shows, the sheer number of observations makes any meaningful engagement with this representation of the data untenable. Figure 7.12c pulls out a single case and plots the relationships among variables along with all observations for the USA. In the data used for our regression analysis, the USA exhibits relatively stable characteristics. There is a change in the proportion of excluded population that corresponds to the enactment of the Civil Rights Act, and some modest variation in GDP per capita and population size (both logged) over the course of 62 years accounted for. The change in excluded population appears to be reflected in a break in the trajectory of the points (each point represents a country-year) near where they meet the line that transects the outcome and the origin. However, the primary change that we see reflected in the movement of observations over time is based on the time control for each observation's year. This is why we see a relatively smooth trajectory across the plot. Figure 7.13 plots the same relationships as are captured in Figure 7.12a–c, but this time with each point representing the average position of each case's observations. As you can see, this plot is more manageable, and better equipped to allow us to explore the relationships among cases.

7.4.2   Deviant Cases

As noted above, Figures 7.12b–c were truncated so that two observations were not shown, these two observations represent a single case (Kosovo), which is also omitted from Figure 7.13. Figure 7.14 plots the regression space with this

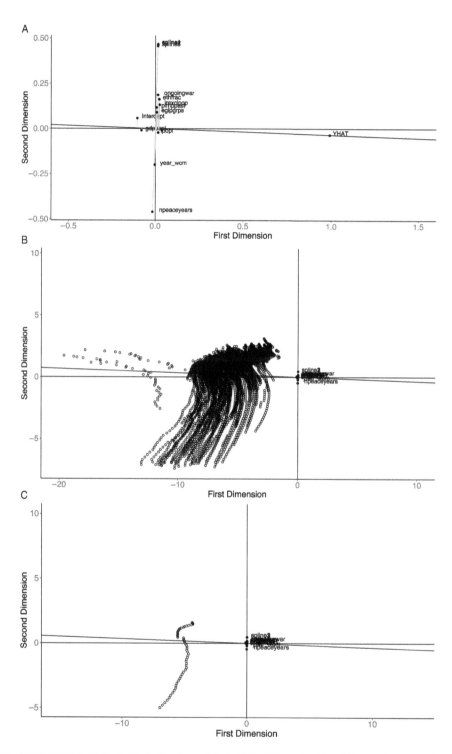

Figure 7.12 Model space for analysis of rebellion by excluded, (a) Variables only, (b) variables and cases, and (c) variables and observations for USA only

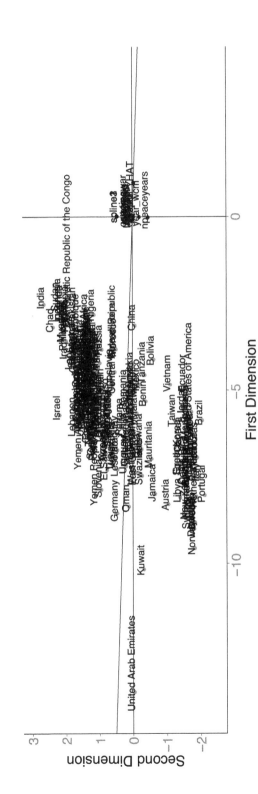

Figure 7.13 Plot of model space with cases aggregated

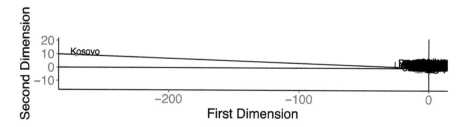

Figure 7.14   Plot of model space with cases aggregated, Kosovo included

case included in the model. As this figure shows, Kosovo is an extreme outlier in our plot, and its inclusion renders the rest of the plot entirely uninterpretable. The reason that Kosovo is such an extreme outlier on this plot is that observations for Kosovo have a predicted probability of armed conflict that is zero. Given that deviant case analysis is intended to assist with (1) amending, extending, or disconfirming existing theories, (2) identifying additional causal pathways, or (3) identifying sources of measurement error, the fact that Kosovo is perfectly predicted raises questions about the data itself. A closer examination reveals that, due to missing data, only two observations from this country are included in our regression model. Its values on the key independent variable are well below the overall mean (8.7% of the population is excluded from political power), and there are no instances of the outcome coded for the two observations included in our data. Thus, Kosovo's identification as a deviant case is actually flagging missing data.

Turning our attention back to Figure 7.13, we can identify additional cases for in-depth analysis. Note in Figure 7.13 that all the cases are to the left of the origin, while the outcome (labeled YHAT) is to the right of the origin. The reason for this is that the model itself does a far better job predicting the absence of war onset than its presence. We can see that there are cases with extreme values on the x-axis, such as the UAE and Kuwait. However, like Kosovo (although to a far lesser degree), these cases are deviant because of their low predicted probabilities. As such, to gain substantive insights, we focus our attention on cases with extreme values on the y-axis.

On the y-axis, the most deviant case is India, which is positioned at the top of the figure in the upper left-hand quadrant. While an in-depth case study of India is beyond the scope of this chapter, examining the data for India included in the EPR reveals meaningful deviations from theoretical expectations. As noted above, the key explanatory variable for rebellion by an excluded group is the size of the excluded population. According to the

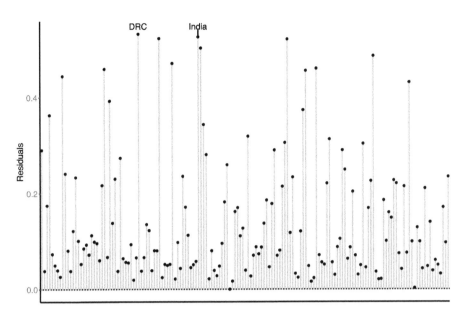

Figure 7.15   Average residuals by country from Table 7.8

data used to estimate our model, India contains 19 politically relevant ethnic groups, but indicates that at no point in the 64 years covered does the share of the population excluded from power exceed 0.07%. For reference, the average share of the excluded population in the entire data set is just under 16%. Despite remarkably low levels of exclusion, this one country – which represents only 0.8% of all observations in the data – accounts for just over 5% of the occurrences of rebellion by an excluded group. This departure from theoretical expectations thus suggests that India is, in fact, a deviant case and that further exploration would be warranted.

To situate what we find using RIO to the conventional approach to identifying deviant cases, Figure 7.15 shows that the average residuals for all observations. As the plot shows, India is among the cases with the highest residuals in the model, exceeded only by the Democratic Republic of Congo (DRC). In contrast, Kosovo (not shown) has the lowest residuals of any case in the entire dataset (followed by the UAE and Kuwait). In analyses of large-N data, it is common to consider more than one case for in-depth analysis, and India is among the best candidates for in-depth analysis based on model residuals. However, it is informative to consider what we might find if we look only at the case with the highest residuals. Like our examination of India and Kosovo, we can briefly explore what insights might be gained from an in-depth analysis of the DRC. In our two-dimensional representation of the regression model, the DRC is in fact positioned close to the margins of the model space. Looking at the raw data for the DRC, there are four instances of onset by an excluded population coded for the DRC (one fewer than in India). Across all years, the average size of the population that is excluded from political power in the DRC is nearly two standard deviations above the population average and exceeds two standard deviations in 41 out of 51 country years. In purely descriptive terms, this aligns particularly well with Wimmer and colleagues (2009) theorization. Moreover, detailed historical analyses similarly suggest that this case broadly conforms with theoretical expectations (Kisangani 2012).

Thinking back to our analysis of Kenworthy's (1999) data where Ireland was flagged as the best candidate for a deviant case but turned out to conform to theoretical expectations, we found that Ireland better matched the criterion for an influential case. Considering this possibility, we can look at whether the DRC is flagged as influential as well. Using Cook's distance, the DRC is in fact identified as influential, as is India. However, unlike India, it appears that despite having high residuals *and* being influential, the DRC better fits the criterion for an influential case rather than a deviant case, whereas the data from India do meaningfully deviate from theoretical expectations.

Comparing what we find by plotting the relationships among cases and variables based on the regression model with what we find by looking at model residuals, we can see that these two approaches leverage distinct information about the model while each also yields useful information. We do not believe that broad conclusions should be drawn about the relative merits of identifying deviant cases based on their position in the model space versus using model residuals, as both cases had extreme values on the residuals as well. Rather, this comparison helps to demonstrate that there is value added in examining the relationship among cases by turning the model inside out.

7.4.3   Most-Similar

Figure 7.16 is a version of our original plot of the baseline regression that is presented in Figure 7.13, with several modifications. First, we removed the majority of case labels from the plot. We then imposed dashed lines from five different points to the origin. By removing the country labels, we can see that many of the cases in our data are extremely close to one another (and in some instances are directly overlapping), indicating an extremely high degree of similarity in

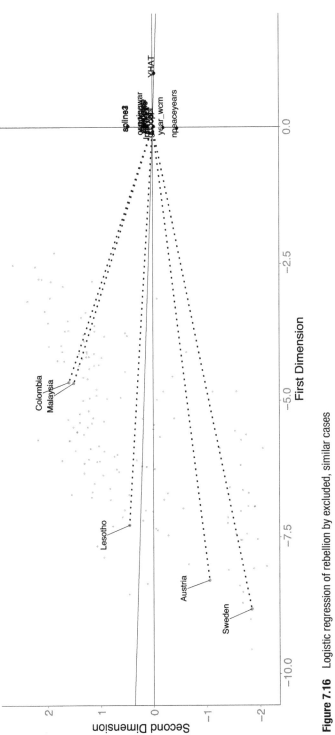

Figure 7.16 Logistic regression of rebellion by excluded, similar cases

the model space. However, there is minimal variation within the overall model space, with all cases positioned in the left two quadrants of the chart and thus no negative or orthogonal relationships. As in our first application, we can use this visual representation to look for cases that are most-similar, most-different, or diverse. Here, we focus on cases that are similar.

While there are a number of candidates for identifying most-similar cases, we selected Colombia and Malaysia. The cosine similarity for these two points is 1.000. Looking at our data on these two countries, neither is coded as having an onset of rebellion by an excluded group during the period covered by these data, yet both had ongoing wars. Both are coded as having two politically relevant excluded groups throughout the entire period covered by the data. They differ in terms of the size of their excluded population, with Colombia having 25.1% and Malaysia 5.9%, but both have high values on their scores for Imperial Past. While these two countries are not identical by any means, these descriptive similarities illustrate their similarity in the overall model space. As noted earlier, rather than taking two random points, visualizing the relationships among cases allows us to start with a single case of interest (i.e., one that we have already collected data on or are quite familiar with) and easily and intuitively select a case that occupies roughly the same position in the model space.

As we emphasized above, using cosine similarity can yield different results from those obtained using other distance/similarity measures. To illustrate, we have highlighted three additional cases in our plot: Sweden, Austria, and Lesotho. Sweden and Austria were identified as the most similar cases using Mahalanobis distance, while Austria and Lesotho were a close second. Because all of the cases in this model are positioned on the opposite side of the origin from the outcome, they all have a reasonably high degree of similarity. While neither Sweden and Austria, nor Austria and Lesotho, are immediately adjacent to one another, all have high cosine similarities. The cosine similarity between Sweden and Austria is 0.996, and 0.982 for Austria and Lesotho. We highlight the different results obtained using these methods to emphasize the point that matching cases by looking at their relationship within the regression model can yield similar information to that provided by Mahalanobis matching, but the two methods rely on different assumptions and can produce inconsistent results. Consequently, researchers should consider the differences between these methods when choosing which method to use, and there may be value in employing both approaches in conjunction. Most importantly, we would contend that neither algorithmic approach should be used to select cases without exploring the nature of the similarities in the data, and the features of the cases themselves.

7.5   Summary

In this chapter, we have detailed how RIO can be used as a gateway for algorithmic case selection. We reviewed common strategies of case selection and illustrated how turning the regression model inside out can contribute to algorithmic approaches to selecting cases based on these strategies. Our point of intervention centers on the contention that there is a basic disconnect between the logic of case studies and the logic of using regression to select cases for in-depth analysis: case studies are intended to shed light on a broader population of cases, while regression sheds light on the relationships among variables. We show how turning the regression model insight out allows us to look at the relationships among cases and variables, and thus gain deeper insight into *how* a given case sheds light on the other cases in the data.

The majority of the chapter centers on two empirical applications that allow us to illustrate the utility of RIO for algorithmic case selection. The first applies RIO to Kenworthy's (1999) examination of whether social welfare policies reduce poverty. This straightforward example builds on an OLS regression of 15 cases, and we use it to illustrate the range of ways that accounting for relationships among cases can complement and extend existing approaches to algorithmic case selection. In doing so, we begin by applying conventional approaches to algorithmic case selection, then use these as our point of departure for exploring the value added by turning the OLS model inside out.

Our second application builds on a logistic regression model based on analyses conducted by Wimmer et al. (2009), with data accounting for 157 cases across 7,725 observations. In this example, we illustrate how RIO facilitates an exploration of cases when each case is characterized by multiple observations. We focus specifically on two forms of case selection and begin by turning the regression model inside out, only later bringing conventional approaches to case selection into dialogue with our findings. Through this example, we highlight key benefits of using RIO, and illustrate useful points of convergence between conventional approaches to algorithmic case selection and turning the regression inside out, as well as noteworthy differences.

8 RIO as a Gateway to Configurational Comparative Analysis

Having explored how RIO facilitates algorithmic case selection, we now turn to a methodological approach that centers on comparisons across multiple cases: configurational comparative analysis. Configurational comparative analysis is designed to facilitate systematic, cross-case comparison while at the same time treating individual cases holistically as complex entities. As Rihoux and Ragin (2008) write, "[the heading Configurational Comparative Methods] indicates that in order to enable the systematic comparative analysis of complex cases, those cases must be transformed into *configurations*" (p. xix; emphasis in original). Configurations are understood as the intersection of multiple properties or characteristics (Ragin 2000: 13). By conceptualizing cases as the intersection of properties or characteristics, researchers can retain the unique characteristics of each individual case because the specific configurations of properties each case possesses (e.g., race, gender, class) can be distinct. At the same time, researchers can systematically compare across cases that exhibit similar configurations, making it possible to identify aggregate patterns. In this way, configurational comparative methods are fundamentally case-oriented, shifting attention from the effects of variables averaged across a population to focus on the way that these conditions combine and interact in cases to affect an outcome.

In this chapter, we demonstrate how turning regression inside out can serve as a gateway between configurational comparative methods and regression analysis by integrating the goals, logic, and mathematics of regression with the case-oriented focus of configurational comparative analysis. The most widely used and well-known configurational comparative method is Qualitative Comparative Analysis (QCA),[1] a set-theoretic

---

[1] Unless otherwise noted, we use the term QCA to refer generally to all iterations of the method, including crisp set, fuzzy set, and multivalue, much as we use the term "regression" as a catch-all that includes OLS, logistic, etc.

approach to social research that is designed to facilitate the identification of necessary and sufficient conditions (Ragin 2014b; Rihoux and Ragin 2008; Schneider and Wagemann 2012). We build our discussion of configurational comparative analysis around QCA because QCA is, as Schneider and Wagemann (2012: 9) observe, "arguably the most formalized and complete set-theoretic method." This formalization has motivated an extensive collection of scholarship comparing QCA and regression, which we build on in our discussion.

To situate our approach, we begin by elaborating the benefits of configurational analysis, then detail differences between QCA and regression. We use this as a point of departure for discussing how turning regression models inside out allows us to integrate the case-oriented logic of configurational comparative analysis into a regression-analytic framework. We then present two empirical applications that illustrate the utility of a configurational comparative approach to regression.

8.1 Comparing QCA and Regression

In 1987, Charles Ragin published the first edition of *The Comparative Method*, which provided a conceptual and analytic foundation for many subsequent developments in configurational comparative analysis. By comparing sets of cases that share common configurations of conditions, QCA assumes that "(1) most often it is a combination of conditions that generate an outcome; (2) several different combinations of conditions may produce the same outcome; and (3) a given condition may have a different impact on the outcome depending on context" (Ragin 2014b: xxii).

Configurational comparative methods are capable of capturing this complexity because treating each case as a complex whole allows for the fact that the causes of a phenomenon may differ from one case to the next. Consequently, analysts can account for the possibility that there is more than one cause to an outcome (referred to as *equifinality*) or that the same condition can contribute to different outcomes in different configurations (referred to as *multifinality*). In addition to allowing for equifinality and multifinality, configurational methods also analytically allow for the possibility that the conditions that lead to the presence of a phenomenon are not the arithmetic inverse of the conditions that lead to its absence (Ragin 2014b). This is referred to as *asymmetric causality* (see Grofman and Schneider 2009; Schneider and Wagemann 2012; Schoon 2014).

The ability to account for these forms of causal complexity, coupled with its high level of formalization and frequent comparisons to regression (e.g., Grofman and Schneider 2009; Ragin 2014b; Rihoux and Ragin 2008), are among the reasons that QCA initially appealed to researchers who use quantitative methods. Yet, QCA represents a holistic approach to social science research, not simply a method of analysis. Grounded in set theory, it is designed to identify relationships of necessity and sufficiency, which are defined by subset and superset relations (Ragin 2014b; Rihoux and Ragin 2008; Schneider and Wagemann 2012). These features of QCA give rise to both conceptual and mathematical differences between QCA and regression. In the revised introduction to *The Comparative Method*, Charles Ragin (2014b) details a series of differences between what he terms the "conventional" (i.e., statistical/experimental) template for social analysis and the "alternate" (i.e., qualitative/comparative) template, which QCA follows. He begins by contrasting variables (conventional template) with sets (alternate template), highlighting how variables are intended to capture some dimension of variation, whereas sets imply membership in a particular category. Ragin explains this distinction, writing:

While a variable can be labeled 'degree of democracy,' a set cannot, because this label does not group cases using membership criteria. However, it is possible to define and construct 'the set of democratic countries' and to list the relevant members of this set. (p. xxiv)

He continues by contrasting measurement (conventional) versus calibration (alternate), dependent variables versus qualitative outcomes, given populations versus constructed populations, correlations versus set-theoretic relations, correlation matrices versus truth tables, and net effects versus causal recipes (for a more detailed discussion of each of these contrasts, see Ragin 2014b).

In addition to these broader conceptual differences, there are also basic mathematical differences between regression and QCA. As Thiem and colleagues (2016) detail, conventional regression analysis relies on the semantics of linear algebra, while QCA relies on that of Boolean algebra. They write, "Boolean algebra provides a self-contained logic of inference … along with mathematical machinery that is neither reducible to nor reconcilable with the logic underlying [Regressional-Analytic Methods]" (p. 745). While the *syntax* of Boolean and linear algebra may be the same, the *semantics* are incompatible. Through formal proofs, Thiem and colleagues show how the laws of (i) distribution, (ii) null elements, and (iii) complementarity are incommensurate across the two algebras. As one example, they show that, "the Boolean operations $x + (-x)$ yields the value 1, but the syntactically identical operation yields the value 0 in the linear case" (p. 748).[2]

Failures to appreciate these foundational differences between QCA and regression have motivated numerous criticisms of QCA for its inability to meet conventional standards for statistical methods (Hug 2013; Lieberson 2004; Lucas and Szatrowski 2014; Seawright 2004). Defenders of QCA routinely contend that these critics either misunderstand or misapply QCA (Fiss, Marx, and Rihoux 2014; Mahoney 2004; Olsen 2014; Ragin 2014a; Ragin and Rihoux 2004; Vaisey 2014), highlighting the kinds of fundamental differences between QCA and regression detailed above. However, even some defenders argue that practitioners of QCA and other configurational comparative methods have contributed to misunderstandings about the two methods by downplaying the differences between them and emphasizing points of similarity (see Thiem, Baumgartner, and Bol 2016).

We note these debates to emphasize two points. First, QCA and regression represent distinct methodological *approaches*, each with its own goals, logic, and mathematics, and each with its own unique value and capacity to advance social research. Second, despite their differences, QCA has a great deal of crossover appeal for regression users. Criticisms of QCA are (often explicitly) motivated by QCA's widespread adoption in areas of scholarship that have long been dominated by statistical methods. Consequently, rather than abandoning QCA for failing to meet conventional statistical standards that it was not designed nor intended to meet, we believe there is a great deal of value in exploring how the two approaches can complement each other in multimethods research, and also how capabilities of QCA that appeal to statistically oriented social scientists can be integrated into regression.

There is already exciting research doing both of these things. Regarding multimethod approaches that incorporate both configurational comparative analysis and regression, multiple studies use the two approaches to address different facets of a single social phenomenon (e.g., Roscigno and Hodson 2004; Schneider and Makszin 2014; Vaisey 2007). For example, in his analysis of the conditions that lead to individuals' experience of *gemeinschaft* (a sense of community belonging, or "we" feeling), Vaisey (2007) uses multiple regression to test a set of hypotheses derived from existing theories on the conditions that influence the experience of gemeinschaft. However, he uses

---

[2] Taking the Boolean operator "+" to imply the union of two sets (each set consisting of 0's and 1's), and "=" to imply the complement of a set (changing 0's to 1's, and 1's to 0's), the union of a set and its complement consists entirely of 1's. By way of contrast, in linear algebra, the addition ("+") of a quantity (x) and its inverse $(-x)$ is 0.

QCA to identify the necessary and sufficient conditions for gemeinschaft. Thus, the regression analysis shows a net effect with a "[significant] association between moral order and we-feeling" (p. 862), whereas the QCA identifies causal recipes, indicating that "moral order is an INUS condition for gemeinschaft – an insufficient but necessary part of all unnecessary but sufficient conditions" (p. 864). Vaisey's conclusions reflect the conceptual differences between QCA and regression (i.e., distinct approaches to causation; see Mahoney and Goertz 2006), leaning on the respective strengths of each methodological approach to advance a broader substantive goal.

There are also exciting methodological advances integrating the logic of comparative analysis and (commensurately) the goals of QCA into a regression-analytic framework. For example, there have been recent efforts to adapt or develop statistical approaches that are capable of accounting for zones of data where no observations occur, in order to identify so-called "floors" and "ceilings," or asymmetric hypotheses, which imply necessary and sufficient conditions (Goertz, Hak, and Dul 2013; Rosenberg, Knuppe, and Braumoeller 2017). These approaches allow researchers using variables and correlational analysis to pursue hypotheses that do not focus on the central tendency of the data.

Our goal for the remainder of this chapter is to contribute to both of these efforts by providing a case-oriented, configurational comparative approach to regression. It is evident that many researchers who are committed to statistical methods are nevertheless interested in the kinds of complexity that are inherent in case-oriented research, and therefore may find value in accounting for these complexities while retaining a focus on variables, correlation, central tendencies, given populations, and net effects.

8.2   RIO as a Gateway to Configurational Comparative Methods

Turning regression inside out does not allow researchers to do QCA. When we turn a regression model inside out, we are working within a regression-analytic framework. We retain variables rather than sets, measurement rather than calibration, dependent variables rather than qualitative outcomes (at least with continuous dependent variables), correlation rather than set relations, and net effects rather than causal recipes. However, similar to configurational comparative analysis, RIO allows us to bring cases to the fore, with each case defined as the intersection of multiple variables.

What does it mean that cases are defined as the intersection of the variables? In Chapters 2 and 3, we demonstrate how RIO allows us to evaluate the relationships among cases and variables, as defined by the regression model. To briefly review, this is accomplished using SVD. SVD generates three matrices: an $n \times p$ matrix of orthogonal row scores (U), a $p \times p$ matrix of orthogonal column scores (V), and a $p \times p$ diagonal matrix of weights (S), where p is the number of predictors (columns) and n is the number of cases (rows; see Appendix 2B). When applied to an independent variable matrix (X), V is a dual set of dimensions pertaining to the variables. To account for the dimensions pertaining to the cases, we postmultiply U by S (calling the result US), which scales the dimensions of the row space (U) by the singular values in S. Thus, we use US to represent the dimensions of the cases and V to represent the dimensions of the variables.

While our SVD makes the row and column spaces orthogonal, as we illustrate with our first example below, each row of US is simply the linear combination of the rows of V, but weighted by the respective (standardized) data value for each row of data on each respective variable (see also discussion of the "transition formulas" in Chapter 9, Section 9.3). In other words, cases are defined as the intersection of the variables, and the variables are defined as the intersection of the cases, reflecting the fundamental duality of cases and variables that is a hallmark of configurational comparative analysis (Breiger 2009).

This understanding of the cases in the regression equation corresponds both conceptually and mathematically with how cases are defined in QCA (see Breiger 2009). From the perspective of providing a gateway to configurational analysis, treating each case as a complex whole makes it possible to adopt a configurational comparative approach to regression: we can account for the fact that the causes of an outcome and the net effect of a particular condition may differ from one case or subset of cases to the next (i.e., equifinality and multifinality), and for the fact that the way certain conditions relate to the presence of an outcome may not simply be the inverse of how they relate to its absence (i.e., asymmetric causality). Turning the regression model inside out also allows us to move seamlessly between aggregate patterns and individual cases such that we can see precisely how each case fits into patterns represented by the regression coefficients, just as QCA methods allow researchers to see precisely how each case fits into the causal recipes identified using truth tables and Boolean minimization.

In these ways, RIO provides a framework for thinking in configurational comparative terms while retaining the analytic and mathematical framework of regression analysis. Much as the tendency of QCA is to complicate and embrace complexity, turning regression inside out allows us to engage with the complexity that is otherwise masked by conventional regression modeling.

Moreover, looking at how cases shape the overall results of the regression model introduces a fundamentally comparative logic. As we detailed in Chapter 5, the intensities of association between cases and variables (i.e., each individual case's contribution to the regression coefficient) are not localized regression coefficients. Rather, they are relative contributions, interpreted not in reference to some external population but in reference to the other cases contributions to the overall model. These differences between RIO and QCA have implications for how we account for key concepts grounded in set theory, such as equifinality, multifinality, and asymmetric causality.

8.2.1   Equifinality and Multifinality in Regression

Within a regression-analytic framework, equifinality and multifinality are mathematically similar to interaction terms, and our approach to account-ing for equifinality and multifinality is consistent with our procedures for detecting interaction terms introduced in Chapter 6. As we illustrate below, to account for equifinality and multifinality, we look at the contributions of cases conditioned on a particular value or set of values. For instance, if we regress self-reported happiness (y) on having an ice cream cone (X_1) and having a hot cup of tea (X_2), using data on a representative sample of the United States, we might have reason to believe that the effects of these two variables will differ across subsets of the population (multifinality) or that different subpopulations will have distinct correlates of happiness (equifi-nality). Using conventional methods, we could include dummy variables measuring residence in Alaska and residence in the Southern United States and interact these dummy variables with our two independent variables to see if the effects of ice cream or hot tea on happiness vary by whether respondents live in a typically hot or typically cold climate. Using RIO, we could instead calculate the contributions of people living in Alaska to the overall regression coefficient, the contributions of people living in the South, and everyone else. If we found antipodal relationships between these two extreme regions (e.g., a positive contribution to the effect of ice cream and a negative contribution to the effect of hot tea for people in Alaska, and the opposite for people living in the South), this would imply more than one pathway to the same outcome.[3]

---

[3] In this example, equifinality necessarily implies multifinality, insofar as the effects of each variable differ across subpopulations. However, we can also imagine a scenario where the contributions of only one variable differs, suggesting multifinality without equifinality.

While meaningful differences in the contributions across these subpopulations would also suggest a likely statistical interaction (see Chapter 6), from a configurational comparative standpoint, there are several benefits of focusing on case contributions rather than simply including interaction terms. First, because RIO allows us to account for contributions down to the level of individual cases, it is capable of capturing a far greater degree of complexity than interaction effects, while also rendering that complexity interpretable. As Ragin (2014b) explains, his efforts to account for complex conjunctural causation began with the use of statistical interaction terms (see Chirot and Ragin 1975). However, as he recounts,

I concluded that working with interaction effects, especially three-way and higher-order terms, was an extremely fragile enterprise. However, this was one of the areas I wanted to explore further, in order to assess the conjecture that there could be mixtures of four, five, or six conditions generating qualitative change (p. xx).

In addition to being statistically fragile due to power and often substantial collinearity between interaction terms and their component parts, the kinds of higher-order interaction terms that are often of interest to case-oriented scholars are both data-intensive and difficult to interpret.

Regarding data requirements, to calculate a higher-order interaction term, all related lower-order interaction terms should also be included in the model (Braumoeller 2004). Consequently, adding a four-way interaction term requires the inclusion of an additional 10 lower-order interaction terms (adding a fifth variable increases the number of lower-order interaction terms to 25, and so forth). Particularly in analyses where the units of observation are individually of interest, such as nations, territories, organizations, or movements, N's are often small and there may not be enough degrees of freedom to estimate so many interaction terms. However, using RIO to assess the contributions of sets of cases representing each possible value of a four-way interaction term requires no more degrees of freedom than are used in the baseline regression model.

Interpreting higher-order interaction terms can also be challenging. While plotting marginal effects of the interaction reduces this burden of interpretation (see Mize 2019), the difficulty of interpretation increases with the inclusion of additional levels of interaction. In contrast, because RIO allows us to build up from individual cases, interpretation is not contingent on the number of variables. Instead, when comparing across sets of cases that represent the different configurations captured by the interaction term, the interpretation of the contributions remains the same regardless of how many sets there are.

This is particularly useful when exploring possible equifinal processes. In a regression context, equifinality implies distinct patterns of association across subsets of a population. If we have two subpopulations that are clearly defined, we can easily decompose all variables in the model into two sets of contributions (as we illustrate below). However, doing the same thing with interaction terms would require interacting every variable in the model with a dummy variable coded for set membership, again consuming degrees of freedom and complicating interpretation.

8.2.2　Asymmetric Causality in Regression

Accounting for asymmetric causality follows the same basic logic as accounting for equifinality or multifinality. However, unlike equifinality and multifinality, where the inclusion of interaction terms could arguably offer similar insights, using RIO to explore causal asymmetries involves partitioning cases' contributions to the overall regression coefficients based on their observed values on the dependent variable. For example, if we used a logistic regression to analyze the determinants of political mobilization (mobilization = 1, no mobilization = 0) by territorially defined linguistic minorities (Ragin 2014b), we might expect that the correlates of nonmobilization are different than those of mobilization. Because regression models the central tendency of the data, there is no way to account for this kind of asymmetry. However, as we illustrate below, a focus on cases' contributions to the overall regression coefficient makes it possible to regress the predictors on this outcome and then examine the nature of the association between predictors and outcomes for subsets of the data based on their values on the dependent variable.

To many readers, the idea that we can partition contributions by their value on the dependent variable will seem jarring, particularly because it may seem to imply that RIO can be used to study only one value for a binary dependent variable without attending to the other. This is not the case. As emphasized throughout the preceding chapters, RIO builds on a regression model, and it is not possible to regress an outcome that exhibits no variation. However, researchers often theorize the association between dependent and independent variables in terms that favor one side of the dependent variable over another. For example, in their widely cited study on ethnicity, insurgency, and civil war, Fearon and Laitin (2003) hypothesize that "the political and military technology of insurgency will be favored, and thus civil war made more likely …" in states where "revenues derive primarily from oil exports" (p. 81). While their theorization associates high oil revenues with insurgency, the regression model imposes the assumption that the inverse is also true – namely, that insurgency is less likely in countries with low oil dependence. It is entirely possible that intensity of association is relatively symmetrical, such that countries that have experienced insurgencies will tend to contribute positively to the regression coefficient for oil revenues while countries without insurgencies contribute negatively. If the effect of oil revenue is significant (which it is, in Fearon and Laitin's analysis), this is the answer assumed by a standard regression model. However, it is also possible that the intensity of association is asymmetrical, such that countries that have experienced civil war contribute positively to the coefficient for oil revenues, while countries that have not experienced civil war are sufficiently heterogeneous that they simply fail to cancel out the association observed among the cases that have experienced insurgency. This possibility would not be inconsistent with the author's theorizing, which focuses entirely on how the characteristics of oil-rich states make them more prone to insurgency. However, the difference between these two possibilities is substantively interesting, and by partitioning the regression coefficient by the dependent variable, we can assess which is most consistent with the data.

It is important to note that in the context of QCA, asymmetric causality is implied by zones with no data, as illustrated in Figure 8.1. From a set-theoretic perspective, the proportion of Xs that are also Ys need not be the same as the proportion of Ys that are also X (see Vaisey 2009). Thus, in Figure 8.1, X is a

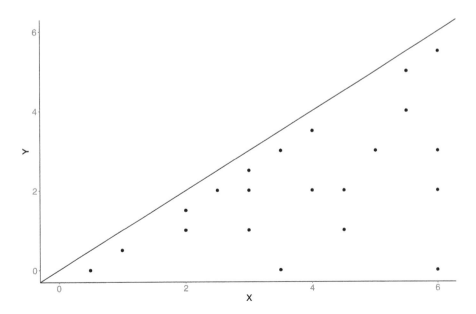

Figure 8.1   Zones of data and no data

necessary condition for Y, whereas Y is a sufficient but unnecessary condition for X. A key concern of QCA is identifying the boundary between these zones with and without data to identify necessary and sufficient conditions, which reflect asymmetric relationships (i.e., having money is a necessary condition for buying a candy bar, but having no money is a sufficient condition for not buying a candy bar).

Asymmetric hypotheses positing zones of no data are quite common in the social sciences, and (as noted above) exciting methodological developments offer a regression-oriented approach to estimating the boundary between zones with data and zones without (see Goertz et al. 2013; Rosenberg, Knuppe, and Braumoeller 2017). Regression inside out is not designed to identify ceilings or floors implied by asymmetric hypotheses. Rather, it allows us to account for asymmetric contributions to the overall regression coefficient, conditional on cases' values on the dependent variable. Differences in these contributions imply different (correlational) causes for the presence versus the absence of an outcome, but they do *not* imply relationships of necessity and sufficiency.

8.3   What Is Configurational Comparative Regression Good For?

A configurational comparative approach to regression is useful when (i) researchers are interested in estimating net effects, and (ii) individual observations (i.e., cases) are theoretically meaningful. Researchers interested in identifying necessary and sufficient conditions, set theoretic relations, case-oriented counterfactual analysis, or small-N comparative analysis are better served by using QCA. Similarly, researchers who are interested in estimating net effects to explore the relationships among variables in contexts where cases are theoretically and methodologically exchangeable (i.e., with data on a representative sample of a real population; Berk 2004) are better served by using conventional regression.

It is often the case, however, that regression is employed to advance claims about the net effect of particular variables even when individual cases are not exchangeable. As noted in preceding chapters, this point has been explicitly made in research on welfare states (e.g., Shalev 2007). Such research often explores the net effects of particular policies on outcomes ranging from life expectancy to voter turnout while acknowledging that the implications of each net effect will vary across cases (or sets of cases), or that important causal heterogeneity is being masked by the net effect. Similarly, analyses of events – ranging from protests to terrorist attacks – routinely recognize that there is a great deal of causal heterogeneity underlying the net effect (see Breiger et al. 2014). While estimating net effects in these contexts still has value, engaging with cases as complex entities is necessary for drawing meaningful conclusions (see Kenworthy 2007).

Case-oriented thinking is also evident in scholarship where individuals are the unit of analysis. For instance, literature on intersectionality posits an "interaction between gender, race, and other categories of difference in individual lives, social practices, institutional arrangements, and cultural ideologies and the outcomes of these interactions in terms of power" (Davis 2008: 68; quoted in Ragin and Fiss 2017: 10). Central to this conceptualization is the understanding that the dynamics of power and inequality vary at the level of individuals based on the intersection of multiple systems of domination (Collins 2002). Consequently, researchers adopting intersectionality as an analytic paradigm focus on individuals as integrated into broader social institutions, requiring attention both to cases as complex wholes and to cross-case patterns (Hancock 2007). Here, configurational comparative regression again offers valuable analytic leverage.

Another context where a configurational comparative approach to regression provides valuable leverage is in mixed-methods research that incorporates both QCA and regression. A configurational approach to regression facilitates integrating insights from QCA into regression analyses in ways that stand to enhance the contributions of each method. Multimethod studies often use different methods for the purpose of triangulation. However, this introduces nontrivial methodological issues when the two methods support divergent conclusions (Seawright 2016). In the context of multimethod research employing QCA and regression, a configurational approach to regression provides a framework for exploring the relationship between the findings produced by each method. It also facilitates a more exploratory approach to regression, but one that allows us to move between cases and variables to improve model specification rather than focusing solely on the addition/subtraction of variables.

In the remainder of this chapter, we illustrate our configurational comparative approach to regression through the reanalysis of two published examples. Our first example comes from Schneider and Makszin's (2014) analysis of how labor protection and social support mediate the effects of education-based inequality in political participation across countries. Our second example comes from Ragin and Fiss's (2017) analysis of the NLSY examining the determinants of poverty. These examples were selected for two reasons. First, they each apply regression and QCA to the same data. This allows us to turn published regression models inside out while also engaging with corresponding published analyses using QCA. Second, these examples differ from one another in their use of QCA. Schnedier and Makszin (2014) apply QCA to a medium-N dataset consisting of country-year observations with the goal of bringing distinguishing features of individual cases to the fore to inform their interpretation of causal processes. In contrast, Ragin and Fiss (2017) apply QCA to large-N data with the goal of accounting for the presence of causal complexity, as implied by an intersectional approach to inequalities.

8.4 Education-Based Participatory Inequality: Reanalyzing Schneider and Makszin (2014)

In our first empirical application, we reanalyze Schneider and Makszin's (2014) study of the determinates of education-based inequality in political participation. With this reanalysis, we have three key goals: (i) to illustrate the duality of cases and variables that undergirds our configurational comparative approach to regression, (ii) to show how turning regression inside out allows us to account for multifinality, and (iii) to demonstrate the utility of RIO for advancing multimethod research that incorporates both regression and QCA. We begin by providing an overview of the original study. We then use a subset of the data from the published article to provide a straightforward illustration of how RIO defines cases as the intersection of variables (and vice versa). Finally, we turn the published regression model inside out to show how this allows us to account for the equifinal processes identified using QCA in the original study and foster dialogue between the two methods.

8.4.1 Overview of the Original Study

In their 2014 article published in *Socio-Economic Review*, Schneider and Makszin employ multiple methods to explore the cross-national determinants of unequal political participation, measured via rates of voter participation. Analyzing data from multiple waves of the Comparative Study of Electoral Systems dataset and the European Social Survey, they show that "in almost all countries, lower educated citizens participate [in elections] less" (Schneider and Makszin 2014: 445). Yet, Schneider and Makszin demonstrate that the degree to which educational inequalities explain differences in electoral participation varies widely across countries, even when controlling for macro-level characteristics, such as the type of electoral system, population size, and a tendency for close elections. These findings set up the central puzzle of their analyses: what explains this cross-national variation in participatory inequality?

Schneider and Makszin make the case that persistent cross-national differences in within-country inequalities are driven by characteristics of each country's system of welfare capitalism. Rather than delineating forms of welfare capitalism according to previously established typologies (e.g., Amable 2003; Bohle and Greskovits 2012; Esping-Andersen 1990; Hall and Soskice 2001; Iversen and Iversen 2005), the authors examine empirically which characteristics (or combination of characteristics) of the welfare capitalist system influence participatory inequality. Building on prior literature, they focus specifically on two sets of conditions: *labor protections* – as indicated by employment protection and union density – and *social support programs* – as indicated by unemployment programs and wage coordination. The authors hypothesize that, "Welfare capitalist systems with higher degrees of labour protection and social support will promote relatively higher engagement and resources for less educated citizens, thereby dampening participatory inequality" (p. 442). They do not propose these as exclusive mechanisms, but rather posit that they can "co-exist and complement each other by increasing the participation of different types of low-educated citizens" (p. 442).

The authors use OLS regression and fuzzy set QCA (fsQCA) to interrogate the relationships between welfare regime types and participatory inequality. First, they use regression to examine which conditions significantly influence levels of participatory inequality. While the regression results partially support their hypotheses, the authors highlight that the models have relatively low overall explanatory power and that the effects of two key variables run counter to their expectation, "thus opening the question [of] whether what matters for participatory inequality are not single welfare capitalist features but rather their combination into distinct welfare regime types" (p. 448). As such, they posit an equifinal process, whereby multiple distinct types of welfare capitalist system – as constituted by different combinations of dimensions of welfare regimes – are causally relevant for explaining participatory inequality.

Schneider and Makszin then use fsQCA to identify three functionally equivalent sets of supportive and protective welfare characteristics associated with low levels of participatory inequality. Consistent with the authors' observation that certain aspects of the capitalist welfare system coexist and complement each other, the countries included in each type are not exclusive to that type, but rather can be more in than out of multiple types (e.g.,

Table 8.1 Summary of Schneider and Makszin's (2014) three welfare types

Type	Attributes	Typical Cases
Protective support	High employment protection; high labor market expenditure	Germany, Netherlands, Norway, Portugal, Spain
Coordinated Support	High labor market expenditure; high-wage coordination	Denmark, Ireland
Unorganized Protection	High employment protection; absence of high union density	Estonia, Korea, Mexico, Portugal

Notes: Detailed information on welfare types and characteristics, along with complete QCA results, can be found in Tables 2–4 of Schneider and Makszin (2014: 450–52).

Germany exhibits features that are consistent with all three types, making it more in than out of all three sets representing the three different types of supportive and protective welfare types). These three types are summarized in Table 8.1. Finally, Schneider and Makszin compare average levels of resources and engagement across countries that are in one of the three sets of supportive and protective welfare types and those that are out to identify mechanisms linking welfare regime type to participatory inequality.

8.4.2 Turning Education-Based Participatory Inequality Inside Out

Our reanalyses centers on Schneider and Makszin's (2014) published regression models. In the original analysis, the authors present four models. The first three models each use multiple waves of data for 37 countries, with an N of 87 country-years. Model 4 analyzes only the final wave of data (collected in 2005), with an N of 30 country-years. The authors include Model 4 to address concerns about their panel data violating regression assumptions. The results presented in Model 4 are substantively consistent with the other models presented.[4] For ease of presentation and discussion, we build on the authors' final model and reanalyze only the final wave of data.

Before turning the published regression model inside out, we will use Schneider and Makszin's data to demonstrate our foundational claim that the cases can be productively understood as the intersection of the variables. For

---

[4] The specification of Schneider and Makszin's Model 4 reproduces the specification of their Model 2. Both models identify the same variables as being statistically significant, and the direction of the effects for statistically significant variables are the same in both models. The primary difference between models is that the coefficients in Model 4 are inflated relative to Model 2, and the direction of the effect for Union Density changes from 0.001 (Model 2) to −0.038 (Model 4), but is nonsignificant in both models.

the sake of simplicity, we demonstrate this using only two variables: Labor market expenditures as % of GDP (scaled) and Social expenditure as % of GDP (scaled). Using SVD, we obtain the matrices **V** (Table 8.2a) and **US** (Table 8.2b).

Using these dimensions, we can see how each row of **US** implies the linear combination of the rows of **V** weighted by the respective (standardized) data value for each row of data on each respective variable (a topic that is further discussed in Section 9.3; see Equation 9.8). For example, Austria's values on our two independent variables are 0.4485 (Labor Market Expenditures) and 1.1972 (Social Expenditures), as shown in Table 8.2b. We first weight each row of **V** (Table 8.2a) by Austria's values on each of the corresponding variables. The weighted values for the first row of **V** are $0.4485 \times -0.7071 = -0.3171$, and $0.4485 \times -0.7071 = -0.3171$. The weighted values for the second row of **V** are $1.1973 \times -0.7071 = -0.8466$ and $1.1973 \times 0.7071 = 0.8466$. Taking the linear sum of the weighted rows of **V**, we arrive at $-0.3171 - 0.8466 = -1.1637$ and $-0.3171 + 0.8466 = 0.5295$, which are Austria's scores on **US** (see Table 8.2b).

With this, we can see how the cases (represented by **US**, the scaled orthogonal row space) can be productively understood as the intersection of the variables (represented by **V**, the orthogonal variable space), and the variables as the intersection of the rows. As detailed in Chapters 2 and 3, these same matrices (**V**, **S**, and **U**) produce the regression coefficients ($\mathbf{b} = \mathbf{VS^{-1}U^T\hat{Y}1}$) and each case's contributions to those coefficients ($\mathbf{VS^{-1}U^T\hat{Y}}$).

Turning our attention to the published regression model, Table 8.3 presents our replication of Schneider and Makszin's original analysis. Consistent with their hypothesis that welfare characteristics associated with social support will reduce participatory inequalities, the model shows a negative effect for labor market expenditures. However, counter to their expectations, the effects of social expenditures are positive. Schneider and Makszin posit that this is likely because the bulk of social expenditures are pension programs, which would not have the hypothesized effect of reducing the impact of educational inequalities in the way that unemployment expenditures might. Regarding their hypothesis that labor market protections will reduce participatory inequalities, again the model offers support for one indicator – employment protection legislation (EPL) – but finds no effect for union density.

Turning this model inside out allows us to account for the multifinality of participatory inequality. As noted above, Schneider and Makszin draw a distinction between countries that have any of the three welfare types identified as being supportive or protective, versus countries that are nonsupportive and nonprotective. Building on their observation that these three types are functionally equivalent and that mechanisms of participation vary based

Table 8.2a–b Matrices V and US for labor market expenditures and social expenditures

a. Scores for variables (**V**)

	Dimensions	
	[1]	[2]
Labor Market Expenditures (scaled)	−0.7071	−0.7071
Social Expenditures (scaled)	−0.7071	0.7071

b. Variable values (scaled) and scores for cases (**US**)

	Labor Market Expenditures (scaled)	Social Expenditures (scaled)	Dimensions	
			[1]	[2]
Austria	0.4485	1.1973	−1.1637	0.5295
Belgium	1.7154	1.0467	−1.9531	−0.4728
Brazil	−0.8798	−1.2285	1.4908	−0.2466
Bulgaria	−0.6168	−0.8270	1.0209	−0.1486
Czech Republic	−0.8448	−0.1244	0.6853	0.5094
Denmark	2.4784	1.2809	−2.6583	−0.8467
Estonia	−1.0810	−1.1616	1.5858	−0.057
Finland	1.2779	0.9129	−1.5492	−0.2581
France	1.0662	1.5988	−1.8844	0.3766
Germany	1.6349	1.2140	−2.0145	−0.2976
Greece	−0.6260	0.0597	0.4005	0.4849
Hungary	−0.5648	0.2772	0.2034	0.5953
Iceland	−0.9848	−0.5593	1.0918	0.3008
Israel	−0.3460	−0.3920	0.5219	−0.0325
Italy	−0.0792	0.6954	−0.4358	0.5477
Japan	−0.6628	−0.3753	0.734	0.2033
Korea	−0.9813	−2.3996	2.3906	−1.0029
Lithuania	−0.9468	−1.0445	1.4081	−0.0691
Mexico	−1.2262	−2.2658	2.4692	−0.7351
Netherlands	1.6699	0.1099	−1.2585	−1.1031
New Zealand	−0.2165	−0.3251	0.383	−0.0768
Norway	−0.1115	0.5114	−0.2827	0.4405
Poland	−0.0695	0.2939	−0.1586	0.257
Portugal	0.2770	0.2270	−0.3563	−0.0354
Slovakia	−0.6453	−0.5091	0.8163	0.0963
Slovenia	−0.6523	0.2604	0.2771	0.6454
Spain	0.6742	0.0764	−0.5308	−0.4227
Sweden	0.9524	1.5486	−1.7685	0.4216
Switzerland	0.0407	−0.0742	0.0237	−0.0812
United Kingdom	−0.7004	−0.0240	0.5122	0.4783

Table 8.3 Replication of Schneider and Makszin's (2014) Table 1, Model 4

Variables	Coefficients (SE)
Union Density	−0.038
	(0.103)
EPL	−7.181**
	(3.094)
Labor market expenditures as % of GDP	−4.481*
	(2.221)
Social expenditure as % of GDP	1.330***
	(0.435)
Wage coordination	−0.461
	(1.781)
Government involvement in wage coordination	5.136*
	(2.560)
Overall electoral turnout	−0.341**
	(0.135)
Intercept	18.124
	(11.798)
N	30
R^2	0.545

Notes: Thresholds for reporting statistical significance follow Schneider and Makszin (2014). All coefficients are unstandardized. ***$p < 0.01$, **$p < 0.05$, *$p < 0.10$.

on whether countries are identified as being supportive and protective versus nonsupportive and protective, we follow their lead and compare cases that exhibit characteristics of these two sets.

Table 8.4 shows the contributions to the overall regression model for these two sets of cases. The contributions to the coefficients sum to the overall coefficients of the analyses presented in Table 8.3 (and the overall contributions of sets are the sums of case's individual contributions), allowing us to move seamlessly between sets of cases and aggregate trends. The differences in contributions between supportive and protective countries versus nonsupportive and nonprotective countries indicate that the conditions associated with electoral inequality meaningfully differ between supportive and protective countries versus nonsupportive and nonprotective (i.e., multifinality). Of the seven variables in the model (excluding the intercept), the direction of the contributions for supportive and protective versus nonsupportive and nonprotective countries is inverse for five: Union Density, EPL, Labor Market

Table 8.4 Contributions of cases more in versus out of sets representing three welfare types

Variables	Supportive and Protective	Nonsupportive and Nonprotective
Union Density	0.076	−0.115
	(0.081)	(0.062)
EPL	4.276	−11.457
	(2.461)	(1.876)
Labor market expenditures as % of GDP	0.889	−5.370
	(1.767)	(1.347)
Social expenditure as % of GDP	0.124	1.207
	(0.346)	(0.263)
Wage coordination	0.977	−1.437
	(1.417)	(1.080)
Government involvement in wage coordination	−1.623	6.759
	(2.035)	(1.55)
Overall electoral turnout	−0.244	−0.098
	(0.107)	(0.082)
Intercept	7.114	11.011
	(9.383)	(7.152)
N	12	18

Notes: Columns represent contributions to coefficients and standard errors in the baseline model, with standard error contributions in parentheses. To calculate the standard errors, we aggregate cases' contributions to the variance and then take the square root of the aggregated contributions.

Expenditures, Wage Coordination, and Government Involvement in Wage Coordination. Of the two variables where the directions of the contributions are the same, we see that one set is driving substantially more of the action than the other. Specifically, 71% of the overall effect of voter turnout is driven by supportive and protective countries, and 90% of the overall effect of social expenditure as a percentage of GDP is driven by nonsupportive and nonprotective countries. This indicates that the conditions associated with electoral inequality are systematically different for cases that exhibit characteristics of supportive and protective welfare regimes versus those that exhibit characteristics of nonsupportive and nonprotective states.

These findings yield novel substantive insights. For example, focusing specifically on the effect of EPL (which is statistically significant in the baseline regression model), the entire effect is driven by the nonsupportive and nonprotective countries, while supportive and protective countries are substantially attenuating this effect. This comparative difference indicates that higher levels of EPL are actually associated with higher rates of participatory inequality in supportive and protective countries when compared with non-supportive and nonprotective countries.

Schneider and Makszin's discussion of EPL helps us to interpret this surprising pattern. The authors detail how higher rates of EPL are associated with less-flexible labor markets, which in turn reduce job turnover. They make the case that lower rates of turnover help to foster networks that would encourage political participation. Based on our reanalysis, it seems plausible that low job turnover simply reduces the stakes at the ballot box for lower educated individuals in countries with supportive and protective welfare regimes. In contrast, the contributions of nonprotective and nonsupportive countries are fully consistent with Schneider and Makszin's hypothesized mechanisms, with higher rates of EPL having a substantial negative effect on participatory inequality.

The comparative contributions to the effects of overall electoral turnout are similarly interesting. Schneider and Makszin control for voter turnout to account for the effects of macro-level factors such as the type of electoral system, the population size, and the degree of fractionalization. As they note, voter turnout is an important structural determinant of participatory inequality "insofar as there is simply less room for participatory inequality with high overall turnout" (p. 439). As noted above, 71% of the effect observed in the baseline regression model is due to variation among countries that are in one or more of the types of protective and supportive welfare regimes. This indicates that there is meaningful variation in participatory inequality among the protective and supportive countries, such that rates of voter turnout matter a great deal for explaining participatory inequalities. In contrast, for the nonprotective and nonsupportive countries, it appears that, relative to the features of the capitalist welfare system, the intensity of the association with voter turnout is minimal. In other words, while variation in welfare provision clearly plays an important role in shaping participatory inequality among nonsupportive and nonprotective countries, the effects of voter turnout suggest that variation in participatory inequality among supportive and protective countries is shaped more by macro-level factors related to the type of electoral system, the population size, and the degree of fractionalization.

Beyond the contributions to coefficients, we also account for contributions to the model variance, which we calculate using the squared residuals approach. As detailed in Chapter 4, there are both methodological and conceptual problems with using inferential statistics to generalize from a single case or subsets of cases; therefore, we cannot treat these contributions to the variance as equivalent to standard errors. However, looking at the distribution of the variance is descriptively informative. Figure 8.2 visually represents the contributions to both the coefficients and variance. For the sake of the visualization, we opted to

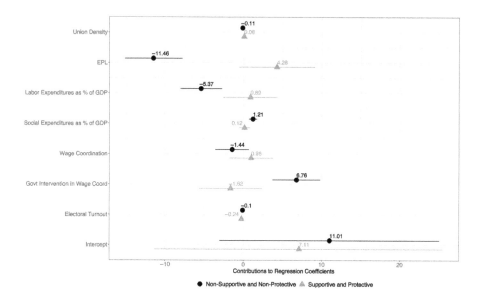

Figure 8.2   Contributions of cases more in versus out of sets representing three welfare types

Notes: Figure shows 95% confidence intervals. These were calculated by first aggregating of each set of cases' contributions to the variance, then taking square root of the aggregated contributions to approximate standard errors. *N* of Supportive/Protective = 12; *N* of Nonsupportive/nonprotective = 18.

present the distribution of the variance as confidence intervals. However, again, these confidence intervals should not be interpreted as conventional indicators of statistical significance. Here we see that a slight majority of the variance is associated with supportive and protective countries (indicated in Figure 8.2 by larger confidence intervals), reinforcing the finding that the nonsupportive and nonprotective countries are better represented by the regression model.

8.4.3   Conclusions

With this example, we have illustrated how cases are productively understood as the intersection of variables (and vice versa) and shown how a case-oriented approach that allows us to account for the divergent effects of dissimilar sets of cases can reveal multifinality within a regression model. To do this, we have put the results of a regression model and fsQCA analysis into direct dialogue with each other. By enhancing the dialogue between methods in this multimethod study, our analysis reinforces and extends Schneider and Makszin's excellent theoretical model and analyses. Schneider and Makszin show that (i) features of the capitalist welfare system matter for participatory inequality, and (ii) that there are multiple pathways to low participatory inequality. Our analysis affirms and extends these findings by showing that, even among nonsupportive and nonprotective countries, variation in the features of the capitalist welfare system still meaningfully explains variation in participatory inequality above and beyond the structurally constraining effects of voter turnout, while macro-level factors linked to voter turnout appear to matter a great deal in countries with supportive and protective welfare regimes.

8.5   The Correlates of Poverty: Reanalyzing Ragin and Fiss (2017)

In our second example, we reanalyze a large dataset with individuals as the unit of analysis: the National Longitudinal Survey of Youth. Our primary goal in this example is to illustrate how turning regression inside out allows us to account for asymmetries in the correlates of being in poverty versus not being in poverty. Here again, we provide an overview of the original study before turning our baseline regression model inside out and showing how our configurational comparative approach to regression can yield insights consistent with findings from Ragin and Fiss's (2017) set-analytic configurational analysis of the same data.

8.5.1   Overview of the Original Study

In their 2017 book, *Intersectional Inequality*, Ragin and Fiss (2017) revisit the controversial findings of Herrnstein and Murray's (1994), *The Bell Curve: Intelligence and Class Structure in American Life*. In *The Bell Curve*, Herrnstein and Murray argue that unequal life chances result from variation in intelligence. They measure intelligence using a standardized test called the Armed Forces Qualification Test (AFQT), which was originally designed as a screening device for the U.S. Armed Services (see Ragin and Fiss 2017: 23). Most controversially, the authors offer a race-based, genetic explanation for differential performance on the standardized test. Herrnstein and Murray's work was criticized on both substantive and methodological grounds, with the most extensive methodological rebuke coming in the form of Fischer and colleagues' (1996) book, *Inequality by Design*. In addition to correcting for technical errors in the original analysis, Fischer and colleagues contend that Herrnstein and Murray's analyses are underspecified. They flesh out the model specification with additional variables measuring attributes of respondents' household and community, their social background, and their living conditions. Their analyses show that the addition of these variables severely attenuates the effects of test scores on outcomes such as poverty, and that differences in test scores are driven by social inequalities, not by genetic differences.

Ragin and Fiss (2017) center their discussion of inequality on these two books and argue that both sets of analyses overlook the fundamentally intersectional dynamics of social inequalities. As they observe, "In almost all known societies, inequalities coincide, compound, and reinforce" (p. 7). They make the case that the cumulative and compounding effect of inequalities has direct methodological implications. Specifically, they argue that the effects of racialized social advantages and disadvantages are not independent of the effects of gender, wealth, or any number of other conditions. Moreover, the conditions that predict the presence of one form of inequality (versus its absence) are not necessarily the same. Thus, Ragin and Fiss highlight a methodological disjuncture between widely accepted theories that recognize the intersectional nature of inequalities, and the net effects methods used by Herrnstein and Murray (1994) and Fischer et al. (1996) to study the causes of social inequalities.

Ragin and Fiss offer a set-theoretic configurational analysis as a corrective to this disjuncture. While it is beyond the scope of this chapter to review all of their methods and findings, to illustrate RIO's capacity to account for asymmetric causality, we draw from two specific elements of their work: (i) a set of baseline logistic regressions, which Ragin and Fiss use to situate their analysis in relation to Herrnstein and Murray's (1994) and Fischer and colleagues' (1996) analyses; and (ii) substantive findings from their configurational analyses regarding the conditions associated with being in poverty versus not being in poverty.

8.5.2   Turning the Correlates of Poverty "Inside Out"

As their point of departure for engaging with Herrnstein and Murray (1994) and Fischer et al. (1996), Ragin and Fiss present a series of logistic regression models. Because configurational methods assess all logically possible conjunctions of conditions, the inclusion of a large number of variables in a configurational analysis is computationally intensive and can be substantively challenging to interpret.[5] As Ragin and Fiss note, in their simplest model, Herrnstein and Murray include only 3 variables, whereas Fischer, et al. (1996) include 29 variables in their fully specified model. Consequently, Ragin and Fiss's first step in their reanalysis is to identify a set of conditions

---

[5] The number of possible conjunctions of conditions is 2^k, where k is the number of conditions/variables included in the analysis. Thus, the inclusion of 5 conditions versus 10 results in an increase from 32 possible combinations of conditions to 1,024 possible combinations of conditions.

that adequately speak to the substance of Fischer and colleagues' critique without replicating Herrnstein and Murray's error of under specification. They identify six variables that together achieve nearly equivalent explanatory power as the logistic regression results presented by Fischer and colleagues.[6] For interested readers, their analyses are presented in Table 3.5 on p. 54 of *Intersectional Inequality* (Ragin and Fiss 2017). Following Fischer and colleagues, Ragin and Fiss present eight different models, running separate analyses for White men, White women, Black men, and Black women. For each population, they ran two models, which differed solely on whether they included respondents' performance on the AFQT. In Table 8.3, we replicate the models that include AFQT, and introduce an additional model analyzing the entire dataset (not broken down by respondents' race and gender).[7]

We turn this additional model (labeled "All" in Table 8.5) inside out. As the results in Table 8.5 show, while effect sizes differ across all models, with

Table 8.5 Logistic regression of likelihood of a person being in poverty

	White Men	White Women	Black Men	Black Women	All
AFQT	−0.021***	−0.018**	−0.016*	−0.021**	−0.019***
	(0.006)	(0.006)	(0.008)	(0.007)	(0.003)
Parental Income	−0.151**	−0.051	−0.121*	−0.121**	−0.110***
	(0.051)	(0.038)	(0.059)	(0.046)	(0.022)
Parental Education	0.036	0.019	−0.028	0.034	0.003
	(0.056)	(0.052)	(0.044)	(0.04)	(0.023)
Respondent Education	−0.212*	−0.256*	−0.340***	−0.480***	−0.296***
	(0.085)	(0.084)	(0.068)	(0.076)	(0.035)
Married	−1.544***	−2.855***	−1.767***	−2.093***	−2.273***
	(0.341)	(0.271)	(0.338)	(0.244)	(0.137)
Children	0.738*	1.745***	0.569*	0.769**	1.236***
	(0.343)	(0.273)	(0.271)	(0.225)	(0.117)
Intercept	1.527	1.953*	3.748***	5.533***	3.004***
	(0.971)	(0.993)	(0.863)	(0.926)	(0.437)
N	1363	1315	732	775	4185

Notes: Thresholds for reporting statistical significance follow Ragin and Fiss (2017). ***$p < 0.001$, **$p < 0.01$, *$p < 0.05$.

[6] See Ragin and Fiss (2017) Chapter 2 for a more detailed discussion of their model specification and analyses.
[7] For ease of presenting multiple models simultaneously, we present the results as a table rather than graphically.

the exception of the intercept for White Men and Parental Income for White Women, the same variables are significant in all models, and the directions of effects are consistent across all models. Thus, our focal model broadly aligns with the findings of each independent model presented in Ragin and Fiss's analysis.

Ragin and Fiss's reanalysis of these data using set-theoretic methods indicates that the determinants of poverty and its absence are causally asymmetric and multifinal. The authors observe highly racialized and asymmetric systems of advantage and disadvantage that cumulatively shape peoples' life chances. For our purposes, we focus specifically on findings from their fifth chapter, where they interrogate the relationship between poverty and two variables that were central to Herrnstein and Murray's *Bell Curve* analysis: the effects of parental income and AFQT scores. Across multiple analyses, Ragin and Fiss show that the conditions used to explain poverty – such as parental income, respondents' education, and test scores – best explain the *absence* of poverty.

More specifically, through their set theoretic analyses, Ragin and Fiss show that both not-low parental income and not-low AFQT scores are strongly associated with *not* being in poverty for White respondents.[8] In other words, White respondents do not have to come from affluent families or have high test scores to avoid poverty, they simply need to *not* be low income or score poorly. In contrast, they observe a "weak to very weak" (p. 86) association for Black respondents. As the authors write, "These results indicate a strong pattern of inheritance of advantage for whites" (Ragin and Fiss 2017: 91). Again, in dialogue with the results of the regression analysis showing that parental income and AFQT scores all have a significant negative effect on the likelihood of poverty, Ragin and Fiss's findings suggest that the negative effect of parental income and AFQT scores on poverty is driven by White respondents who are not in poverty.

Table 8.6 presents the overall analysis turned inside out, with cases' contributions clustered by values of the outcome (in poverty = 1, not in poverty = 0). The results show that, in the aggregate, the effects observed in the logistic regression model are driven by respondents who are *not* in poverty. As noted earlier in

---

[8] The specification of "not low parental income" and "not low AFQT scores" follow the logic of set-theoretic analyses, with sets defined based on qualitative membership criteria. To illustrate why this specification is important, imagine that we set a threshold for "low" income as being less than $20,000/year and "high" income as being greater than $250,000/year. This leaves everyone with incomes between $20,000 and $250,000 unaccounted for if our sets are defined as "high income" or "low income." Consequently, "not low income" is intended to refer to anyone with an income above $20,000, while "not high income" would include everyone with an income below $250,000.

Table 8.6 Contributions of respondents by poverty status

	In Poverty	Not in Poverty
AFQT	0.000	−0.020
	(0.140)	(0.131)
Parental Income	0.000	−0.111
	(0.380)	(0.355)
Parental Education	−0.003	0.006
	(0.385)	(0.359)
Respondent Education	−0.007	−0.290
	(0.477)	(0.446)
Married	−0.028	−2.244
	(0.939)	(0.877)
Children	0.063	1.173
	(0.869)	(0.811)
Intercept	−0.002	3.006
	(1.678)	(1.567)
N	564	3,621

Notes: Columns represent contributions to coefficients and standard errors in the baseline model, with standard error contributions in parentheses. To calculate the standard errors, we aggregate cases' contributions to the variance and then take the square root of the aggregated contributions.

this chapter, this does not mean that respondents who are in poverty are not contributing anything to the model. Rather, their contributions are sufficiently heterogeneous that they simply cancel one another out when aggregated in this way. Focusing on the two variables that Ragin and Fiss treat as substantively consequential (parental income and AFQT), not only do those who are in poverty make no aggregate contribution to the overall regression coefficients, but the contributions of those who are not in poverty are nearly identical to the overall regression coefficients reported in Table 8.5. While the difference is not quite as stark, the same generally holds true for all other variables as well. Substantively, given that parental income and test scores are significant in the overall model and we see here that they are driven entirely by respondents who are not in poverty, we could reasonably conclude that these variables best explain the *absence* of poverty. This is entirely consistent with Ragin and Fiss's conclusions based on their set-theoretic configurational analysis.

As in our reanalysis of Schneider and Makszin's data, we again report contributions to the standard errors using the squared residuals approach, and

Table 8.7 Contributions of respondents by poverty status and race

	White/ In Poverty	Black/ In Poverty	White/ Not in Poverty	Black/ Not in Poverty
AFQT	−0.001	0.001	−0.034	0.015
	(0.113)	(0.083)	(0.105)	(0.078)
Parental Income	−0.003	0.003	−0.147	0.036
	(0.307)	(0.224)	(0.245)	(0.211)
Parental Education	−0.001	−0.002	0.000	0.006
	(0.311)	(0.227)	(0.288)	(0.214)
Respondent Education	0.009	−0.016	−0.061	−0.229
	(0.385)	(0.281)	(0.358)	(0.266)
Married	0.028	−0.056	−1.704	−0.541
	(0.758)	(0.554)	(0.704)	(0.523)
Kids	−0.013	0.077	0.887	0.286
	(0.701)	(0.513)	(0.651)	(0.483)
Intercept	−0.131	0.129	1.346	1.660
	(1.355)	(0.990)	(1.259)	(0.934)
N	190	374	2,488	1,113

Notes: Columns represent contributions to coefficients and standard errors in the baseline model, with standard error contributions in parentheses.

again we first take the sum of the contributions based on whether they are in poverty or not and then take the square root of the additive contributions. Consistent with the fact that most of the effects reflected in the coefficients are associated with people who are not in poverty, slightly more of the variance is being driven by people who are in poverty. On a purely descriptive level, this suggests that there is somewhat more noise than signal among respondents who are in poverty, and vice versa for those who are not in poverty.

Yet, Ragin and Fiss's published configurational analyses suggest something more complex, namely that the results are not simply driven by those who are not in poverty, but that they are driven by White respondents who are not in poverty. To examine this possibility in the regression model, we cluster the contributions of cases by respondent's coding on the outcome *and* respondent's race. Results are presented in Table 8.7.

Several interesting features emerge from these configurations of cases. First, heterogeneity among respondents who are in poverty starts to emerge, as we see divergent contributions to multiple variables among respondents who are White and in poverty versus Black and in poverty. Second, consistent with the findings above, respondents who are in poverty contribute only nominally to the effect of any variable from the overall model. However, homing in on the respondents who are not in poverty, we see that there are important differences between respondents who are White versus Black. For example, the negative effects of AFQT scores reported in Table 8.5 are driven entirely by White respondents, with 97% of the negative contribution coming from those who are White and not in poverty. In contrast, Black respondents contribute positively to the overall regression coefficient for AFQT scores.

This is instructive when we contrast it with the strategy adopted by Herrnstein and Murray, Fischer and colleagues, and Ragin and Fiss, which was to run separate regression models for Black and White men and women, respectively. As shown in Table 8.5, the effects of each variable are largely consistent when regressions are run separately for each subpopulation. This highlights how the results presented in Table 8.5 show the effect of AFQT scores on variation *within* limited subpopulations. In contrast, taking the overall model and looking at the contributions of configurations of cases shows the effect of AFQT for Black respondents *compared* to the effect of AFQT for White respondents. Understanding these results as comparisons across cases rather than simply regression coefficients for a subpopulation of the data, the results show that the Black population's contribution to the overall regression coefficient is a substantial attenuation of the effect of AFQT. Situated in terms of Ragin and Fiss's finding that Black people are systematically and cumulatively disadvantaged, these findings indicate that higher AFQT scores among Black respondents are associated with a higher likelihood of poverty *compared to* White respondents with equivalent AFQT scores.

Turning to the effects of parental income, we see a similar pattern. The negative effect shown in Table 8.5 is entirely driven by White respondents who are not in poverty. The positive contribution of Black respondents who are not in poverty again shows that these respondents attenuate the overall effect of parental income. Again, respondents who are in poverty do not meaningfully contribute to the overall regression coefficients. The fact that Black and White respondents who are not in poverty consistently have nontrivial contributions to the overall regression coefficient reinforces the notion that the model is best at predicting the determinants of *not* being in poverty, while adding depth to our initial analysis by showing that Black respondents fare more poorly than equivalent White respondents in terms of the impact of things like parental income, test scores, and education.

We fully expect that more complexity would emerge if we further subdivided these sets of cases. Here, we are clustering case contributions based on two variables (race and poverty), but as we noted earlier in this chapter, we can continue to explore differences down to the level of individual cases and incorporate additional information that is exogenous to the model itself. This ability to move seamlessly between individual cases and aggregate patterns is a hallmark of configurational comparative methods, and a key benefit of turning regression models inside out.

8.5.3 Conclusions

With this example, we have shown how a configurational comparative approach to regression can be productively used to account for causal asymmetries. We demonstrated this through an application to large-N data with individuals as the unit of analysis. Comparing cases' contributions based solely on whether respondents are in poverty versus not in poverty indicates that the effects of the overall model are driven by those who are *not* in poverty. As noted earlier in this chapter, it is important to remember that this does not mean that respondents who are coded as being in poverty are not contributing to the model. The intensities of association are fundamentally comparative and cannot be interpreted as localized regression coefficients. Breaking these comparisons down further to compare across cases by race and poverty shows positive contributions by Black respondents who are not in poverty. Broadly, turning the regression model inside out suggests that, while there are common conditions that predict the absence of poverty, the causes of poverty are multiple, and at a minimum, vary by race. Thus, much as previous research shows that there are widely varying reasons that violence may be considered legitimate but there are a few common reasons that violence is considered illegitimate (Schoon 2014), or that there are multiple causes of failure in academia but a few common pathways to success (Bornmann and Marx 2012), our analysis indicates that there is a common pathway to avoiding poverty, but comparatively more and more varied pathways into poverty. These results point to important scope conditions for common explanations of poverty, and suggest that additional (nonsymmetric) theorizing is required to understand the causes of poverty as opposed to its absence.

8.6 Summary

Our goal in this chapter was to illustrate how RIO can serve as a gateway to configurational comparative analysis. We detailed how turning regression models inside out offers a fundamentally case-oriented approach that, like configurational comparative methods, treats individual cases (i.e., observations) holistically as complex entities. The ability to retain the complexities of individual cases – which are defined as the intersection of distinct configurations of variables – allows us to account for the complexities that are commonly accounted for in existing configurational comparative methods.

We situate our approach to configurational comparative analysis by detailing key differences between regression and QCA, the most widely known and formalized approach to configurational comparative analysis. In doing so, we make the case that these two approaches to social research are fundamentally different, but configurational comparative analysis has a great deal of crossover appeal for users of regression. With this as our point of departure, we elaborate both mathematically and conceptually the logic of a configurational comparative approach to regression that can be achieved by turning regression inside out.

Finally, we demonstrate the utility of our configurational comparative approach to regression by reanalyzing two published regression models. These reanalyses allow us to demonstrate how we can use regression to account for multifinality and asymmetric causality. We also highlight the benefits of using RIO as a bridge between QCA and regression in multimethod research.

9   RIO as a Gateway to Field Theory

Broadly construed, field theory encompasses an approach to social research that focuses on the role of social fields in shaping the dynamics of action and interaction. As Martin (2003) details, there are several varieties of field theory, but all share common characteristics, such as a focus on how change occurs via interaction between a field and its elements, an understanding that the elements (e.g., individuals, institutions, etc.) have particular attributes that make them more or less susceptible to field effects, and recognition that fields are organized and differentiated. The best-known and most influential proponent of a field-theoretic approach to social research is Pierre Bourdieu, who conceived of fields as nested, hierarchical social contexts, each with specific rules defined by field-specific forms of capital (Bourdieu 1983, 1984). Bourdieu conceptualized a superordinate field of power, and both theorized and empirically explored subordinate fields, ranging from the field of class relations to the field of cultural production. As we detail below, in his theorization of fields, Bourdieu was particularly interested in methods for their formal analysis via methods of geometric data analysis (GDA).

In this chapter, we develop and illustrate our contention that RIO provides a gateway to field theory, and in particular to GDA – a connection that we introduce in Sections 9.2–9.4. In doing so, we recognize that our conception of field theory captures only some limited ways in which Bourdieu and others have developed the concept of fields. For example, Bourdieu and others have explicitly introduced practice, performativity, and agency into the rather austere structuralist aspects of his theory on which both we and the GDA analysts focus, though our approach is not incompatible with these other aspects. We recognize as well that we are not working directly within the GDA tradition; however, we have been inspired by that analytical tradition, and we see our work as providing a gateway to that body of work.

We develop these ideas in dialogue with two empirical examples. First, we extend the reanalysis of Kenworthy (1999) that we developed in Chapter 2. A limitation of our presentation in Chapter 2 is that it was confined to only two independent variables; therefore, the geometry could be represented with no distortion in two-dimensional diagrams. Here we do not draw diagrams, but we show how our geometric thinking yields precise algebraic results with any number of independent variables (dimensions). New results include a novel decomposition of "leverage" (the cells on the diagonal of the Hat matrix), which shows leverage as a function of each predictor variable in the regression model. Second, we reanalyze a dataset on the average savings rate across 50 countries. These data, originally published as a didactic example by Belsley, Kuh, and Welsch (2004), are a classic example in regression diagnostics and provide an excellent basis for illustrating how RIO can serve as a gateway to field theory, while also substantially recasting and broadening the analysis of diagnostics to include the study of the structuring of the entire network among the cases that underlie every regression model.

We begin by providing a review of existing efforts to formalize field theory. Each successive section addresses a key idea implicated in Pierre Bourdiue's theorization of fields. These ideas are (1) social logics, (2) the co-constitution of institutions and their properties, and (3) networks.

9.1   The Formalization of Social Fields

At the core of Pierre Bourdieu's theorization of social fields is a vision of social and institutional life as fundamentally relational in nature. Bourdieu, whose sociology of fields today remains of immense importance in the social sciences (Medvetz and Sallaz 2018), felt tempted to

twist Hegel's famous formula and say that *the real is the relational*: what exists in the social world are relations—not interactions between agents or intersubjective ties between individuals, but objective relations which exist 'independently of individual consciousness and will,' as Marx said (Bourdieu and Wacquant 1992).[1]

Some key ideas implicated by Bourdieu's theorization of fields include networks, social logics, and the co-constitution (or duality) of institutions and properties. As to networks, Bourdieu writes that, "in analytic terms, a field may be defined as a network, or configuration, of objective relations between positions" (Bourdieu and Wacquant 1992), and fields are amenable to study, in part, on the basis of methods developed by social network analysts (Martin 2003). As to logics, fields are "spaces of objective relations that are the site of

---

[1] In Hegel's formula, "the real is the rational" (Vandenberghe 1999).

a logic and a necessity that are *specific and irreducible* to those that regulate other fields" (Bourdieu and Wacquant 1992). As for the duality of institutions and properties, Bourdieu's fields foreground the co-constitution of classes and classification.[2]

In recent years, there has been increased appreciation for the extent to which Bourdieu's concepts of field and social space are linked to specific formal techniques of analysis, going under the general name of GDA, developed in particular by several generations of French mathematicians, statisticians, and social scientists whose work has been innovative and generative both of formal–methodological and theoretical insight (Duval 2018; Lebaron 2009; Lebaron and Le Roux 2018; Rouanet, Ackermann, and Le Roux 2000; Schmidt-Wellenburg and Lebaron 2018).

In important respects, Bourdieu's field theory was developed in opposition to the regression modeling that is so pervasive in the social sciences. What Bourdieu had against regression modeling is that the particular relations between a dependent variable and an independent variable "tend to mask the complete system of relationships which constitutes the true principle of the specific strength and form of the effects registered in any particular correlation" or coefficient (Bourdieu 1984). Unlike in regression analysis, the analyst should focus simultaneously on three mutually implicated systems of relations: those among all the variables, those among all the actors (whether the latter be individuals, groups, classes, or organizations), and those linking variables and actors. Indeed, "the most independent of 'independent' variables conceals a whole network of statistical relations which are present, implicitly, in the relationship with any given opinion or practice" (Bourdieu 1984). Bourdieu "consciously" found an alternative to regression modeling (and related dominant quantitative methods in the social sciences) by making use of the geometric modeling of data, which he practiced for some three decades beginning in the 1970s (Lebaron 2009). In Bourdieu's final lecture at the College de France, in 2001, he reiterated, with reference to a central technique of GDA: "Those who know the principles of multiple correspondence

---

[2] Concerning the latter idea, "if, for example, my task is to analyze various combat sports (wrestling, judo, aikido, boxing, etc.), or different institutions of higher learning, or different Parisian newspapers," Bourdieu tells his graduate students (Bourdieu and Wacquant 1992), "I will enter each of these institutions on a line and I will create a new column each time I discover a property necessary to characterize one of them." This very simple table "has the virtue of forcing you to think relationally both about the social units under consideration and their properties" (Bourdieu and Wacquant 1992). The idea of co-constitution ("duality") of institutions and properties has been understood to be theoretically and methodologically central to Bourdieu's approach (Breiger 2000; Lee and Martin 2018; see also Mützel and Breiger 2020).

analysis will grasp the affinities between this method of mathematical analysis and the thinking in terms of field" (quoted in Lebaron 2009).

And yet, it would not be quite true to assert that there have been no openings to bridging regression modeling with Bourdieu's field theory and with the techniques of GDA. Despite his principled commitment to GDA, Bourdieu "was enthusiastic about the possibility of future integration of regression into the framework of geometric data analysis" (Lebaron 2009). Of greatest importance was a paper of "reflections and suggestions" on regression modeling and GDA authored by Rouanet et al. (2002), a paper demonstrating the visualization of the results of regression analysis by projecting the multidimensional space constructed from the independent variables of the model and representing the regression outcome as a supplementary variable (see also the approach of Robette and Roueff 2019), similar in important respects to, but predating, the RIO framework we introduced in Part I of this book.

Now we develop some additional consequences of RIO that assist an analyst in moving from a variables-centered modeling approach to one focused simultaneously on cases, variables, and their interrelations. We make use of the dimensions of the space of variables, the space of cases, and the joint space of case-variable affiliations, dimensions that derive naturally from the SVD of a data matrix.[3]

9.2   Social Logics: A Decomposition of Leverage in the Hat Matrix

In this section, we show how a decomposition of the Hat matrix allows us to identify the broader social logic of an institutional field. Data points that exercise considerable influence on the fitted regression model are called *leverage points*. A particular matrix, called the Hat matrix (or sometimes the projection matrix) has diagonal values that are taken as measures of leverage. Values close to 1 indicate that the corresponding case exerts strong influence on the regression fit; values close to zero indicate only slight influence (Belsley et al. 2004).

We begin with a novel decomposition of the "leverage" of observations, that is, their values on the diagonal of the Hat matrix. So as to have an example that the reader can easily reproduce, we illustrate using Kenworthy's (1999) dataset that has provided a running example through several chapters of this

---

[3] For a brief introduction to SVD, see Appendix B.

book. Unlike the limitation of our discussion in Chapter 2, however, where our two-dimensional diagrams could not be extended precisely to datasets having more than two independent variables, here we use Kenworthy's full dataset, and we show that the results we present in this chapter are not constrained by numbers of variables (or numbers of cases) in a dataset. Chapter 7, on case selection, also used Kenworthy's full dataset, and our analyses in this chapter will extend the insights obtained previously. The variables, in scaled (Z-score) form, are given in Table 9.1. The regression model is that used in Chapter 7 (Table 7.2).

Working with the dimensions that underly both SVD and regression modeling, we begin by computing the SVD of our matrix of independent variables. Referring to our scaled matrix of independent variables ($\mathbf{Z_X}$, Table 9.1) as matrix $\mathbf{X}$, we use SVD to decompose it into the three matrices given in Table 9.2.

$$\mathbf{X} = \mathbf{U\,S\,V}^\mathrm{T} \tag{9.1}$$

As reviewed in Appendix B, we interpret any value in matrix $\mathbf{U}$ as the coordinate of a particular country on a particular dimension (respectively) of a three-dimensional "space for countries." We interpret any value in matrix $\mathbf{V}$ as the coordinate of one of the three independent variables on one of the

Table 9.1 Matrix $\mathbf{Z_X}$ (three variables) and $\mathbf{Z_Y}$ from Kenworthy (1999)

	Matrix $\mathbf{Z_X}$			$\mathbf{Z_Y}$
Nation	Transfers (scaled)	GDP/ capita (scaled)	Pretax/ transfer Poverty (scaled)	Posttax/ transfer Poverty (scaled)
AUS	−1.383	0.154	−0.005	0.376
BEL	1.515	−0.567	0.398	−0.465
CAN	−0.851	0.233	−0.098	−0.393
DNK	0.114	0.015	0.352	−0.479
FIN	−0.634	−0.834	−1.321	−0.793
FRA	1.152	−0.235	1.472	0.077
DEU	0.428	−0.329	−0.940	−0.707
IRL	−0.610	−1.718	1.829	2.871
ITA	0.356	−0.935	0.848	0.718
NLD	2.046	−0.014	−0.144	−0.279
NOR	0.090	−0.446	−1.632	−1.078
SWE	0.380	0.268	0.041	−0.493
CHE	−0.876	1.956	−1.252	−0.778
GBR	−0.707	0.275	0.722	1.075
USA	−1.020	2.177	−0.271	0.348

Table 9.2 SVD for matrix Z_X of Table 9.1

a) Matrix **U** (15 nations × 3 dimensions)

Nation	[,1]	[,2]	[,3]
	Dimension		
AUS	−0.174	0.309	0.139
BEL	0.292	−0.257	−0.118
CAN	−0.137	0.170	0.066
DNK	0.053	0.040	−0.084
FIN	−0.114	−0.088	0.548
FRA	0.335	0.020	−0.358
DEU	−0.020	−0.266	0.206
IRL	0.384	0.514	0.200
ITA	0.268	0.097	0.047
NLD	0.211	−0.489	−0.235
NOR	−0.124	−0.317	0.408
SWE	0.010	−0.084	−0.128
CHE	−0.512	−0.075	−0.178
GBR	−0.030	0.290	−0.115
USA	−0.441	0.137	−0.399

b) Matrix **S** (3 dimensions × 3 dimensions)

	[,1]	[,2]	[,3]
	Dimensions		
[1,]	4.718	0.000	0.000
[2,]	0.000	3.398	0.000
[3,]	0.000	0.000	2.863

c) Matrix **V** (3 variables × 3 dimensions)

	[,1]	[,2]	[,3]
	Dimensions		
Transfers	0.522	−0.768	−0.371
GDP	−0.642	−0.067	−0.764
Pre-pov	0.562	0.637	−0.528

three dimensions. And we interpret the three values in matrix **S** as reflecting the relative weight of each respective dimension. The matrices **U**, **S**, and **V** are given in Table 9.2.[4]

---

[4] The numbers in Table 9.2 are different from those presented in Table 2.9 because Table 2.9 reports the SVD of a reduced data matrix with only two predictors.

One advantage of our focus on the dimensions that underly the regression model is a straightforward formula for the Hat matrix ($\mathbf{H}$):

$$\mathbf{H} = \mathbf{U}\,\mathbf{U}^{\mathrm{T}} \tag{9.2}$$

where the right-hand side references matrix multiplication of $\mathbf{U}$ (given in Table 9.2) by its transpose. We also have (Belsley et al. 2004):

$$\hat{\mathbf{y}} = \mathbf{H}\,\mathbf{y} \tag{9.3}$$

which we discussed in Section 2.5. From Equation 9.3 we see that each case's estimated value ($\hat{y}_i$) is a linear combination of every case's observed value on $\mathbf{y}$. Therefore, a case with a high value on the diagonal of $\mathbf{H}$ tends to strongly influence the fit. And from Equation 9.2, we see that any cell on the diagonal of $\mathbf{H}$ has a geometric representation as the square of the distance of its respective point from the origin. This is true for any dimensionality (here, a three-dimensional space).[5]

The diagonal values of the Hat matrix ($\mathbf{H}$) are often used in their own right as measures of leverage, and they also form an integral component of most measures used in regression diagnostics. In addition to all this, however, our RIO approach that focuses on dimensions allows us to decompose the leverage measure for each case according to each respective variable in the regression model. Considering matrices $\mathbf{U}$ and $\mathbf{V}$ in Table 9.2, we form the matrix product

$$\mathbf{U}\,\mathbf{V}^{\mathrm{T}} \tag{9.4}$$

Then, the sum of squares across any row of this matrix yields the respective value on the diagonal of the Hat matrix ($\mathbf{H}$).[6] This decomposition is illustrated in Table 9.3, where the final column (labeled h_i) gives the diagonal values of the Hat matrix, and the sum of the first three columns (one for each variable in the regression model) equals h_i. In this summing, we ignore the parentheses around certain cells in Table 9.3. Those parentheses indicate entries in Equation 9.4 that are negative in value.

Nations in Table 9.3 are sorted in descending order according to their leverage (column h_i). Each cell in the first three columns is the square of the corresponding cell in $\mathbf{UV}^{\mathrm{T}}$. This table aids us substantially in turning regression inside out in order to study cases. Consistent with our discussion of these data in Chapter 7, in the first row of the table we see that Ireland has the highest

---

[5] For example, from matrix $\mathbf{U}$ in Table 9.2, the squared distance of Australia from the origin in three-dimensional space is $(-0.174^2) + (0.309^2) + (0.139^2) = 0.145$, which is the diagonal value of $\mathbf{H}$ for Australia (given in the ninth row of Table 9.3).

[6] For example, for Ireland in Table 9.3, we have that $0.072 + 0.188 + 0.192 = 0.452$.

Table 9.3 Decomposing leverage (h_i) by squares of cells in $\mathbf{UV}^T$

	Transfers	GDP	Pre-pov	Hat Matrix h_i
IRL	(0.072)	(0.188)	0.192	0.452
USA	(0.035)	0.335	0.002	0.373
NLD	0.328	0.006	(0.005)	0.339
FIN	(0.038)	(0.115)	(0.168)	0.321
CHE	(0.021)	0.220	(0.058)	0.300
NOR	0.001	(0.045)	(0.237)	0.283
FRA	0.085	0.003	0.152	0.240
BEL	0.155	(0.006)	0.004	0.165
AUS	(0.144)	0.000	0.001	0.145
DEU	0.014	(0.016)	(0.084)	0.114
GBR	(0.038)	0.008	0.052	0.098
ITA	0.002	(0.046)	0.035	0.083
CAN	(0.051)	0.001	0.000	0.052
SWE	0.014	0.009	0.000	0.023
DNK	0.001	0.001	0.010	0.011

Notes: Diagonal cells of the Hat matrix $\left(h_i\right)$ are sums across the first 3 columns (ignoring parentheses). Parentheses indicate negative values in $\mathbf{UV}^T$. Rows are ordered by descending values of h_i.

leverage, and that this leverage is due about equally to its (quite high) poverty before taxes and transfers ("pre-pov") and to its (quite low) GDP per capita. The USA has the next-highest leverage. Table 9.3 calls our attention to the sharp differences between these two cases (Ireland and the U.S.) that have the highest leverage. We see that the high leverage of the U.S. is due overwhelmingly (0.335/0.373, or 90%) to its high GDP per capita, much less (0.035/0.373, or 9%) to its low rate of transfers, and essentially not at all (0.002/0.373 = 1%) to its rate of poverty prior to taxes and transfers. Contrast both of these cases with that of the Netherlands, in the third row of Table 9.3: its leverage is due overwhelmingly to its high rate of transfers (0.328/0.339 = 97%). The decomposition of leverage in Table 9.3 thus has great descriptive value to aid in our understanding of why some countries stand out, with respect to the predictor variables in our model and the cases' leverage in the regression model.[7] In this way, we are able to better understand the social logic undergirding the system of relationships represented by the regression model.

[7] By convention, h_i values are considered large if they are greater than $2p/n$, where we have p variables and n cases (here, $p = 3$ and $n = 15$; $2p/n = 0.4$). However, this very rough rule of thumb is based on

9.3 The Co-constitution of Institutions and Properties

The results presented in this section are well known to every student of correspondence analysis, where they often go under the name of transition formulas (see Le Roux and Rouanet 2004). We nonetheless review them here because they illuminate, within a regression context, a geometry according to which the positioning of the cases, and that of the predictor variables used in regression, co-constitute each other. In the context of field theory, this allows us to account for the duality of institutions and properties, as detailed earlier. As we discuss in Chapter 7, this notion has also been elaborated as "the duality of cases and variables" (Breiger 2009; see also Martin 2018).

Matrix V (Table 9.2) consists of the coordinates of each predictor variable in a multidimensional space (here, a space of three dimensions). Remarkably, we can write these coordinates as a function of the coordinates for the cases (displayed in matrix U), weighted by the "profile" of a predictor variable, where a variable's "profile" is simply the observed data on that variable for all the cases. In other words, the variable *is* the cases that comprise it. The multidimensional coordinates of the variable are functions of the coordinates of the cases, and vice versa.

Let us illustrate, by computing an entry in the first row ("Transfers") of matrix V (Table 9.2). To compute the coordinate on dimension 1 for "Transfers" (which, as we see from Table 9.2, is 0.522), we simply find the sum of cross-products of the coordinates of all the *cases* on dimension 1 (i.e., the first column of matrix U), weighting each case's coordinate by its observed data value (i.e., the "Transfers" column in the data matrix in Table 9.1), obtaining:

$$(-0.174 \times -1.383) + (0.292 \times 1.515) + \ldots + (-0.441 \times -1.020) = 2.4612 \qquad (9.5)$$

Dividing this sum by the singular value for dimension 1 (the first entry in matrix S in Table 9.2) gives us 2.4612/4.718 = 0.522, which is what we were looking for: the coordinate on dimension 1 for the variable Transfers. In matrix notation, we find the coordinates for all variables on all dimensions (i.e., matrix V) by the matrix product

$$V = X^T U S^{-1} \qquad (9.6)$$

assumptions of independence among cases and a multivariate Gaussian distribution among predictor variables (Belsley et al. 2004), assumptions that are clearly ludicrous with respect to the present dataset, where descriptive analysis nonetheless seems productive. Development of permutation tests and other forms of combinatorial inference are promising (Le Roux, Bienaise, and Durand 2019).

Where **X** denotes the matrix of predictors in Table 9.1, and **U**, **S**, and **V** are the matrices of the SVD (Table 9.2). And, dually, to compute the coordinates of the cases in a multidimensional space:

$$\mathbf{U} = \mathbf{X} \, \mathbf{V} \, \mathbf{S}^{-1} \tag{9.7}$$

Notice that, by postmultiplying each side of Equation 9.7 by matrix **S**, we have

$$\mathbf{U} \, \mathbf{S} = \mathbf{X} \, \mathbf{V} \tag{9.8}$$

Equation 9.7 provides the rationale for plotting matrices **US** and **V** in the same space in Chapter 2 (e.g., Figures 2.3, 2.4 and 2.5). We have also made use of this equation in our discussion of education-based participatory inequality (Section 7.4.2). This type of representation is known as "barycentric," and the dual barycentric representation is given by postmultipying Equation 9.6 by **S** (see Breiger 2009).

9.4   A Network Approach to Field Analysis of Regression

Near the beginning of this chapter, we mentioned Bourdieu's comment that, "in analytic terms, a field may be defined as a network, or configuration, of objective relations between positions" (Bourdieu and Wacquant 1992). Several researchers have produced studies that combine aspects of networks and fields (or closely related aspects of GDA); see, for example, de Nooy (2003) and Denord (2015). Here we introduce our RIO approach as a gateway to a form of network analysis that we see as underlying regression modeling as the modeling of a field of relations among cases and variables.

The key to our approach is the recognition by a generative theorist of social fields (Martin 2003) that the empirical specification of field position involves a reduction of myriad relationships to a manageable position. "In sum, ... we may say that a field exists when a set of analytic elements are aligned in such a way that it is parsimonious to describe their current state in terms of position vis-à-vis one another" (Martin 2003: 41–42). An appealing criterion for identifying positions in fields (DiMaggio and Powell 1983; Martin 2003) is the network concept of structural equivalence, according to which elements are grouped together in the same network position if they have highly similar relations to all elements in the system (Dabkowski, Fan, and Breiger 2020; White, Boorman, and Breiger 1976). Structural equivalence (as well as generalized forms of equivalence) has been applied to identify positions in networks of relations by means of methods going under the name of blockmodels. As methodological sophistication in network analysis has increased, the variety of strategies for defining and implementing blockmodels on networks has expanded (Doreian, Batagelj, and Ferligoj 2020). We will demonstrate the relevance for regression modeling of one form of blockmodel.

For our example, we use classic data (Belsley et al. 2004) on 50 countries and 4 predictor variables in order to study (as the outcome variable) the average aggregate personal savings rate in each country over a 20-year period. According to the "life cycle" hypothesis that informed the original analysis, savings rates should be smaller if nonmembers of the labor force constitute a large part of the population. Two predictor variables measure (respectively) the average percentage of the population under 15 years of age across the study period, as well as the average percentage over 75 years of age. Income (average level of real per-capita disposable income in each country during the study period) is included in the model, as is income growth (the average percentage growth rate of disposable income over the study period).

The regression modelers (Belsley et al. 2004) were particularly interested in the Hat matrix associated with their regression model. However, they were interested primarily in values on the diagonal of this matrix, due to their goal of identifying a relatively small number of cases (outliers, for example, and those exhibiting high leverage) that didn't fit the general pattern of the regression model.[8] In contrast, with our network approach, we will consider the Hat matrix as a network.[9] We analyze this network in order to identify an overall patterning among the 50 countries with respect to the variables at issue.

In our analysis of the network underlying the above-mentioned regression model, we will apply to the Hat matrix an analog to a model known in the networks literature as a degree-corrected stochastic blockmodel (Karrer and Newman 2011). In a stochastic blockmodel, nodes (in our example, the

---

[8] Belsley et al. (2004) also devoted great attention to "multiple-row diagnostics," developing innovative insights about the mathematics of the regression model. However, subsequent analyses of regression diagnostics have tended not to adopt this aspect of their work, continuing to treat each observation (case) in relative isolation from the others. Our approach, by contrast, emphasizes, not the identification of small numbers or sets of cases that don't fit a regression model, but rather the overall structure and patterning of cases that underlies any regression model.

[9] One productive way to begin to think of the Hat matrix as a network is suggested by its definition (Equation 9.3). In a regression model, the vector of fitted values ($\hat{y}$) is selected so as to maximize its correlation with the observed outcome (y). From Equation 9.3, we see that the Hat matrix (H) is the network among the predictor variables that, when postmultiplied by y, maximizes the correlation. Moreover, if y consisted of some different data, H would remain the same, because H depends only on relations among the predictor variables, and not on the outcome. In this sense (because it maximizes the correlation between the observed and the fitted values, no matter what values y consists of), H may be understood as an optimal network among the predictor variables.

nations in the study) are deemed to be similar (and candidates to be placed within a common position or "block") if they connect to equivalent nodes with equal probability, and if they connect to nodes in other blocks in an equivalent way (Rosvall et al. 2019). More precisely, the probability of a connection between two nodes, u and v, belonging (respectively) to block c_u and block c_v (where c_u may equal c_v), is determined by a single parameter specific to the intersection of c_u and c_v. In our analog of this model that is applicable to the Hat matrix, we will use cosine similarities rather than probabilities.

The literature on stochastic blockmodels is large. Although such models are usually applied to conventional network data (often, to a network of connections considered only "present" or "absent"), the idea of stochastic equivalence has been generalized to tables of counts (e.g., Breiger and Mohr 2004) and to weighted networks. As we here consider extensions to regression modeling contexts, we note that one idea of particular interest in the literature on stochastic blockmodels is that stochastic equivalence (as described above) may be, in part, a function of nodes receiving (and/or sending) differential numbers of network connections or ties. Network *degree* refers to the volume of ties sent from (and/or received by) any node. Degree is measured by the row-sums (and/or column-sums) of the matrix representation of the network. Therefore, the motivation for a "degree-corrected" stochastic blockmodel is that the underlying pattern of connections among stochastically equivalent sets (or "blocks") of nodes should be sought *after* removing the effect of nodal degree (Karrer and Newman 2011).

The Hat matrix ($\mathbf{H} = \mathbf{U}\mathbf{U}^\mathrm{T}$ from Equation 9.2) represents a special network. Controlling for "degree" would make no sense because all row- and column-sums of the Hat matrix are 1. For the Hat matrix, the crucial feature to "correct for" is the diagonal. We would like to know the influence of one case (row or column of $\mathbf{H}$) on another – we are concerned with off-diagonal entries – and we would like to understand this network of influence "controlling for" the overall distinctiveness of each individual node. Any cell on the diagonal of $\mathbf{H}$ is the square of the distance of the corresponding row in matrix $\mathbf{U}$ (as introduced earlier in Chapter 2, Section 2.5) from the origin.

Following from this discussion, let us define a diagonal matrix $\mathbf{D}$ that contains the diagonal of the Hat matrix. Then (in analogy to an equation used in "degree-corrected" stochastic blockmodels; Rosvall et al. 2019), for country i in block $\mathbf{u}$ and country j in block $\mathbf{v}$ (where $\mathbf{u}$ and $\mathbf{v}$ might be the same), we should like to study similarities among these countries with respect to a model matrix $\mathbf{B}$ such that

$$\mathbf{B}_{ij} = \mathbf{D}^{-1/2}\left(\mathbf{U}\mathbf{U}^\mathrm{T}\right)\mathbf{D}^{-1/2} = \Omega_{\mathbf{uv}} \tag{9.9}$$

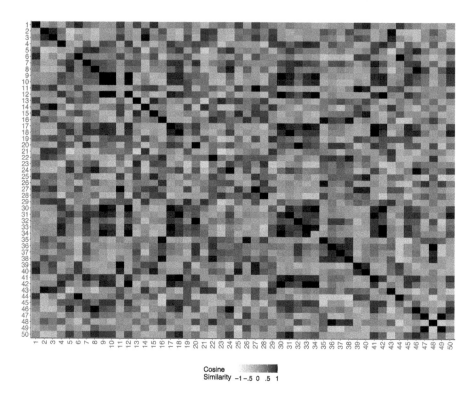

Cosine
Similarity −1 −.5 0 .5 1

Figure 9.1   The matrix cos(**UU**ᵀ)

Pre- and postmultiplying the Hat matrix by $\mathbf{D}^{-1/2}$ transforms it to a matrix of cosines, **B**. The Ω term specifies that all cosines should have the *same* value for the influence of any country i in block **u** on any country j in block **v**.

To examine the pattern inside the Hat matrix, we remove the effect of the diagonal cells (our alternative to network "degree"), and we focus on the similarities in the cosine matrix. To show this matrix compactly, we use the visualization in Figure 9.1, where rows and columns are arranged in their original (and arbitrary) order.

We produced a blocking (a partition of the rows and, simultaneously, the columns) of Figure 9.1 by use of the CONCOR algorithm, which is widely applied in network analysis (Wasserman and Faust 1994). We emphasize, however, that RIO is not about finding a partition, which might arise from any other inductive procedure or (as illustrated in Chapter 7) from an a priori hypothesis or theory.

The four-block partition of the 50 countries is applied in Figure 9.2. This figure contains the same data as the previous one, but here the rows and columns are rearranged according to the partition we are working with.

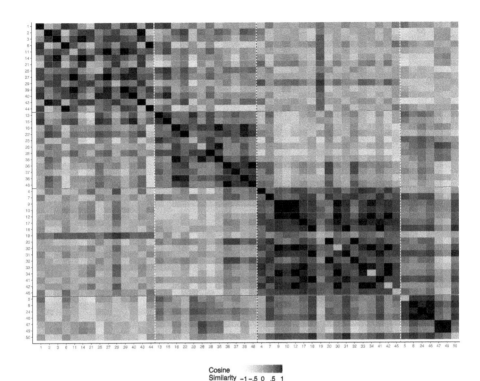

Cosine
Similarity −1 −.5 0 .5 1

Figure 9.2   Blocked matrix cos(**UU**ᵀ)

We see from Figure 9.2 that our inductive procedure has indeed revealed a patterning of the cosines in the cosine matrix. The mean density[10] within each of the 4 × 4 submatrices of Figure 9.2 is presented in Table 9.4.

As seen above and in Figure 9.2, the mean cosine within a block is not less than 0.532. Blocks 3 and 4 are somewhat similar (the mean cosine similarity connecting countries in Block 3 with those in Block 4 is 0.345), but all others are much less similar (the next-highest mean cosine is 0.171).

In a stochastic blockmodel, each pair of equivalent nodes has an identical probability of having a connection to all nodes, based on their block membership. Our analogy to probability is cosine similarity. Our model for Figure 9.2 is that every cell within a submatrix has *the same* value, given by the blocked means reported above. Therefore, our blockmodel (Equation 9.9) is the one

---

[10] Density is the sum of entries in a submatrix, divided by the number of cells in that submatrix. Hence, it is the mean cosine of the cells within each submatrix (diagonal cells are excluded from both the numerator and the denominator of density).

Table 9.4 Mean density within each of 4 × 4 submatrices of Figure 9.2

	B1	B2	B3	B4
B1	0.532	0.170	0.063	−0.100
B2	0.170	0.591	0.000	0.171
B3	0.063	0.000	0.741	0.345
B4	−0.100	0.171	0.345	0.698

Notes: B refers to block.

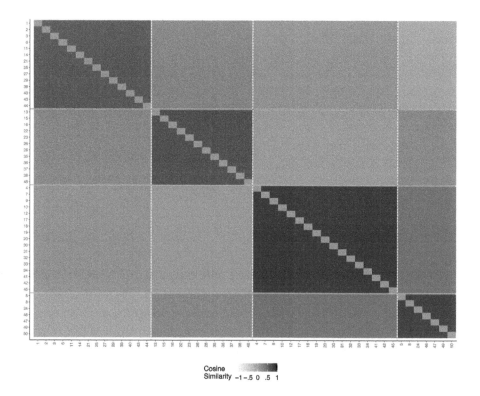

Figure 9.3   The blockmodel for the partition shown in Figure 9.2

reported in Figure 9.3.[11] Here, every cell is assigned the mean density of its submatrix.

Our model does not, of course, fit perfectly. Residuals (defined as the values in Figure 9.2 minus those in Figure 9.3) are reported in Figure 9.4.

---

[11] Notice that blocked densities in Figure 9.3 are, by construction, the same as those reported in the 4 × 4 matrix above.

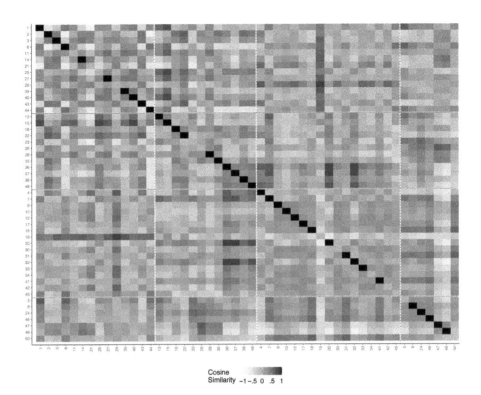

Cosine
Similarity −1 −.5 0 .5 1

Figure 9.4   Residuals from the model of Figure 9.3

The patterning of residuals is not entirely random (see, e.g., case 19), and this might lead us to further investigate the residuals in ways proposed earlier. However, by construction, there is no patterning of the residuals by block, in the specific sense that the mean residual in each of the 16 sub-matrices of Figure 9.4 is zero. The combination of strong equivalence in the blockmodel (Figure 9.3) and more modest patterning in the residuals (Figure 9.4) suggests that our blockmodel provides a compelling identification of positions within the Hat matrix, once that matrix is "corrected" for the volumes of its individual nodes (here, the leverage values of the 50 countries).

In order to descriptively assess the fit of our blockmodel, we can examine several features. Ignoring the 50 cells on the diagonal, the sum of squares of the cosines in the full matrix $\cos(UU^T)$ of Figure 9.1 (and therefore also Figure 9.2) is 62.6041. The sum of squares of cosines for the blockmodel of Figure 9.3 is 40.0448. In analogy to the analysis of variance, the latter number is the "between-block" sum of squares, obtained at the expense of just 10 of the 1,225 degrees of freedom.[12] The "within" sum of squares of the residuals (Figure 9.4) is 62.6041 − 40.0448 = 22.5593. Thus, the "between-block" sum of squares (Figure 9.3) is 64% (= 40.0448/62.6041) of the total (Figures 9.1 and 9.2), at the expense of just 10 degrees of freedom.

We can also examine the fit of the blockmodel descriptively by partitioning the fitted values (the $\hat{\mathbf{y}}$) from the usual regression model into two sets of numbers: one by approximating the Hat matrix using the modeled data (Figure 9.3), the other by using the residuals in Figure 9.4. (These two sets of numbers sum to the $\hat{\mathbf{y}}$ from the conventional regression model.) We will define a matrix $\mathbf{D}^{1/2}$ to be a matrix with entries of the square root of d_i (see Equation 9.9) on its diagonal and 0s elsewhere. We will refer to the matrix in Figure 9.3 as "cosUUt.blocked" and to the matrix in Figure 9.4 as "cosUUt.resid." Then we will define two vectors, as follows:

$$\text{model.yhat.1} = \mathbf{D}^{1/2}\,\text{cosUUt.blocked}\,\mathbf{D}^{1/2}\mathbf{y} \tag{9.10a}$$

$$\text{model.yhat.2} = \mathbf{D}^{1/2}\,\text{cosUUt.resid}\,\mathbf{D}^{1/2}\mathbf{y} \tag{9.10b}$$

Notice (from Equation 9.9) that model.yhat.1 + model.yhat.2 equals the vector of $\hat{\mathbf{y}}$ values from the usual regression equation. How well does equation 9.10a do in predicting the regression model's $\hat{\mathbf{y}}$ values? Across the 50 cases, the correlation of the modeled $\hat{\mathbf{y}}$ values (model.yhat.1) with $\hat{\mathbf{y}}$ from the usual regression model is +0.592. The correlation of the modeled $\hat{\mathbf{y}}$ from the residualized matrix is, descriptively, lower (+0.272).

These results are descriptive in nature. We have not developed a formal means of assessing fit. We have nonetheless illustrated the potential of this particular form of network analysis (blockmodels) to identify positions in the field of positioning that underlies every regression model. Among the useful next steps will be developing a framework for partition distributions to move toward combinatorial inference (Le Roux, Bienaise, and Durand 2019).

9.5 Summary

In this chapter, we have shown how RIO provides a gateway between regression and field theory. Focusing on key ideas that are implicated in Bourdieu's theorization of fields, we demonstrate how RIO allows us to identify and

[12] To fit the blockmodel in Figure 9.3, we estimate one number for each of the 4 sets of countries, and 6 additional numbers for all pairs of blocks, for a total of 10 degrees of freedom. At the level of countries (Figure 9.1 or Figure 9.2), the number of cosines is ½×50 × 49 = 1,225 degrees of freedom.

explore social logics via an extension of earlier analyses of Kenworthy's (1999) study of the determinants of poverty. Building on this example, we further illustrate the duality of institutions and their properties. We then introduce a network approach to field analysis of regression. Drawing a parallel between positions in fields and the network concept of structural equivalence, we demonstrate the relevance of RIO for blockmodeling and field theory. In this latter example, we reanalyze data on the average savings rate across 50 countries. Taken together, this chapter illustrates how homologies between the underlying mathematics of GDA and regression allow us to integrate key elements of the logic of field theory into regression modeling.

10 Conclusion

In this book, we have presented a methodology for turning regression models "inside out." RIO brings cases to the fore, making it possible to better account for and engage with the kinds of complexities that serious attention to cases introduces into any analysis. By design, regression summarizes the relationships among variables, and our interpretation of these summaries depends on the assumption that observations are exchangeable. This is why much of standard regression theory focuses on issues related to sampling fluctuation. Yet, regression is routinely applied to data where the observations are not exchangeable because they represent meaningful cases that are of theoretical interest in their own right.

Particularly in the social sciences, analyses where cases are neither substantively nor theoretically exchangeable are remarkably common. For example, statistical analyses of the determinants of civil war may include data on nearly every country in the world across many years, but analysts would never claim that Canada in 1997 and Papua New Guinea in 1956 (or any other pair of countries and years) are exchangeable or even functionally equivalent. An analysis of corporate practices might use data on Fortune 500 companies, but no reasonable analyst would consider Walmart or Amazon as exchangeable with Williams-Sonoma or Cincinnati Financial. Datasets on social movement organizations include both the NAACP and the Ku Klux Klan; again, these groups are hardly exchangeable. Even in instances where our observations are statistically exchangeable, important theoretical and epistemological commitments may push researchers to treat case-level differences as meaningful variation that should not simply be absorbed into the error term (e.g., Crenshaw 1989; Hancock 2007; Ragin and Fiss 2017). When individual observations are theoretically or substantively interesting, understanding how they fit into, inform, and potentially alter the stories we tell with our regression models becomes essential for effective research.

In this way, RIO is a powerful tool that allows us to expand *what* we learn from a regression model by rethinking *how* we learn from a regression model.

As noted in the introduction to this book, the ability to interpret the results of a regression model is typically taken for granted in scholarship that either uses or advances statistical methods. Yet, as we have shown, the summaries produced by our regression models (such as coefficients and standard errors) do not always provide a complete picture of our data. As we show in Chapter 5, not all observations matter equally, even when they are technically unproblematic from the perspective of regression theory. A failure to account for this basic fact increases the risk that researchers will draw conclusions that do not generalize, or overlook the presence of multiple distinct patterns within the data that each tell a distinct but equally valid story. While there are a variety of methods available that allow researchers to account for these kinds of complexity – from case studies and other forms of qualitative research to machine learning – RIO enables researchers to engage with these complexities in the context of what is arguably the most widely taught and applied methodological tool in the social sciences.

As we conclude this book, we want to reemphasize the unique theoretical, methodological, and substantive benefits of employing a case-oriented approach to regression. Theoretically, the case-oriented logic of RIO allows us to relax many of the philosophical assumptions embedded in regression analysis. For example, Abbott (1988) emphasizes that within a regression framework, attributes' causal meanings cannot depend on its context, shifting based on its position within the attribute space of the model. Yet, by revealing how individual cases come together in the linear model, RIO allows us to explore discontinuities in the causal meanings of particular variables and capture these kinds of contextual variations, accounting for the ways that a variable's location in the attribute space influences its interpretation and how the causal importance of attributes changes from one observation to the next. For example, in our analysis of the correlates of dog ownership in Chapter 5, we find that the effect of race on dog ownership varies across subpopulations of the larger dataset, such that the effect of race is different for people at the lowest income levels compared with other respondents. Similarly, Abbott (1988: 170) also notes that the "past path of an entity through the attribute space (its history) can have no influence on its future path." Here again, we are able to account for the movement of an observation through the attribute space, thereby observing how its history influences its future path. We show this in Chapter 7 in our reanalysis of Wimmer, Cederman, and Min's (2009) Ethnic Power Relation's dataset, plotting the trajectory of individual cases over time (which, in this dataset, are represented by multiple observations) in relation to the model specification (see Figure 7.12). This allows us to see the effect of case-specific contingencies on cases' relationship to the model, as illustrated by the United States (Figure 7.12c) where we see a distinct break corresponding to the enactment of the Civil Rights Act in the otherwise reasonably stable trajectory of this country across the model space over time. In these and other ways, RIO allows us to relax many of the constraints of a general linear reality.

RIO also enables us to incorporate both logics and insights from methodological approaches that are conventionally understood as distinct from regression. Regression analysis is routinely invoked as a point of reference for clarifying the unique perspectives and contributions of qualitative, case-oriented, and relational methods. However, as we have shown in the preceding chapters, turning regression models inside out allows us to incorporate the logic of cases into regression analysis, making it possible to directly apply case-based, qualitative insights in the interpretation of model outputs and advance a fundamentally relational understanding of social phenomena. Building on the mathematical homologies between regression and an array of other methods ranging from network analysis and correspondence analysis to Qualitative Comparative Analysis (QCA), RIO provides a foundation for bridging gaps between regression and these other methodological approaches. For example, we show how the basic mathematics underlying regression allows us to conceive of the rows of the data matrix as co-constituted by the columns of the data matrix (Chapter 8), just as they are understood and explicitly theorized in QCA. This opens the door for moving seamlessly between cases and variables in the analysis of aggregate patterns in our data to account for causal complexities that are typically lost in run-of-the-mill regression models. Similarly, the ability to map the attribute space of regression models opens the door for a fundamentally relational approach to regression. In doing so, we are able to incorporate tools and theories associated with both correspondence analysis and network analysis – from geometric data analysis to blockmodels – into a regression framework (see Chapter 9).

As we have shown with our empirical illustrations throughout the book, these theoretical and methodological advances often yield novel substantive insights. For example, in Chapter 7, we show how RIO can help us to make sense of seemingly contradictory results that emerge from existing approaches to algorithmic case selection. In our analysis of Kenworthy's (1999) study of the effects of welfare spending on poverty, we show how conventional approaches to algorithmic case selection identify Ireland as both a deviant case and an influential case in the context of the model. These two types of cases (i.e., deviant and influential) have theoretically inconsistent purposes in the context of case study research. Turning the model inside out reveals that, while Ireland is identified as a deviant case, it is actually an extreme illustration of the theorized process, thus suggesting that Ireland is more productively treated as an influential case. Similarly, in Chapter 8, we show how RIO facilitates dialogue between QCA and regression in ways that yield novel substantive insights. For example, in our exploration of Schneider and Makszin's (2014) analysis of how labor protections and social support mediate the effects of education-based inequality in political participation, we extend their original findings. In their original analyses, the authors show that features of the capitalist welfare system matter for participatory inequality, and that there are multiple pathways to low participatory inequality. By turning their regression model insight out, we affirm their findings, while also demonstrating that variation in the features of the capitalist welfare system still meaningfully explain variation in participatory inequality above and beyond the structurally constraining effects of voter turnout, while macro-level factors linked to voter turnout appear to matter a great deal in countries with supportive and protective welfare regimes. In these and other examples, we show how turning attention to cases adds depth and detail to our interpretation of the phenomena under examination and, in some instances, upends established findings (see, e.g., Chapter 5, Section 5.5).

It bears reemphasizing here that RIO differs from common methods for regression diagnostics in its orientation toward cases. Within a conventional regression framework, cases are generally only taken seriously in the context of diagnostics. However, as we noted in Chapter 1, diagnostics are oriented toward identifying problematic cases, with the goal of altering – and thereby improving – a regression model. Common diagnostic methods, such as Cook's distance or DFBETA, flag cases to be removed from the model because they exert disproportionate influence. RIO enables analysts to look inside the space of the model and discern how the cases relate to one another and to the effects of the variables.

While it is not the goal of RIO to imply or identify a better fitting model in terms of either variables or cases, gaining a deeper understanding of a regression model may motivate respecification. We illustrate this in Chapter 6 by showing how RIO can be used to detect statistically significant interaction terms. In most instances, the inclusion of interaction terms will be guided by theory. However, theory can have blind spots, and an important goal of testing and applying theory across disparate contexts is to identify deviations from established expectations. Consequently, an exploratory approach to identifying interaction terms can be beneficial. However, simply plugging in every possible interaction term is both time consuming and prone to user error. By turning the model inside out and using the relationships among cases to identify interaction terms, RIO provides both a systematic and efficient approach to identifying statistically significant interaction terms with exceptional accuracy.

From expanding the ways that regression can inform theory to creating new substantive insights from the inside of a model space, we contend that RIO stands to enhance research in a variety of contexts and a variety of ways. Regression is a powerful tool for reducing data and summarizing the average associations with an outcome. While some researchers use regression to understand relationships among variables, regression is often employed to gain knowledge or make claims about the cases that constitute our data. By unmasking these critical inputs, RIO allows researchers to directly interrogate the link between their regression models and the cases that constitute those models, learning more about both in the process.

10.1   Opportunities for Further Methodological Development

The work covered in this book is a summary of our efforts to date to develop the logic and applications of RIO, but there is much left to explore. For example, there is a great deal of room for future work to extend both the logic and mathematics of RIO to additional types of regression models, such as event history models or structural equation models. In Chapter 3, we described the vital role of the link function in visualizing models with noncontinuous outcomes. In particular, the linear relationship between the predictors and the outcome must be maintained in order to visualize the regression results. We illustrated this with logistic regression, Poisson regression, and negative binomial regression. Subsequent work should explore how to turn multinomial or rare event models, for example, inside out. Another common outcome type is the alternative-specific outcome that is typically fit with conditional logistic regression (Allison 2009). RIO generalizations in the context of conditional logistic regression could shed light on case contributions to the likelihood of selecting particular outcome categories. There are also exciting possibilities for RIO to improve machine learning models, which rely on variables to make case-based predictions.

In Chapter 3, we described how to turn random intercept linear mixed models inside out and provided an example in Chapter 5. Extending this to random slopes only entails altering the weight matrix in the linear solution to the coefficients (Littell et al. 2006). Such an extension would be imminently useful because of the scale of multilevel data. Often multilevel data structures are complex and large (e.g., the European Social Survey), making an understanding of the model even more important and challenging. Growth curve models, which entail a random component on (at least) the linear effect of time, summarize trajectories over countless units. RIO plots of the trajectories could be compared to interrogate observed patterns beyond the mean tendencies reported in the regression coefficients themselves. Other contributions to RIO in the context of mixed models include generalizing the methods to cross-classified data, addressing case contributions to the variance in the context of mixed models, or extensions to limited dependent variables.

Visualization is central to much of what we have presented in the preceding chapters, and we also believe there are exciting opportunities for further development in this area. In Chapter 2, we show how RIO can be used to visualize the model space of a regression, but throughout the book, we only present two-dimensional representations of the model space. With continuing advances in data visualization, there may be opportunities to expand this to multidimensional representations that provide a more complete and complex representation of the regression space. That is, plotting three or even four dimensions of the data may become easier with software improvements.

While we present two possibilities for decomposing variance, there is a great deal more room for development in this area. Even in the context of linear outcomes, alternative methods of variance decomposition warrant further consideration. Some promising work illustrates, for example, how to visualize t-ratios in regression biplots (Ter Braak and Looman 1994). By including t-ratios, the graph conveys information about both the average effect of predictor variables (vis-à-vis the variable's relation to the outcome in the plot) and the consistency of that effect across cases. These methods could be integrated with RIO to show t-ratios when variables are included in the plots.

In addition to technical advances, we see exciting possibilities for developing RIO as a gateway to other methodological approaches. While Chapters 7 and 8 point to ways that RIO can enrich multimethod research, these treatments only scratch the surface of the possibilities that exist within the vibrant and rapidly growing literature on this topic (Creswell and Clark 2017; Greene 2007; Greene, Caracelli, and Graham 1989; Lieberman 2005; Seawright 2016a, 2016b; Small 2011; Tashakkori, Johnson, and Teddlie 2020; Tashakkori, Teddlie, and Teddlie 1998; Weller and Barnes 2016). Moreover, while we offer a suggestive introduction to how RIO allows us to think of the relationships among cases defined by a regression model in network terms, we believe a great deal more can be done to expand in these directions. As well, in parallel to our formulation of individual and cluster contributions to regression coefficients, we take note of other researchers' identification of individual, within-group, and between-group components to inequality coefficients such as the Gini coefficient (Liao 2019) and to network centrality measures such as eigenvector and betweenness centrality (Everett and Borgatti 2012).

Of course, we hope that readers will also use RIO to enhance substantive and theoretical research of all kinds. The examples that we have provided in the preceding pages are drawn from the areas of scholarship that are most familiar to us, and thus tend to focus on issues related to inequality and politics. Yet, for any research question that can be explored using regression, RIO can be used to look inside the model and explore the possibility that there are multiple stories, meaningful cases, or significant interactions. We believe that this kind of exploration has the potential to deepen and enhance our understanding of the phenomena we study, whatever they may be.

10.2 Summary

This book provides a technical and conceptual foundation for rethinking regression in terms that reflect the growing recognition that a firm divide between case-oriented and variables-oriented approaches is both methodologically and theoretically untenable. Regression remains an essential tool for scientific research. It is a simple but powerful way to synthesize vast amounts of data and identify trends that offer valuable insights into the world around us and allow us to make meaning out of a wide array of inputs. However, by rendering cases invisible, conventional regression analysis risks homogenizing the phenomena we study and supporting an unnecessarily narrow approach to understanding the world around us. By making the cases visible, RIO allows us to retain the strengths of regression while facilitating meaningful dialogue between theory and evidence.

Appendix A
A Brief Introduction to Matrices and Matrix Multiplication

We offer this quick sketch as an introduction to matrices and to matrix multiplication for readers with little or no background on these topics, but who would like to understand how matrix multiplication, and a few related concepts, "work." More complete treatments may be found in a variety of textbooks (including Draper and Smith 1998), and even by searching for "matrix multiplication" on the Internet.

A *matrix* is a collection of numbers arranged in an array of rows and columns. If the matrix has n rows and p columns, it is called a matrix of order $n \times p$. Here are four matrices:

$$\mathbf{A} = \begin{pmatrix} 6 & 5 \\ 2 & 3 \\ 4 & 8 \\ 1 & 7 \end{pmatrix}$$
$$\mathbf{B} = \begin{pmatrix} 4 & 20 & 10 \\ 7 & 19 & 11 \end{pmatrix}$$
$$\mathbf{C} = \begin{pmatrix} 8 & 0 & 0 \\ 0 & 11 & 0 \\ 0 & 0 & 18 \end{pmatrix}$$
$$\mathbf{I} = \begin{pmatrix} 1 & 0 & 0 \\ 0 & 1 & 0 \\ 0 & 0 & 1 \end{pmatrix}$$

(A.1)

Matrix $\mathbf{A}$ is of order 4×2, matrix $\mathbf{B}$ is of order 2×3, and matrices $\mathbf{C}$ and $\mathbf{I}$ are both *square* matrices of order 3×3.

Numbers (or elements) within a matrix are often indexed with respect to their row number and their column number. Thus, the "8" in matrix $\mathbf{A}$ is at the intersection of row 3 and column 2. We might refer to this number's location within the matrix as "cell (3,2)" and to the number 8 itself as $A_{3,2}$. More generally, the letter i is often used to index row numbers, and j is often used for column numbers. So, cell (i,j) of matrix A is "5" when $i = 1$ and $j = 2$, and is "8" when $i = 3$ and $j = 2$.

The *transpose* of a matrix interchanges its rows and its columns. That is, the number in cell (i,j) of matrix $\mathbf{M}$ is in cell (j,i) of the transpose of $\mathbf{M}$, which we denote with a superscript T, as in $\mathbf{M}^T$. Here is a concrete example; the transpose of matrix A above is

$$\mathbf{A}^T = \begin{pmatrix} 6 & 2 & 4 & 1 \\ 5 & 3 & 8 & 7 \end{pmatrix} \tag{A.2}$$

Notice (once again) that rows of $\mathbf{A}$ are columns of $\mathbf{A}^T$, and vice versa.

Each row of a matrix is also called a row *vector*, and each column is often referred to as a column *vector*. If two vectors are of the same length, we can *multiply* them by summing the products of the corresponding cells. For example, let's call the first row of matrix $\mathbf{A}$ the vector $v_1 = <6, 5>$. And let's refer to the third column of matrix B as $v_2 = <10, 11>$. Then the product $v_1 \times v_2$ is $v_1 \times v_2 = (6 \times 10) + (5 \times 11) = 60 + 55 = 115$.

Now we can define the *matrix multiplication* of two matrices, A and B, as the array of the product of all row vectors of A with all column vectors of B. For the specific matrices $\mathbf{A}$ and $\mathbf{B}$ in (A.1), the matrix product is

$$\mathbf{AB} = \begin{pmatrix} (6\times4+5\times7) & (6\times20+5\times19) & (6\times10+5\times11) \\ (2\times4+3\times7) & (2\times20+3\times19) & (2\times10+3\times11) \\ (4\times4+8\times7) & (4\times20+8\times19) & (4\times10+8\times11) \\ (1\times4+7\times7) & (1\times20+7\times19) & (1\times10+7\times11) \end{pmatrix}$$

$$= \begin{pmatrix} 59 & 215 & 115 \\ 29 & 97 & 53 \\ 72 & 232 & 128 \\ 53 & 153 & 87 \end{pmatrix} \tag{A.3}$$

Here, $\mathbf{A}$ is of order 4×2, $\mathbf{B}$ is of order 2×3, and the product $\mathbf{AB}$ (shown directly above) is of order 4×3. In general, for matrix multiplication to be defined, the number of columns in A and the number of rows in B must be equal (so that a row vector of A and a column vector of B are of the same length, here length 2). Also, in general, if matrix $\mathbf{A}$ is of order $n \times p$, and matrix $\mathbf{B}$ is of order $p \times m$, then the matrix product $\mathbf{AB}$ is of order $n \times m$ (because all rows of $\mathbf{A}$ must be multiplied by all columns of $\mathbf{B}$).

A *square* matrix has the same number of rows as columns. The *diagonal* of a square matrix $\mathbf{M}$ of order $n \times n$ consists of the vector of numbers $< \mathbf{M}_{11}, \mathbf{M}_{22}, \ldots, \mathbf{M}_{nn} >$.

By the above definition of matrix multiplication, the product of the transpose of a matrix $\mathbf{A}$ with matrix $\mathbf{A}$ itself – here we can consider specifically the product $\mathbf{A}^{T}\mathbf{A}$ for the matrices shown above – is a square matrix of sums of squares (on its diagonal) and sums of cross-products (in the off-diagonal cells). For matrix $\mathbf{A}$ given above,

$$\mathbf{A}^{T}\mathbf{A} = \begin{pmatrix} 57 & 75 \\ 75 & 147 \end{pmatrix} \tag{A.4}$$

where 57 is the sum of squares of the numbers in the first column of $\mathbf{A}$, 147 is the sum of squares of the numbers in the second column, and 75 is the vector product of the two columns of numbers in $\mathbf{A}$.

A special case of the above is that, for a matrix $\mathbf{M}$ of order $n \times p$ in which all columns are mean-centered, the product $\mathbf{M}^{T}\mathbf{M}$ is a square matrix (of order $p \times p$) each of whose diagonal cells is $(n - 1)$ times the variance of the respective column of $\mathbf{M}$, and each of whose off-diagonal cells $[i,j]$ is $(n - 1)$ times the covariance of columns i and j.

Matrix $\mathbf{I}$ in (Equation A.1) is an example of an *Identity matrix*, defined as a square matrix with 1's on the diagonal and 0's elsewhere. For an identity matrix $\mathbf{I}$ and any real-valued matrix $\mathbf{M}$ (of the appropriate order), the product $\mathbf{IM}$, and the product $\mathbf{MI}$, both equal $\mathbf{M}$ itself. Thus, the Identity matrix plays the same role as the number "1" does in everyday arithmetic multiplication.

The *inverse* of a matrix $\mathbf{M}$, denoted $\mathbf{M}^{-1}$, or $\mathbf{M}$ to the -1 power, is defined as the matrix that, when pre- or postmultiplied by $\mathbf{M}$, yields the identity matrix $\mathbf{I}$. Here we will not discuss inverse matrices in general, but we will mention a special case that appears often in this book and that is simple to compute. If a matrix is square and diagonal – consider as an example matrix $\mathbf{C}$ in (A.1) – then its inverse is a diagonal matrix each of whose entries $[i,i]$ is just the reciprocal of cell $[i,i]$ in $\mathbf{C}$. For our matrix C, for example, the matrix product $\mathbf{C}^{-1}\mathbf{C}$ is

$$\mathbf{C}^{-1}\mathbf{C} = \begin{pmatrix} 1/8 & 0 & 0 \\ 0 & 1/11 & 0 \\ 0 & 0 & 1/18 \end{pmatrix} \begin{pmatrix} 8 & 0 & 0 \\ 0 & 11 & 0 \\ 0 & 0 & 18 \end{pmatrix} = \begin{pmatrix} 1 & 0 & 0 \\ 0 & 1 & 0 \\ 0 & 0 & 1 \end{pmatrix} = \mathbf{I} \tag{A.5}$$

Matrix multiplication is *associative*. For matrices $\mathbf{U}$, $\mathbf{V}$, and $\mathbf{W}$, $(\mathbf{UV})\mathbf{W} = \mathbf{U}(\mathbf{VW})$. However, matrix multiplication is not in general *commutative*. $\mathbf{UW} \neq \mathbf{WU}$.

Appendix B

Computation of the Singular Value Decomposition (SVD)

Here we provide details of computation for readers who want to get their "hands on" the equations in Chapter 2. With respect to the matrix of scaled independent variables in our Table 2.1 (15 nations by 2 variables), which we will label as matrix $\mathbf{X}$, we make use of a classic decomposition that can be applied to it, the singular value decomposition, or (as some mathematicians refer to it owing to its bountiful theory and applications) "the extraordinary SVD" (Martin and Porter 2012). Our matrix $\mathbf{X}$ (in fact, any real-valued matrix) can be decomposed or "factored" into a singular value decomposition (SVD)

$$\mathbf{X} = \mathbf{U}\mathbf{S}\mathbf{V}^{\mathrm{T}} \tag{B.1}$$

where $\mathbf{U}$ and $\mathbf{V}$ are orthogonal matrices (the sum of cross-products of any two columns of $\mathbf{U}$ is 0, and similarly for $\mathbf{V}$) and $\mathbf{S}$ is diagonal with $d = rank(X)$ leading positive diagonal entries (Martin and Porter 2012). The SVD decomposes our Chapter 2 data matrix $\mathbf{X}$ (of size $n = 15$ cases by $p = 2$ variables) into a multiplicative product of three objects:

- a set of $d = 2$ dimensions pertaining to the cases, represented by matrix $\mathbf{U}$ (of size n cases by d dimensions),
- a dual set of dimensions pertaining to the variables, encoded in matrix $\mathbf{V}$ (of size p cases by d dimensions), and
- a matrix $\mathbf{S}$ (of size d by d dimensions) that has values of 0 everywhere except on its diagonal; the diagonal entries are called the singular values of $\mathbf{X}$, and they are ordered from highest to lowest magnitude.

As mentioned in the text, computing the SVD of a matrix is usually entrusted to statistical packages, as we will do throughout the rest of this book subsequent to Chapter 2. However, in the special case we have here – the matrix $\mathbf{Z_X}$ comprised of exactly two variables, both of which are in scaled (Z-score) form – we can use simple arithmetic to compute the matrices $\mathbf{U}$, $\mathbf{S}$, and $\mathbf{V}$ of the SVD. We now show how.

Denoting the two columns of our data matrix (Z_X in Table 2.1) as Z_1 (the variable *transfers*) and Z_2 (the variable *pov1*) respectively, we can define orthogonal combinations of these, as follows:

$$U_1 = (Z_1 + Z_2) \Big/ \sqrt{\sum(Z_1 + Z_2)^2} \tag{B.2}$$

$$U_2 = (Z_1 - Z_2) \Big/ \sqrt{\sum(Z_1 - Z_2)^2} \tag{B.3}$$

Then U_1 and U_2 are the columns of matrix U (one column for each dimension of what we will call "the space of countries"), a key matrix of the SVD of matrix Z_X. As an example of computation, consider the second-listed country (Belgium) in Table 2.1. For Belgium, $(Z_1 + Z_2)$ is the sum of 1.51 and 0.40, which is 1.91. Squaring this number, doing the same for all 15 countries, and summing the squares yield 32.976, so the denominator of Equation (B.2) is the square root of 32.976, or 5.742. For Belgium, dividing the numerator (1.91) by this denominator (5.742) yields 0.333, which is indeed the matrix U coordinate of Belgium with respect to dimension 1 of the SVD. (The number 0.333 is given in Table 2.6 in the text.)

To compute values for the second column (corresponding to the second dimension) of matrix U, we sum the squares of *differences* of the variables in Z_X. Again from Table 2.1, for Belgium, the difference is 1.51 – 0.40, which is 1.11. Summing the squared differences across all 15 countries yields 23.024. So the value of Belgium on dimension 2 of matrix U is 1.11/sqrt(23.024) = 0.233, which is reported in Table 2.6 as Belgium's coordinate on the second dimension.[1]

We can also compute the other quantities of the SVD (namely, the matrices S and V that appear in Equation B.1) using simple arithmetic (for this special case in which the data matrix has exactly two variables, both in Z-score form). Matrix S is a diagonal matrix (that is, only cells [1,1] and [2,2] are nonzero). The values on the diagonal may be computed as follows.

$$S_{1,1} = \sqrt{\frac{1}{2}\sum(Z_1 + Z_2)^2} \tag{B.4}$$

$$S_{2,2} = \sqrt{\frac{1}{2}\sum(Z_1 - Z_2)^2} \tag{B.5}$$

As we saw above, the sum of squares in Equation B.2 is 32.976, so the value for dimension 1 (often called its *singular value*) is the square root of (0.5 ×

---

[1] In illustrating this computation, we ignore slight rounding error in the third decimal place. (Using the R script and the unrounded data that we provide as supplementary materials to this book, rounding error is not an issue.)

Table B.1 Signs of the entries in matrix V

	Dim 1	Dim 2
Transfers	1	1
Pretax/transfer Poverty	1	−1

32.976), which computes to 4.061. This is the first value in matrix **S**, as shown in Table 2.6. Likewise, we saw previously that the sum of squared differences in Equation B.3 is 23.024. Therefore, the singular value for the second dimension is the square root of (0.5×23.024), which is 3.393 (which is also reported for matrix **S** in Table 2.6). We interpret any value in matrix **U** as the coordinate of a particular country on dimension 1 or dimension 2 (respectively) of a two-dimensional "space for countries." We interpret the two values in matrix **S** as the relative weight of each respective dimension.

Moving on to the third key matrix in the SVD, matrix **V** has one row for each variable (here, the variables are *transfers* and *pov1*), and it has one column for each of the two dimensions. Thus, matrix **V** can be interpreted as a "space for variables" (a dual counterpart to the "space for countries" encoded in matrix **U**). Because we have exactly two variables, the magnitude of each entry in matrix V is $1/\mathrm{sqrt}(2)$, which is 0.707. The signs of the entries in matrix **V** are presented in Table B.1.

The first column (for dimension 1) shows that, when we have been dealing with dimension 1 (see Equations B.2 and B.4), we have **summed** the variables (Z_1 *plus* Z_2). The second column reflects that, when considering the second dimension (Equations B.3 and B.5), we have **subtracted** Z_2 from Z_1 (Z_1 *minus* Z_2). Now combining magnitude and sign, we compute matrix **V** as

$$V = \begin{pmatrix} 0.707 & 0.707 \\ 0.707 & -0.707 \end{pmatrix} \tag{B.6}$$

as is also reported in Table 2.6.

Appendix C
Variance for Binomial and Count Outcomes

In the case of OLS regression, we decompose each case's contribution to the *MSE* and then multiply that by the variance/covariance matrix for the model. Here we describe the necessary steps to extend our approach to binomial and count outcomes, providing a descriptive assessment of each case's contribution to the variance of each variable. Both the *MSE* and the variance/covariance matrix are different when the outcome is nonlinear.

As described in Section 3.3 of Chapter 3, the variance/covariance matrix for logistic regression coefficients is defined as $\left(\mathbf{X}^{\mathsf{T}}\mathbf{W}\mathbf{X}\right)^{-1}$, where $\mathbf{W}$ is a weight matrix. This form of the standard error is identical for logistic, Poisson, and negative binomial regression models. The only difference is the definition of the diagonal entries in the weight matrix. For logistic regression, the diagonal of the weight matrix is defined as $\pi_i\left(1-\pi_i\right)$, for Poisson regression the diagonal entries are defined as $\hat{y}$, and for negative binomial regression the diagonal entries are defined as $\hat{y}_i \Big/ \left(1+\hat{y}_i/\theta\right)$ (θ refers to the overdispersion term; Hilbe 2011).

In the models under consideration, there is no *MSE* to weight the variance/covariance matrix as we did in the case of OLS. Our solution is to weight the observed variance/covariance matrix proportional to the case's contribution to the mean squared error (*MSE*). While the *MSE* is not used in computing the variance/covariance matrix for the model coefficients, we employ the same logic, weighting cases contributions to variance by their contribution to the average model error. As in the case of OLS regression, the *MSE* is defined as $e_i^{\mathsf{T}}e_i \Big/ n-p$, except here the definition of the model residual is the working response or pseudovalues minus the linear predictors. The pseudovalues are defined in Equations C1–C2 and the subsequent case-level decomposition to the coefficient variance is presented in C3. C1 defines the pseudovalues for logistic regression (Hosmer and Lemeshow 2000: 129), and C2 defines them for Poisson and negative binomial regression (Hilbe 2011: 52) – the difference is in the definition of the fitted values, with the latter including the overdispersion term.

$$z_i = \mathbf{X}\beta + \mathbf{W}^{-1}\left(y_i - \hat{\pi}\right) \tag{C.1}$$

$$z_i = \mathbf{X}\beta + \left(y_i - \hat{y}_i\right)/\hat{y}_i \tag{C.2}$$

$$var_i\left(\hat{\beta}_i\right) = {MSE_i}\Big/{MSE} \times \left(\mathbf{X}^\mathsf{T}\mathbf{W}\mathbf{X}\right)^{-1} \tag{C.3}$$

Appendix D
Compositional Effects in Using RIO to Detect Statistical Interactions

In this appendix, we present the results of simulations showing that compositional effects can drive whether interaction effects are identified when using RIO to identify interaction terms. Below is a function that simulates data. It simulates an outcome and two predictors – one continuous and one binary – with a given parameter vector and a given size of the groups for the binary variable. In the function, *nobs* is N (number of observations), *xv* is a parameter vector, and *p* is the proportion of the dummy variable predictor that is coded 1. The function returns a data matrix with an outcome, and two predictors. The predictors have xv effect on the outcome (the first term in xv is the constant, the second is the main effect of predictor 1, the third is the main effect of predictor 2, and the fourth is the interaction between 1 and 2).

```
contin_syn1 <- function(nobs = 200, xv =c (1,.33,-.33,0),p = .5){
X1<-c(rep(1,p*nobs),rep(0,(1-p)*nobs))
X2<-rnorm(nobs)
X<-cbind(1,X1,X2,X1*X2)
xb<-X %*% xv
py<-rnorm(nobs,xb)
out<-data.frame(cbind(py,X[,–1]))
names(out)<-c("py","x1","x2","x1x2")
return(out)}
```

Simulation 1: .25/.75 Group Composition

Below we simulate two different data sets. In the first, the interaction effect is 1. In the second, the interaction is 0. In addition to estimating the regression model, the code below also turns the regression coefficients inside out, and then aggregates the rows by the binary variable (x1). When the interaction is present, we expect the effect of x2 to vary by states of x1. So we want to focus on the extent to which there is variation in the effect of x2 by x1.

```
dat <- contin_syn1(nobs=10000,xv=c(1,.5,.5,1),p=.25)
summary(lm (py ~ x1 + x2 + x1x2 ,data=dat))
##
## Call:
## lm(formula = py ~ x1 + x2 + x1x2, data = dat)
##
## Residuals:
##      Min       1Q    Median       3Q      Max
## -3.5009   -0.6817   -0.0036   0.6629   3.9049
##
## Coefficients:
##                Estimate Std. Error t value Pr(>|t|)
## (Intercept) 1.00383    0.01160   86.53   <2e-16 ***
## x1          0.48847    0.02320   21.05   <2e-16 ***
## x2          0.50037    0.01159   43.18   <2e-16 ***
## x1x2        1.00986    0.02300   43.91   <2e-16 ***
## ---
## Signif. codes:  0 '***' 0.001 '**' 0.01 '*' 0.05 '.' 0.1 ' ' 1
##
## Residual standard error: 1.005 on 9996 degrees of freedom
## Multiple R-squared:   0.4487, Adjusted R-squared:   0.4485
## F-statistic:   2712 on 3 and 9996 DF,   p-value: < 2.2e-16
X <- as.matrix(cbind(1,dat[,2:3]))
y <- dat[,1]
b.long1<-solve(t(X) %*% X) %*% t(X) %*% diag(y)
rowSums(b.long1) # Regression coefficients
##         1        x1        x2
## 1.0007285 0.5068087 0.7567763
a1.1<-aggregate(t(b.long1),by=list(dat[,2]),FUN=sum) # aggregating
by x1, the binary variable
b1.1<-aggregate(t(b.long1),by=list(dat[,2]),FUN=mean)

dat <- contin_syn1(nobs=10000,xv=c(1,.5,.5,0),p=.25)
summary(lm (py ~ x1 + x2 + x1x2 ,data=dat))
##
## Call:
## lm(formula = py ~ x1 + x2 + x1x2, data = dat)
```

```
##
## Residuals:
##     Min        1Q     Median       3Q      Max
## -3.5468   -0.6686   -0.0192   0.6697   3.8959
##
## Coefficients:
##                  Estimate Std. Error t value Pr(>|t|)
## (Intercept) 1.00475      0.01158   86.732    <2e-16 ***
## x1             0.51059      0.02317   22.038    <2e-16 ***
## x2             0.48611      0.01160   41.904    <2e-16 ***
## x1x2           0.03960      0.02354    1.682    0.0926 .
## ---
## Signif. codes:   0 '***' 0.001 '**' 0.01 '*' 0.05 '.' 0.1 ' ' 1
##
## Residual standard error: 1.003 on 9996 degrees of freedom
## Multiple R-squared:   0.2243, Adjusted R-squared:   0.2241
## F-statistic: 963.4 on 3 and 9996 DF,   p-value: < 2.2e-16
X <- as.matrix(cbind(1,dat[,2:3]))
y <- dat[,1]
b.long2<-solve(t(X) %*% X) %*% t(X) %*% diag(y)
rowSums(b.long2) # Regression coefficients
##         1          x1          x2
## 1.0046826  0.5105695  0.4957299
a1.2<-aggregate(t(b.long2),by=list(dat[,2]),FUN=sum)
b1.2<-aggregate(t(b.long2),by=list(dat[,2]),FUN=mean)
```

The results below are when we SUM the subsets (as defined by x1). The difference between the subsets is larger when the interaction is set to zero. That is incorrect.

```
a1.1[,4] # When the interaction is included
## [1] 0.3733291 0.3834472
a1.2[,4] # When the interaction is set to zero
## [1] 0.3680748 0.1276550
```

The results below are when we AVERAGE the subsets (as defined by x1). The difference between the subsets is larger when the interaction is set to 1, as we expect when an interaction is present.

```
round(b1.1[,4],6)   # When the interaction is included
## [1] 0.000050 0.000153
```

```
round(b1.2[,4],6) # When the interaction is set to zero
## [1] 4.9e-05 5.1e-05
```

The difference above is what we would expect, but the magnitude is hard to discern at that scale. For ease of interpretation, we graph the differences between subsets.

In Figure D.1 (when the interaction is in the data), the difference in the averages by groups is relatively large compared to the distribution of case contributions to the coefficient. In Figure D.2 (when the interaction is set to zero), the difference in the averages by groups is the same as the average of the distribution of case contributions to the coefficient.

```
pdat1<-tibble(x1=t(b.long1)[,3])
ggplot(data=pdat1,aes(x=x1)) + geom_density() + theme_classic() +
    geom_vline(xintercept=b1.1[2,4]-b1.1[1,4], linetype="dashed",
                    color = "red", size = .5)
```

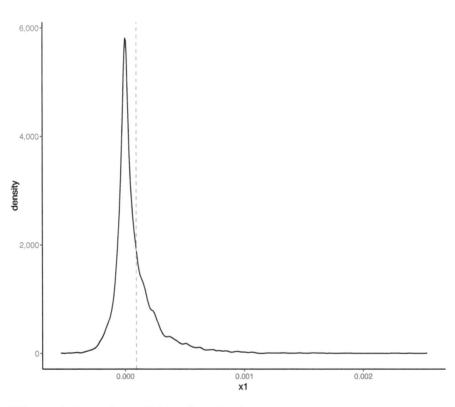

Figure D.1　Differences between subsets with interaction included

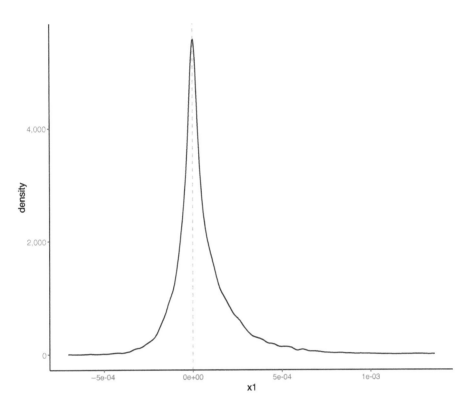

Figure D.2   Differences between subsets without interaction

```
pdat2<-tibble(x1=t(b.long2)[,3])
ggplot(data=pdat2,aes(x=x1)) + geom_density() + theme_classic() +
    geom_vline(xintercept=b1.2[2,4]-b1.2[1,4], linetype="dashed",
                color = "red", size=.5)
```

Simulation 2: .50/.50 Group Composition

In our second simulation (Figure D.3), we set group composition to .50/.50. In this case, both the sum and the average correctly point to an interaction in the first specification.

```
dat <- contin_syn1(nobs=10000,xv=c(1,.5,.5,1),p=.5)
summary(lm (py ~ x1 + x2 + x1x2 ,data=dat))
##
## Call:
## lm(formula = py ~ x1 + x2 + x1x2, data = dat)
```

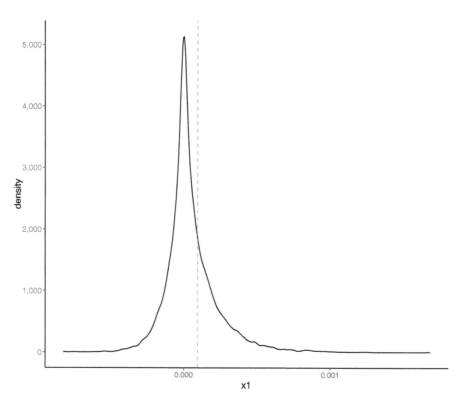

Figure D.3   Differences between subsets with interaction

```
##
## Residuals:
##     Min        1Q    Median      3Q      Max
## -4.1077   -0.6685    0.0071   0.6762   3.3774
##
## Coefficients:
##               Estimate Std. Error t value Pr(>|t|)
## (Intercept)   0.99071    0.01418   69.85   <2e-16 ***
## x1            0.50067    0.02006   24.96   <2e-16 ***
## x2            0.49841    0.01431   34.83   <2e-16 ***
## x1x2          1.00426    0.02007   50.03   <2e-16 ***
## ---
## Signif. codes:   0 '***' 0.001 '**' 0.01 '*' 0.05 '.' 0.1 ' ' 1
##
## Residual standard error: 1.003 on 9996 degrees of freedom
## Multiple R-squared:   0.569,   Adjusted R-squared:   0.5689
## F-statistic:   4399 on 3 and 9996 DF,   p-value: < 2.2e-16
```

```
X <- as.matrix(cbind(1,dat[,2:3]))
y <- dat[,1]
b.long1<-solve(t(X) %*% X) %*% t(X) %*% diag(y)
rowSums(b.long1) # Regression coefficients
##         1          x1          x2
## 0.9851491 0.5036100 1.0086835
a2.1<-aggregate(t(b.long1),by=list(dat[,2]),FUN=sum) # aggregating by
x1, the binary variable
b2.1<-aggregate(t(b.long1),by=list(dat[,2]),FUN=mean)

dat <- contin_syn1(nobs=10000,xv=c(1,.5,.5,0),p=.5)
summary(lm (py ~ x1 + x2 + x1x2 ,data=dat))
##
## Call:
## lm(formula = py ~ x1 + x2 + x1x2, data = dat)
##
## Residuals:
##     Min      1Q  Median      3Q     Max
## -4.1483  -0.6728   0.0010  0.6734  3.5564
##
## Coefficients:
##              Estimate Std. Error t value Pr(>|t|)
## (Intercept) 0.988826   0.014221  69.534  <2e-16 ***
## x1          0.513809   0.020110  25.550  <2e-16 ***
## x2          0.484972   0.014273  33.977  <2e-16 ***
## x1x2        0.003746   0.020210   0.185  0.853
## ---
## Signif. codes:   0 '***' 0.001 '**' 0.01 '*' 0.05 '.' 0.1 ' ' 1
##
## Residual standard error: 1.005 on 9996 degrees of freedom
## Multiple R-squared:   0.2304, Adjusted R-squared:   0.2301
## F-statistic: 997.3 on 3 and 9996 DF,   p-value: < 2.2e-16
X <- as.matrix(cbind(1,dat[,2:3]))
y <- dat[,1]
b.long2<-solve(t(X) %*% X) %*% t(X) %*% diag(y)
rowSums(b.long2) # Regression coefficients
##         1          x1          x2
## 0.9888601 0.5137686 0.4868403
a2.2<-aggregate(t(b.long2),by=list(dat[,2]),FUN=sum)
b2.2<-aggregate(t(b.long2),by=list(dat[,2]),FUN=mean)
a2.1
```

```
##    Group.1          1          xl          x2
## 1       0   0.993476947  -0.992175  0.2451597
## 2       1  -0.008327821   1.495785  0.7635239
a2.2
##    Group.1          1          xl          x2
## 1       0  0.984439627  -0.9835479  0.2430757
## 2       1  0.004420458   1.4973165  0.2437646
round(b2.1,6)
##    Group.1        1          xl          x2
## 1       0   0.000199  -0.000198  0.000049
## 2       1  -0.000002   0.000299  0.000153
round(b2.2,6)
##    Group.1        1          xl        x2
## 1       0  0.000197  -0.000197  4.9e-05
## 2       1  0.000001   0.000299  4.9e-05
```

Again for ease of interpretation, we graph the differences between subsets (Figures D.4 and D.5).

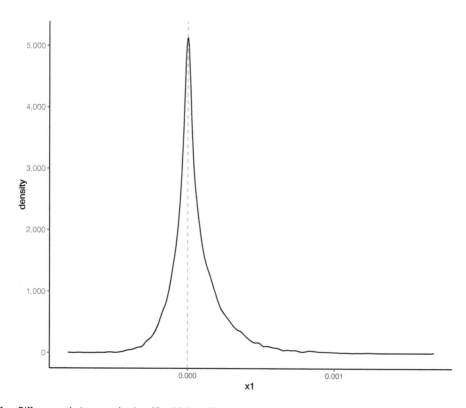

Figure D.4   Differences between subsets without interaction

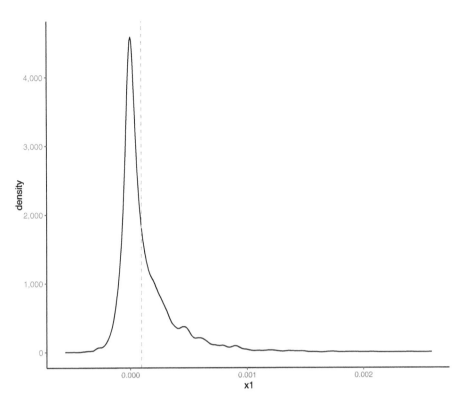

Figure D.5   Differences between subsets with interaction

```
pdat3<-tibble(x1=t(b.long2)[,3])
ggplot(data=pdat3,aes(x=x1)) + geom_density() + theme_classic() +
    geom_vline(xintercept=b1.1[2,4]-b1.1[1,4], linetype="dashed",
               color = "red", size=.5)

pdat4<-tibble(x1=t(b.long2)[,3])
ggplot(data=pdat4,aes(x=x1)) + geom_density() + theme_classic() +
    geom_vline(xintercept=b1.2[2,4]-b1.2[1,4], linetype="dashed",
               color = "red", size=.5)
```

Simulation 3: .75/.25 Group Composition

In our third simulation (Figure D.4), we set group composition to 0.75/0.25. In this case, the SUM indicates (incorrectly) that there is an interaction effect present in both models (Figure D.6). The average finds the same result as above, indicating that it works as we would hope.

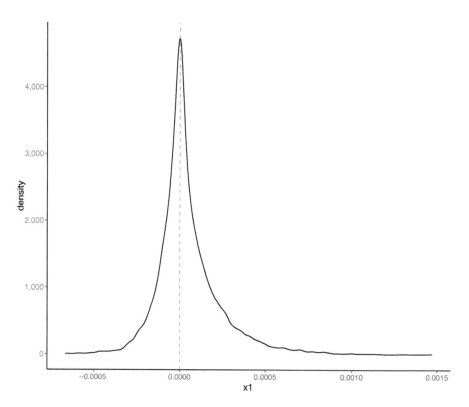

Figure D.6   Differences between subsets without interaction

dat <- contin_syn1(nobs=10000,xv=c(1,.5,.5,1),p=.75)
summary(lm (py ~ x1 + x2 + x1x2 ,data=dat))
\#\#
\#\# Call:
\#\# lm(formula = py ~ x1 + x2 + x1x2, data = dat)
\#\#
\#\# Residuals:
\#\#   Min   1Q   Median   3Q   Max
\#\# -3.8888 -0.6653   0.0015   0.6722   3.8772
\#\#
\#\# Coefficients:
\#\#   Estimate Std. Error t value Pr(>|t|)
\#\# (Intercept) 0.99687   0.01991   50.08   <2e-16 ***
\#\# x1   0.50964   0.02299   22.17   <2e-16 ***
\#\# x2   0.51154   0.01988   25.74   <2e-16 ***
\#\# x1x2   0.98690   0.02297   42.97   <2e-16 ***

```
## ---
## Signif. codes:   0 '***' 0.001 '**' 0.01 '*' 0.05 '.' 0.1 ' ' 1
##
## Residual standard error: 0.9954 on 9996 degrees of freedom
## Multiple R-squared:   0.6437, Adjusted R-squared:   0.6436
## F-statistic:   6020 on 3 and 9996 DF,   p-value: < 2.2e-16
X <- as.matrix(cbind(1,dat[,2:3]))
y <- dat[,1]b.long1<-solve(t(X) %*% X) %*% t(X) %*% diag(y)
rowSums(b.long1) # Regression coefficients
##           1         x1         x2
## 0.9956376 0.5081393 1.2504903
a3.1<-aggregate(t(b.long1),by=list(dat[,2]),FUN=sum) # aggregating by x1,
the binary variable
b3.1<-aggregate(t(b.long1),by=list(dat[,2]),FUN=mean)

dat <- contin_syn1(nobs=10000,xv=c(1,.5,.5,0),p=.75)
summary(lm (py ~ x1 + x2 + x1x2 ,data=dat))
##
## Call:
## lm(formula = py ~ x1 + x2 + x1x2, data = dat)
##
## Residuals:
##    Min       1Q  Median      3Q     Max
## -3.5681  -0.6704  -0.0048  0.6545  3.9298
##
## Coefficients:
##               Estimate Std. Error t value Pr(>|t|)
## (Intercept) 0.97515    0.01980   49.250  <2e-16 ***
## x1          0.52235    0.02286   22.848  <2e-16 ***
## x2          0.48931    0.01983   24.670  <2e-16 ***
## x1x2        0.01443    0.02288    0.631   0.528
## ---
## Signif. codes:   0 '***' 0.001 '**' 0.01 '*' 0.05 '.' 0.1 ' ' 1
##
## Residual standard error: 0.9898 on 9996 degrees of freedom
## Multiple R-squared:   0.2377, Adjusted R-squared:   0.2375
## F-statistic:   1039 on 3 and 9996 DF,   p-value: < 2.2e-16
X <- as.matrix(cbind(1,dat[,2:3]))
y <- dat[,1]b.long2<-solve(t(X) %*% X) %*% t(X) %*% diag(y)
```

```
rowSums(b.long2) # Regression coefficients
##         1         x1         x2
## 0.9753821 0.5221639 0.5001551
a3.2<-aggregate(t(b.long2),by=list(dat[,2]),FUN=sum)
b3.2<-aggregate(t(b.long2),by=list(dat[,2]),FUN=mean)
a3.1
##    Group.1            1          x1         x2
## 1        0   0.99751193 -0.996094 0.1285224
## 2        1  -0.00187436  1.504233 1.1219678
a3.2
##    Group.1            1          x1         x2
## 1        0  0.967161237 -0.9688113  0.1215730
## 2        1  0.008220889  1.4909752  0.3785822
round(b3.1,6)
##    Group.1        1         x1       x2
## 1        0 0.000399 -0.000398 5.1e-05
## 2        1 0.000000  0.000201 1.5e-04
round(b3.2,6)
##    Group.1        1         x1       x2
## 1        0 0.000387 -0.000388 4.9e-05
## 2        1 0.000001  0.000199 5.0e-05

pdat5<-tibble(x1=t(b.long1)[,3])
ggplot(data=pdat5,aes(x=x1)) + geom_density() + theme_classic() +
   geom_vline(xintercept=b1.1[2,4]-b1.1[1,4], linetype="dashed",
              color = "red", size=.5)
pdat6<-tibble(x1=t(b.long2)[,3])
ggplot(data=pdat6,aes(x=x1)) + geom_density() + theme_classic() +
   geom_vline(xintercept=b1.2[2,4]-b1.2[1,4], linetype="dashed",
              color = "red", size=.5)
```

Appendix E
Monte Carlo Simulation Detecting Interactions by Regressing on Rows of P

The following is the code used to conduct the Monte Carlo simulation that demonstrates the effectiveness of regressing on rows of **P** to detect statistically significant interaction effects, as discussed in Chapter 6. We begin by simulating data with 11 predictors, and an interaction between predictors 10 and 11 (other interactions are set to zero). The following is a function to produce these data:

```
contin_syn1 <- function(nobs = 200, xv =c (0,.1,-.1,.2,-.2,.3,-.3,.4,-.4,.5,-
.5,.6,rep(0,54),-.6)){

p<-length(xv)-55
X<-cbind(matrix(rnorm(nobs * (p-1)),ncol = p-1))
# X[,2]<-(X[,2]>0)*1
#X[,3]<-(X[,3]>0)*1
#X[,4]<-(X[,4]>0)*1
p<-p-1
#Int 1 x 2
X2<-cbind(X,X[,p-10]*X[,p-9])
#Int 1 x 3
X3<-cbind(X2,X2[,p-10]*X2[,p-8])
#Int 1 x 4
X4<-cbind(X3,X3[,p-10]*X3[,p-7])
#Int 1 x 5
X5<-cbind(X4,X4[,p-10]*X4[,p-6])
#Int 1 x 6
X6<-cbind(X5,X5[,p-10]*X5[,p-5])
#Int 1 x 7
X7<-cbind(X6,X6[,p-10]*X6[,p-4])
#Int 1 x 8
X8<-cbind(X7,X7[,p-10]*X7[,p-3])
#Int 1 x 9
X9<-cbind(X8,X8[,p-10]*X8[,p-2])
```

```
#Int 1 x 10
X10<-cbind(X9,X9[,p-10]*X9[,p-1])
#Int 1 x 11
X11<-cbind(X10,X10[,p-10]*X10[,p])

#Int 2 x 3
X12<-cbind(X11,X11[,p-9]*X11[,p-8])
#Int 2 x 4
X13<-cbind(X12,X12[,p-9]*X12[,p-7])
#Int 2 x 5
X14<-cbind(X13,X13[,p-9]*X13[,p-6])
#Int 2 x 6
X15<-cbind(X14,X14[,p-9]*X14[,p-5])
#Int 2 x 7
X16<-cbind(X15,X15[,p-9]*X15[,p-4])
#Int 2 x 8
X17<-cbind(X16,X16[,p-9]*X16[,p-3])
#Int 2 x 9
X18<-cbind(X17,X17[,p-9]*X17[,p-2])
#Int 2 x 10
X19<-cbind(X18,X18[,p-9]*X18[,p-1])
#Int 2 x 11
X20<-cbind(X19,X19[,p-9]*X19[,p])

#Int 3 x 4
X21<-cbind(X20,X20[,p-8]*X20[,p-7])
#Int 3 x 5
X22<-cbind(X21,X21[,p-8]*X21[,p-6])
#Int 3 x 6
X23<-cbind(X22,X22[,p-8]*X22[,p-5])
#Int 3 x 7
X24<-cbind(X23,X23[,p-8]*X23[,p-4])
#Int 3 x 8
X25<-cbind(X24,X24[,p-8]*X24[,p-3])
#Int 3 x 9
X26<-cbind(X25,X25[,p-8]*X25[,p-2])
#Int 3 x 10
X27<-cbind(X26,X26[,p-8]*X26[,p-1])
#Int 3 x 11
X28<-cbind(X27,X27[,p-8]*X27[,p])
```

```
#Int 4 x 5
X29<-cbind(X28,X28[,p-7]*X28[,p-6])
#Int 4 x 6
X30<-cbind(X29,X29[,p-7]*X29[,p-5])
#Int 4 x 7
X31<-cbind(X30,X30[,p-7]*X30[,p-4])
#Int 4 x 8
X32<-cbind(X31,X31[,p-7]*X31[,p-3])
#Int 4 x 9
X33<-cbind(X32,X32[,p-7]*X32[,p-2])
#Int 4 x 10
X34<-cbind(X33,X33[,p-7]*X33[,p-1])
#Int 4 x 11
X35<-cbind(X34,X34[,p-7]*X34[,p])

#Int 5 x 6
X36<-cbind(X35,X35[,p-6]*X35[,p-5])
#Int 5 x 7
X37<-cbind(X36,X36[,p-6]*X36[,p-4])
#Int 5 x 8
X38<-cbind(X37,X37[,p-6]*X37[,p-3])
#Int 5 x 9
X39<-cbind(X38,X38[,p-6]*X38[,p-2])
#Int 5 x 10
X40<-cbind(X39,X39[,p-6]*X39[,p-1])
#Int 5 x 11
X41<-cbind(X40,X40[,p-6]*X40[,p])

#Int 6 x 7
X42<-cbind(X41,X41[,p-5]*X41[,p-4])
#Int 6 x 8
X43<-cbind(X42,X42[,p-5]*X42[,p-3])
#Int 6 x 9
X44<-cbind(X43,X43[,p-5]*X43[,p-2])
#Int 6 x 10
X45<-cbind(X44,X44[,p-5]*X44[,p-1])
#Int 6 x 11
X46<-cbind(X45,X45[,p-5]*X45[,p])

#Int 7 x 8
X47<-cbind(X46,X4[,p-4]*X46[,p-3])
```

```
#Int 7 x 9
X48<-cbind(X47,X47[,p-4]*X47[,p-2])
#Int 7 x 10
X49<-cbind(X48,X48[,p-4]*X48[,p-1])
#Int 7 x 11
X50<-cbind(X49,X49[,p-4]*X49[,p])

#Int 8 x 9
X51<-cbind(X50,X50[,p-3]*X50[,p-2])
#Int 8 x 10
X52<-cbind(X51,X51[,p-3]*X51[,p-1])
#Int 8 x 11
X53<-cbind(X52,X52[,p-3]*X52[,p])

#Int 9 x 10
X54<-cbind(X53,X53[,p-2]*X53[,p-1])
#Int 9 x 11
X55<-cbind(X54,X54[,p-2]*X54[,p])

#Int 10 x 11
X56<-cbind(X55,X55[,p-1]*X55[,p])
X56<-cbind(1,X56)
xb<-X56 %*% xv
py<-rnorm(nobs,xb)
out<-data.frame(cbind(py,X56[,-1]))
names(out)<-
c("py","x1","x2","x3","x4","x5","x6","x7","x8","x9","x10","x11","x1x2","x1x3","x1x4",
"x1x5","x1x6","x1x7","x1x8","x1x9","x1x10","x1x11","x2x3","x2x4","x2x5","x2x6",
"x2x7","x2x8","x2x9","x2x10","x2x11","x3x4","x3x5","x3x6","x3x7","x3x8","x3x9",
"x3x10","x3x11","x4x5","x4x6","x4x7","x4x8","x4x9","x4x10","x4x11","x5x6",
"x5x7","x5x8","x5x9","x5x10","x5x11","x6x7","x6x8","x6x9","x6x10","x6x11",
"x7x8","x7x9","x7x10","x7x11","x8x9","x8x10","x8x11","x9x10","x9x11","x10x11")
return(out)
}
```

Before conducting the Monte Carlo simulation, we run a basic test:

```
E1<- contin_syn1(nobs = 5000, xv =c (.1,.1,.1,.1,.1,.1,.1,.1,.1,.1,.1,rep(0,54),.1))

y<-E1[,1]
X<-as.matrix(scale(E1[,-1]))

m1<-lm(y ~ X -1)
summary(m1)
```

```
##
## Call:
## lm(formula = y ~ X - 1)
##
## Residuals:
##     Min       1Q   Median      3Q     Max
## -3.6683  -0.5679   0.0641  0.7501  3.3217
##
## Coefficients:
##              Estimate Std. Error t value Pr(>|t|)
## Xx1         0.1205186  0.0143302  8.410   < 2e-16 ***
## Xx2         0.1067502  0.0143907  7.418 1.39e-13 ***
## Xx3         0.0848867  0.0143312  5.923 3.37e-09 ***
## Xx4         0.0921261  0.0143703  6.411 1.58e-10 ***
## Xx5         0.0760078  0.0143211  5.307 1.16e-07 ***
## Xx6         0.1155132  0.0143631  8.042 1.09e-15 ***
## Xx7         0.1417589  0.0143092  9.907   < 2e-16 ***
## Xx8         0.0959873  0.0142970  6.714 2.11e-11 ***
## Xx9         0.0986346  0.0142796  6.907 5.56e-12 ***
## Xx10        0.0870802  0.0143076  6.086 1.24e-09 ***
## Xx11        0.0979852  0.0143458  6.830 9.50e-12 ***
## Xx1x2       0.0116480  0.0143881  0.810   0.4182
## Xx1x3       0.0262749  0.0142919  1.838   0.0661.
## Xx1x4       0.0008117  0.0143594  0.057   0.9549
## Xx1x5       0.0035248  0.0143233  0.246   0.8056
## Xx1x6       0.0020466  0.0143194  0.143   0.8864
## Xx1x7      -0.0027848  0.0143727 -0.194   0.8464
## Xx1x8       0.0157844  0.0143215  1.102   0.2705
## Xx1x9       0.0059699  0.0143480  0.416   0.6774
## Xx1x10      0.0148930  0.0143496  1.038   0.2994
## Xx1x11      0.0047509  0.0143457  0.331   0.7405
## Xx2x3       0.0041297  0.0144070  0.287   0.7744
## Xx2x4       0.0002197  0.0144200  0.015   0.9878
## Xx2x5       0.0106476  0.0143562  0.742   0.4583
## Xx2x6       0.0061833  0.0144187  0.429   0.6681
## Xx2x7       0.0011029  0.0143556  0.077   0.9388
## Xx2x8       0.0252029  0.0143413  1.757   0.0789.
## Xx2x9      -0.0177719  0.0144216 -1.232   0.2179
## Xx2x10      0.0101763  0.0143415  0.710   0.4780
## Xx2x11     -0.0076053  0.0143783 -0.529   0.5969
```

```
## Xx3x4      -0.0137371   0.0143373   -0.958    0.3380
## Xx3x5      -0.0049154   0.0143783   -0.342    0.7325
## Xx3x6       0.0074084   0.0143075    0.518    0.6046
## Xx3x7       0.0077435   0.0143381    0.540    0.5892
## Xx3x8      -0.0202256   0.0143691   -1.408    0.1593
## Xx3x9      -0.0154567   0.0143133   -1.080    0.2802
## Xx3x10      0.0114000   0.0143147    0.796    0.4258
## Xx3x11      0.0120973   0.0143606    0.842    0.3996
## Xx4x5       0.0076279   0.0143522    0.531    0.5951
## Xx4x6      -0.0102014   0.0143542   -0.711    0.4773
## Xx4x7       0.0313178   0.0143544    2.182    0.0292 *
## Xx4x8       0.0089793   0.0143386    0.626    0.5312
## Xx4x9      -0.0030960   0.0143577   -0.216    0.8293
## Xx4x10      0.0088441   0.0143243    0.617    0.5370
## Xx4x11     -0.0197388   0.0144047   -1.370    0.1707
## Xx5x6       0.0235594   0.0143646    1.640    0.1010
## Xx5x7       0.0160640   0.0142877    1.124    0.2609
## Xx5x8      -0.0049940   0.0143023   -0.349    0.7270
## Xx5x9       0.0166924   0.0143444    1.164    0.2446
## Xx5x10      0.0152000   0.0143285    1.061    0.2888
## Xx5x11      0.0017781   0.0143354    0.124    0.9013
## Xx6x7      -0.0083726   0.0143401   -0.584    0.5593
## Xx6x8       0.0105445   0.0143543    0.735    0.4626
## Xx6x9      -0.0293456   0.0143531   -2.045    0.0410 *
## Xx6x10     -0.0001714   0.0143458   -0.012    0.9905
## Xx6x11     -0.0145682   0.0144003   -1.012    0.3117
## Xx7x8       0.0052908   0.0143029    0.370    0.7115
## Xx7x9      -0.0139859   0.0143283   -0.976    0.3291
## Xx7x10      0.0197514   0.0143405    1.377    0.1685
## Xx7x11      0.0247430   0.0143919    1.719    0.0856.
## Xx8x9       0.0199247   0.0143142    1.392    0.1640
## Xx8x10     -0.0123678   0.0143058   -0.865    0.3873
## Xx8x11      0.0074309   0.0143799    0.517    0.6053
## Xx9x10      0.0281502   0.0143198    1.966    0.0494 *
## Xx9x11     -0.0049599   0.0143591   -0.345    0.7298
## Xx10x11     0.0921072   0.0143479    6.420 1.49e-10 ***
## ---
## Signif. codes:   0 '***' 0.001 '**' 0.01 '*' 0.05 '.' 0.1 ' ' 1
##
```

```
## Residual standard error: 1.005 on 4934 degrees of freedom
## Multiple R-squared:   0.1202, Adjusted R-squared:   0.1084
## F-statistic: 10.21 on 66 and 4934 DF,   p-value: < 2.2e-16
b.long<-solve(t(X) %*% X) %*% t(X) %*% diag(y)
# Regress the row in b.long corresponding to variable #11 on the others
int.m1<-lm(b.long[11,] ~ X[,1:10] -1)
# What's the largest t-value?
m1<-max(abs(((coef(int.m1)/sqrt(diag(vcov(int.m1))))[1:10])))
# Which variable has the largest t-value?
m2<-which(abs((coef(int.m1)/sqrt(diag(vcov(int.m1)))))[1:10]==m1)
# Is the variable with the largest t-value variable 10?
m3<-1*(m2==10)
# Is it greater than 2 (i.e., significantly different from zero)
m3<-ifelse(m1>2,m3,0)
#does.it.work.2[1,i]<-m3
```

Now we will run the simulation to test how often our approach identifies an interaction in the data when one is present:

```
num.right <- rep(NA,1000)
for(i in 1:1000){
E1<- contin_syn1(nobs = 5000, xv =c (.1,.1,.1,.1,.1,.1,.1,.1,.1,.1,.1,rep(0,54),.1))
y<-E1[,1]
X<-as.matrix(scale(E1[,-1]))
b.long<-solve(t(X) %*% X) %*% t(X) %*% diag(y)
# Regress the row in b.long corresponding to variable #11 on the others
int.m1<-lm(b.long[11,] ~ X[,1:10] -1)
# What's the largest t-value?
m1<-max(abs(((coef(int.m1)/sqrt(diag(vcov(int.m1))))[1:10])))
# Which variable has the largest t-value?
m2<-which(abs((coef(int.m1)/sqrt(diag(vcov(int.m1)))))[1:10]==m1)
# Is the variable with the largest t-value variable 10?
m3<-1*(m2==10)
# Is it greater than 2 (i.e., significantly different from zero)
m3<-ifelse(m1>2,m3,0)
num.right[i]<-m3}
sum(num.right)
## [1] 1000
```

The results show that we identify the relevant interactions 1000 out of 1000 times.

References

Abbott, Andrew. 1988. "Transcending General Linear Reality." *Sociological Theory* 6(2):169–86. doi: 10.2307/202114.

Ai, Chunrong, and Edward C. Norton. 2003. "Interaction Terms in Logit and Profit Models." *Economic Letters* 80(1):123–9.

Allison, Paul D. 2009. *Fixed Effects Regression Models*. SAGE Publications.

Amable, Bruno. 2003. *The Diversity of Modern Capitalism*. Oxford: Oxford University Press.

Ansari, Aziz, and Eric Klinenberg. 2015. *Modern Romance*. Penguin.

Asal, Victor H., R. Karl Rethemeyer, and Eric W. Schoon. 2019. "Crime, Conflict, and the Legitimacy Trade-Off: Explaining Variation in Insurgents' Participation in Crime." *The Journal of Politics* 81(2):399–410. doi: 10.1086/701492.

Beckfield, Jason. 2004. "Does Income Inequality Harm Health? New Cross-National Evidence." *Journal of Health and Social Behavior* 45(3):231–48. doi: 10.1177/002214650404500301.

Beckfield, Jason. 2006. "European Integration and Income Inequality." *American Sociological Review* 71(6):964–85. doi: 10.1177/000312240607100605.

Belsley, David A., Edwin Kuh, and Roy E. Welsch. 2004. *Regression Diagnostics: Identifying Influential Data and Sources of Collinearity*. John Wiley & Sons.

Berk, Richard A. 2004. *Regression Analysis: A Constructive Critique*. SAGE Publications.

Berry, William D. 1993. *Understanding Regression Assumptions*. SAGE Publications.

Bezerra, Paul, Jacob Cramer, Megan Hauser, Jennifer L. Miller, and Thomas J. Volgy. 2015. "Going for the Gold versus Distributing the Green: Foreign Policy Substitutability and Complementarity in Status Enhancement Strategies." *Foreign Policy Analysis* 11(3):253–72. doi: 10.1111/fpa.12061.

Bohle, Dorothee, and Béla Greskovits. 2012. *Capitalist Diversity on Europe's Periphery*. Cornell University Press.

Bornmann, Lutz, and Werner Marx. 2012. "The Anna Karenina Principle: A Way of Thinking about Success in Science" *Journal of the American Society for Information Science and Technology* 63(10):2037–51.

Bourdieu, Pierre. 1983. "The Field of Cultural Production, Or: The Economic World Reversed." *Poetics* 12(4):311–56. doi: 10.1016/0304-422X(83)90012-8.

Bourdieu, Pierre. 1984. *Distinction: A Social Critique of the Judgement of Taste*. Cambridge, MA: Harvard University Press.

Bourdieu, Pierre, and Loïc J. D. Wacquant. 1992. *An Invitation to Reflexive Sociology*. Chicago: University of Chicago Press.

Braumoeller, Bear F. 2004. "Hypothesis Testing and Multiplicative Interaction Terms." *International Organization* 58(4):807–20.

Breiger, Ronald L. 2000. "A Tool Kit for Practice Theory." *Poetics* 27(2–3):91–115. doi: 10.1016/S0304-422X(99)00026-1.

Breiger, Ronald L. 2009. "On the Duality of Cases and Variables: Correspondence Analysis (CA) and Qualitative Comparative Analysis (QCA)." pp. 243–59 in *The SAGE Handbook of Case-Based Methods*, edited by D. Byrne and C. C. Ragin. London: SAGE Publications.

Breiger, Ronald L., Gary A. Ackerman, Victor Asal, et al. 2011. "Application of a Profile Similarity Methodology for Identifying Terrorist Groups That Use or Pursue CBRN Weapons." pp. 26–33 in *Social Computing, Behavioral-Cultural Modeling and Prediction, Lecture Notes in Computer Science*, edited by J. Salerno, S. J. Yang, D. Nau, and S.-K. Chai. Berlin, Heidelberg: Springer.

Breiger, Ronald L., and David Melamed. 2014. "The Duality of Organizations and Their Attributes: Turning Regression Modeling 'Inside Out'." *Research in the Sociology of Organizations* 40:263–75. doi: 10.1108/S0733-558X(2014)0000040013.

Breiger, Ronald L., Eric Schoon, David Melamed, Victor Asal, and R. Karl Rethemeyer. 2014. "Comparative Configurational Analysis as a Two-Mode Network Problem: A Study of Terrorist Group Engagement in the Drug Trade." *Social Networks* 36:23–39. doi: 10.1016/j.socnet.2013.04.002.

Breiger, Ronald, and John W. Mohr. 2004. "Institutional Logics from the Aggregation of Organizational Networks: Operational Procedures for the Analysis of Counted Data." *Computational & Mathematical Organization Theory* 10(1):17–43. doi: 10.1023/B:CMOT.0000032578.16511.9d.

Burawoy, Michael. 1989. "Two Methods in Search of Science." *Theory and Society* 18:759–805.

Burke, Kenneth. 1969. *A Grammar of Motives*. University of California Press.

Chatterjee, Samprit, and Ali S. Hadi. 1988. "Impact of Simultaneous Omission of a Variable and an Observation on a Linear Regression Equation." *Computational Statistics & Data Analysis* 6(2):129–44. doi: 10.1016/0167-9473(88)90044-8.

Chirot, Daniel, and Charles Ragin. 1975. "The Market, Tradition and Peasant Rebellion: The Case of Romania in 1907." *American Sociological Review* 40(4):428–44. doi: 10.2307/2094430.

Coleman, James S. 1994. *Foundations of Social Theory*. Harvard University Press.

Collier, Paul, and Nicholas Sambanis. 2005. *Understanding Civil War: Evidence and Analysis, Volume 2. Europe, Central Asia, and Other Regions*. Washington, DC: World Bank.

Collins, Patricia Hill. 2002. *Black Feminist Thought: Knowledge, Consciousness, and the Politics of Empowerment*. Routledge.

Cook, R. Dennis. 1977. "Detection of Influential Observation in Linear Regression." *Technometrics* 19(1):15–18. doi: 10.1080/00401706.1977.10489493.

Cook, R. Dennis, and Sanford Weisberg. 1999. "Graphs in Statistical Analysis: Is the Medium the Message?" *The American Statistician* 53(1):29–37. doi: 10.1080/00031305.1999.10474426.

Cornell, Svante, and Michael Jonsson. 2014. "The Nexus of Crime and Conflict." pp. 1–22 in *Conflict, Crime, and the State in Postcommunist Eurasia*, edited by S. Cornell and M. Jonsson. University of Pennsylvania Press.

Crenshaw, Kimberle. 1989. "Demarginalizing the Intersection of Race and Sex: A Black Feminist Critique of Anti-Discrimination Doctrine, Feminist Theory and Anti-Racist Politics." *The University of Chicago Legal Forum* 140:139.

Crenshaw, Kimberle. 1991. "Mapping the Margins: Intersectionality, Identity Politics, and Violence Against Women of Color." *Stanford Law Review* 43(6):1241–99.

Creswell, John W., and Vicki L. Plano Clark. 2017. *Designing and Conducting Mixed Methods Research*. SAGE Publications.

Dabkowski, Matthew F., Neng Fan, and Ronald Breiger. 2020. "Finding Globally Optimal Macrostructure in Multiple Relation, Mixed-Mode Social Networks." *Methodological Innovations* 13(3):1–17. doi: 10.1177/2059799120961693.

Dafoe, Allan, and Nina Kelsey. 2014. "Observing the Capitalist Peace: Examining Market-Mediated Signaling and Other Mechanisms." *Journal of Peace Research* 51(5):619–33. doi: 10.1177/0022343314536423.

Davis, Kathy. 2008. "Intersectionality as Buzzword: A Sociology of Science Perspective on What Makes a Feminist Theory Successful." *Feminist Theory* 9(1):67–85. doi: 10.1177/1464700108086364.

Denord, François. 2015. "Géométrie Des Reseaux Sociaux." pp. 59–78 in *La méthodologie de Pierre Bourdieu en action*, edited by F. Lebaron and B. Le Roux. Paris: Dunod.

DiMaggio, Paul J., and Walter W. Powell. 1983. "The Iron Cage Revisited: Institutional Isomorphism and Collective Rationality in Organizational Fields." *American Sociological Review* 48(2):147–60. doi: 10.2307/2095101.

Doreian, Patrick, Vladimir Batagelj, and Anuška Ferligoj, eds. 2020. *Advances in Network Clustering and Blockmodeling*. 1st ed. Hoboken, NJ: Wiley.

Draper, Norman R., and Harry Smith. 1998. *Applied Regression Analysis*. 3rd ed. New York: Wiley.

Dufur, Mikaela J., Toby L. Parcel, and Kelly P. Troutman. 2013. "Does Capital at Home Matter More than Capital at School? Social Capital Effects on Academic Achievement." *Research in Social Stratification and Mobility* 31:1–21. doi: 10.1016/j.rssm.2012.08.002.

Duncan, Otis Dudley. 1984. *Notes on Social Measurement: Historical and Critical*. Russell Sage Foundation.

Duval, Julien. 2018. "Correspondence Analysis and Bourdieu's Approach to Statistics: Using Correspondence Analysis within Field Theory." pp. 512–27 in *The Oxford Handbook of Pierre Bourdieu*, edited by T. Medvetz and J. J. Sallaz. New York: Oxford University Press.

Efron, B., and C. Stein. 1981. "The Jackknife Estimate of Variance." *The Annals of Statistics* 9(3):586–96.

Elman, Colin, John Gerring, and James Mahoney. 2016. "Case Study Research: Putting the Quant into the Qual." *Sociological Methods & Research* 45(3):375–91. doi: 10.1177/0049124116644273.

Emigh, Rebecca Jean. 1997. "The Power of Negative Thinking: The Use of Negative Case Methodology in the Development of Sociological Theory." *Theory and Society* 26(5):649–84.

Emirbayer, Mustafa. 1997. "Manifesto for a Relational Sociology." *American Journal of Sociology* 103(2):281–317. doi: 10.1086/231209.

Ermakoff, Ivan. 2014. "Exceptional Cases: Epistemic Contributions and Normative Expectations." *European Journal of Sociology* 55(2):223–43. doi: 10.1017/S0003975614000101.

Esping-Andersen, Gøsta. 1990. *The Three Worlds of Welfare Capitalism*. Cambridge: Polity.

Esping-Andersen, Gosta. 1999. *Social Foundations of Postindustrial Economies*. Oxford University Press.

Everett, Martin G., and Stephen P. Borgatti. 2012. "Categorical Attribute-Based Centrality: E-I and G-F Centrality." *Social Networks* 34(4): 269–562. doi: 10.1016/j.socnet.2012.06.002.

Fearon, James D., and David D. Laitin. 2003. "Ethnicity, Insurgency, and Civil War." *American Political Science Review* 97(1):75–90.

Fearon, James D., and David D. Laitin. 2011. "Integrating Qualitative and Quantitative Methods." *The Oxford Handbook of Political Science*. Retrieved June 16, 2022 (www.oxfordhandbooks .com/view/10.1093/oxfordhb/9780199604456.001.0001/oxfordhb-9780199604456-e-052).

Fischer, Claude S., Michael Hout, Martín Sánchez Jankowski, Samuel R. Lucas, Ann Swidler, and Kim Voss. 1996. *Inequality by Design: Cracking the Bell Curve Myth*. Princeton University Press.

Fiss, Peer C., Axel Marx, and Benoît Rihoux. 2014. "Comment: Getting QCA Right." *Sociological Methodology* 44(1):95–100. doi: 10.1177/0081175014542079.

Fox, John. 2019. *Regression Diagnostics: An Introduction*. SAGE Publications.

Freedman, David A. 1991. "Statistical Models and Shoe Leather." *Sociological Methodology* 21:291–313. doi: 10.2307/270939.

van de Geer, Johannes Petrus. 1971. *Introduction to Multivariate Analysis for the Social Sciences*. San Francisco: W. H. Freeman.

Gelman, Andrew, Jennifer Hill, and Aki Vehtari. 2020. *Regression and Other Stories*. Cambridge University Press.

George, Alexander L., and Andrew Bennett. 2005. *Case Studies and Theory Development in the Social Sciences*. Illustrated ed. Cambridge, MA: The MIT Press.

Gerring, John. 2017. *Case Study Research: Principles and Practices*. Cambridge University Press.

Gerring, John, and Lee Cojocaru. 2016. "Selecting Cases for Intensive Analysis: A Diversity of Goals and Methods." *Sociological Methods & Research* 45(3):392–423. doi: 10.1177/0049124116631692.

Goertz, Gary. 2017. *Multimethod Research, Causal Mechanisms, and Case Studies: An Integrated Approach*. Princeton University Press.

Goertz, Gary, Tony Hak, and Jan Dul. 2013. "Ceilings and Floors: Where Are There No Observations?" *Sociological Methods & Research* 42(1):3–40. doi: 10.1177/0049124112460375.

Goodman, Leo A. 1996. "A Single General Method for the Analysis of Cross-Classified Data: Reconciliation and Synthesis of Some Methods of Pearson, Yule, and Fisher, and Also Some Methods of Correspondence Analysis and Association Analysis." *Journal of the American Statistical Association* 91(433):408–28. doi: 10.1080/01621459.1996.10476702.

Goodman, Leo A. 2007. "Otis Dudley Duncan, Quantitative Sociologist Par Excellence: Path Analysis, Loglinear Methods, and Rasch Models." *Research in Social Stratification and Mobility* 25(2):129–39. doi: 10.1016/j.rssm.2007.05.005.

Gray, J. Brian, and Robert F. Ling. 1984. "K-Clustering as a Detection Tool for Influential Subsets in Regression." *Technometrics* 26(4):305–18.

Greene, Jennifer C. 2007. *Mixed Methods in Social Inquiry*. John Wiley & Sons.

Greene, Jennifer C., Valerie J. Caracelli, and Wendy F. Graham. 1989. "Toward a Conceptual Framework for Mixed-Method Evaluation Designs." *Educational Evaluation and Policy Analysis* 11(3):255–74. doi: 10.3102/01623737011003255.

Greenland, Sander, Stephen J. Senn, Kenneth J. Rothman, John B. Carlin, Charles Poole, Steven N. Goodman, and Douglas G. Altman. 2016. "Statistical Tests, P Values, Confidence Intervals, and Power: A Guide to Misinterpretations." *European Journal of Epidemiology* 31(4):337–50. doi: 10.1007/s10654-016-0149-3.

Grofman, Bernard, and Carsten Q. Schneider. 2009. "An Introduction to Crisp Set QCA, with a Comparison to Binary Logistic Regression." *Political Research Quarterly* 62(4):662–72. doi: 10.1177/1065912909338464.

Habshah, M., M. R. Norazan, and A. H. M. Rahmatullah Imon. 2009. "The Performance of Diagnostic-Robust Generalized Potentials for the Identification of Multiple High Leverage Points in Linear Regression." *Journal of Applied Statistics* 36(5):507–20. doi: 10.1080/02664760802553463.

Hall, Peter A., and David Soskice. 2001. *Varieties of Capitalism: The Institutional Foundations of Comparative Advantage*. Oxford: Oxford University Press.

Hancock, Ange-Marie. 2007. "Intersectionality as a Normative and Empirical Paradigm." *Politics & Gender* 3(2):248–54. doi: 10.1017/S1743923X07000062.

Herrnstein, Richard J., and Charles Murray. 1994. *The Bell Curve: Intelligence and Class Structure in American Life*. Simon & Schuster.

Hicks, Alexander, and Lane Kenworthy. 2003. "Varieties of Welfare Capitalism." *Socio-Economic Review* 1(1):27–61. doi: 10.1093/soceco/1.1.27.

Hilbe, Joseph M. 2011. *Negative Binomial Regression*. Cambridge University Press.

Horwitz, Ilana M., Kaylee T. Matheny, Krystal Laryea, and Landon Schnabel. 2022. "From Bat Mitzvah to the Bar: Religious Habitus, Self-Concept, and Women's Educational Outcomes." *American Sociological Review* 87(2):336–72. doi: 10.1177/00031224221076487.

Hosmer, David W., and Stanley Lemeshow. 2000. *Applied Logistic Regression*. New York: John Wiley & Sons.

Hotelling, Harold, Walter Bartky, W. Edwards Deming, Milton Friedman, and Paul Hoel. 1948. "The Teaching of Statistics: A Report of the Institute of Mathematical Statistics Committee on the Teaching of Statistics." *The Annals of Mathematical Statistics* 19(1):95–115.

Hothorn, Torsten, and Brian S. Everitt. 2006. *A Handbook of Statistical Analyses Using R*. New York: Chapman and Hall/CRC.

Hug, Simon. 2013. "Qualitative Comparative Analysis: How Inductive Use and Measurement Error Lead to Problematic Inference." *Political Analysis* 21(2):252–65. doi: 10.1093/pan/mps061.

Ikeda, Nayu, Eiko Saito, Naoki Kondo, Manami Inoue, Shunya Ikeda, Toshihiko Satoh, Koji Wada et al. 2011. "What Has Made the Population of Japan Healthy?" *The Lancet* 378(9796):1094–1105.

Iversen, Torben, and Professor Torben Iversen. 2005. *Capitalism, Democracy, and Welfare*. Cambridge University Press.

Jick, Todd D. 1979. "Mixing Qualitative and Quantitative Methods: Triangulation in Action." *Administrative Science Quarterly* 24(4):602–11. doi: 10.2307/2392366.

Karrer, Brian, and M. E. J. Newman. 2011. "Stochastic Blockmodels and Community Structure in Networks." *Physical Review E – Statistical, Nonlinear, and Soft Matter Physics* 83(1):016107. doi: 10.1103/PhysRevE.83.016107.

Kennedy, Peter E. 2002. "Sinning in the Basement: What Are the Rules? The Ten Commandments of Applied Econometrics." *Journal of Economic Surveys* 16(4):569–89. doi: 10.1111/1467-6419.00179.

Kenworthy, Lane. 1999. "Do Social-Welfare Policies Reduce Poverty? A Cross-National Assessment." *Social Forces* 77(3):1119–39.

Kenworthy, Lane. 2007. "Toward Improved Use of Regression in Macro-Comparative Analysis." pp. 261–308 in *Comparative Social Research*, edited by Lars Mjøset and Tommy H. Clausen. Vol. 24. Bingley: Emerald (MCB UP).

Kersbergen, Kees van. 2003. *Social Capitalism: A Study of Christian Democracy and the Welfare State*. Routledge.

Kisangani, Emizet F. 2012. *Civil Wars in the Democratic Republic of Congo, 1960–2010*. Lynne Rienner Publishers.

Kondo, Naoki, Grace Sembajwe, Ichiro Kawachi, Rob M. van Dam, S. V. Subramanian, and Zentaro Yamagata. 2009. "Income Inequality, Mortality, and Self Rated Health: Meta-Analysis of Multilevel Studies." *BMJ* 339:b4471. doi: 10.1136/bmj.b4471.

Korpi, Walter, and Michael Shalev. 1980. "Strikes, Power, and Politics in the Western Nations, 1900–1976." *Political Power and Social Theory* 1:301–334.

Kutner, Michael H., Chris Nachtsheim, and John Neter. 2004. *Applied Linear Regression Models*. McGraw-Hill/Irwin.

Ladurie, Emmanuel Le Roy. 1978. *Montaillou: The Promised Land of Error*. G. Braziller.

Le Roux, Brigitte, Solène Bienaise, and Jean-Luc Durand. 2019. *Combinatorial Inference in Geometric Data Analysis*. Boca Raton, FL: CRC Press.

Le Roux, Brigitte, and Henry Rouanet. 2004. *Geometric Data Analysis: From Correspondence Analysis to Structured Data Analysis*. Springer Science & Business Media.

Lebaron, Frédéric. 2009. "How Bourdieu 'Quantified' Bourdieu: The Geometric Modelling of Data." pp. 11–29 in *Quantifying Theory: Pierre Bourdieu*, edited by K. Robson and C. Sanders. Dordrecht: Springer Netherlands.

Lebaron, Frédéric, and Brigitte Le Roux. 2018. "Bourdieu and Geometric Data Analysis." pp. 503–511 in *The Oxford Handbook of Pierre Bourdieu*, edited by T. Medvetz and J. J. Sallaz. New York: Oxford University Press.

Lee, Monica, and John Levi Martin. 2018. "Doorway to the Dharma of Duality." *Poetics* 68:18–30. doi: 10.1016/j.poetic.2018.01.001.

Li, Xinru, Elise Dusseldorp, and Jacqueline J. Meulman. 2019. "A Flexible Approach to Identify Interaction Effects between Moderators in Meta-Analysis." *Research Synthesis Methods* 10(1):134–52. doi: 10.1002/jrsm.1334.

Liao, Tim Futing. 2019. "Individual Components of Three Inequality Measures for Analyzing Shapes of Inequality." *Sociological Methods & Research* 51(3):1325–56. doi: 10.1177/0049124119875961

Lieberman, Evan S. 2005. "Nested Analysis as a Mixed-Method Strategy for Comparative Research." *American Political Science Review* 99(3):435–52. doi: 10.1017/S0003055405051762.

Lieberson, Stanley. 2004. "Comments on the Use and Utility of QCA." *Qualitative Methods: Newsletter of the American Political Science Association Organized Section on Qualitative Methods* 2(2):13–14.

Lim, Michael, and Trevor Hastie. 2015. "Learning Interactions via Hierarchical Group-Lasso Regularization." *Journal of Computational and Graphical Statistics* 24(3):627–54. doi: 10.1080/10618600.2014.938812.

Littell, Ramon C., George A. Milliken, Walter W. Stroup, Russell D. Wolfinger, and Oliver Schabenberger. 2006. *SAS for Mixed Models*. 2nd ed. SAS Institute.

Loh, Wei-Yin. 2002. "Regression Tress with Unbiased Variable Selection and Interaction Detection." *Statistica Sinica* 12(2):361–86.

Long, John Scott. 1997. *Regression Models for Categorical and Limited Dependent Variables*. 1st ed. Thousand Oaks: SAGE Publications, Inc.

Lucas, Samuel R., and Alisa Szatrowski. 2014. "Qualitative Comparative Analysis in Critical Perspective." *Sociological Methodology* 44(1):1–79. doi: 10.1177/0081175014532763.

Lynd, Robert Staughton, and Helen Merrell Lynd. 1957. *Middletown: A Study in American Culture*. Harcourt, Brace.

Mahoney, James. 2004. "Reflections on Fs/QCA." *Qualitative Methods: Newsletter of the American Political Science Association Organized Section on Qualitative Methods* 2(2):17–21.

Mahoney, James. 2021. *The Logic of Social Science*. Princeton University Press.

Mahoney, James, and Gary Goertz. 2006. "A Tale of Two Cultures: Contrasting Quantitative and Qualitative Research." *Political Analysis* 14(3):227–49.

Martin, Carla D., and Mason A. Porter. 2012. "The Extraordinary SVD." *American Mathematical Monthly* 119(10):838–51. doi: 10.4169/amer.math.monthly.119.10.838.

Martin, John Levi. 2003. "What Is Field Theory?" *American Journal of Sociology* 109(1):1–49.

Martin, John Levi. 2018. *Thinking through Statistics*. Chicago: University of Chicago Press.

McKendall, Marie A., and John A. Wagner. 1997. "Motive, Opportunity, Choice, and Corporate Illegality." *Organization Science* 8(6):624–47. doi: 10.1287/orsc.8.6.624.

McShane, Blakeley B., and Andrew Gelman. 2017. "Abandon Statistical Significance." *Nature* 551(7682):557–59. doi: 10.1038/d41586-017-07522-z.

Medvetz, Thomas, and Jeffrey J. Sallaz. 2018. *The Oxford Handbook of Pierre Bourdieu*. New York: Oxford University Press.

Melamed, David, Ronald L. Breiger, and Eric Schoon. 2013. "The Duality of Clusters and Statistical Interactions." *Sociological Methods & Research* 42(1):41–59. doi: 10.1177/00491241 12464870.

Mill, John Stuart. 1869. *A System of Logic, Ratiocinative and Inductive: Being a Connected View of the Principles of Evidence and the Methods of Scientific Investigation*. Harper and Brothers.

Mize, Trenton D. 2019. "Best Practices for Estimating, Interpreting, and Presenting Nonlinear Interaction Effects." *Sociological Science* 6:81–117. doi: 10.15195/v6.a4.

Morgan, James N., and John A. Sonquist. 1963. "Some Results from a Non-Symmetrical Branching Process That Looks for Interaction Effects." *Young* 8(5):40–53.

Mosteller, Frederick, and John Wilder Tukey. 1977. *Data Analysis and Regression: A Second Course in Statistics*. Addison-Wesley Publishing Company.

Mützel, Sophie, and Ronald L. Breiger. 2020. "Duality beyond Persons and Groups: Culture and Affiliation." pp. 392–413 in *The Oxford Handbook of Social Networks*, edited by R. Light and J. Moody. New York: Oxford University Press.

Nelsen, Roger B. 2020. "Titu's Lemma." *Mathematics Magazine* 93(1):70. doi: 10.1080/ 0025570X.2020.1682745.

Neter, John, Michael H. Kutner, Christopher Nachtsheim, and William Wasserman. 1996. *Applied Linear Statistical Models*. Boston: McGraw Hill.

Nielsen, Richard A. 2016. "Case Selection via Matching." *Sociological Methods & Research* 45(3):569–97. doi: 10.1177/0049124114547054.

de Nooy, Wouter. 2003. "Fields and Networks: Correspondence Analysis and Social Network Analysis in the Framework of Field Theory." *Poetics* 31(5–6):305–27. doi: 10.1016/S0304-422X(03)00035-4.

Olsen, Wendy. 2014. "Comment: The Usefulness of QCA under Realist Assumptions." *Sociological Methodology* 44(1):101–7. doi: 10.1177/0081175014542080.

Pacewicz, Josh. 2020. "What Can You Do With a Single Case? How to Think About Ethnographic Case Selection Like a Historical Sociologist." *Sociological Methods & Research* 51(3):931–962. doi: 10.1177/0049124119901213.

Pattison, Philippa E., and Ronald L. Breiger. 2002. "Lattices and Dimensional Representations: Matrix Decompositions and Ordering Structures." *Social Networks* 24(4):423–44. doi: 10.1016/S0378-8733(02)00015-1.

Pickett, Kate E., and Richard G. Wilkinson. 2015. "Recalibrating Rambotti: Disentangling Concepts of Poverty and Inequality." *Social Science & Medicine (1982)* 139:132–34. doi: 10.1016/j.socscimed.2015.07.005.

Pregibon, Daryl. 1981. "Logistic Regression Diagnostics." *The Annals of Statistics* 9(4):705–24. doi: 10.1214/aos/1176345513.

Ragin, Charles C. 2000. *Fuzzy-Set Social Science*. Chicago: University of Chicago Press.

Ragin, Charles C. 2006. "The Limitations of Net-Effects Thinking." pp. 13–41 in *Innovative Comparative Methods for Policy Analysis*, edited by B. Rihoux and H. Grimm. Boston: Kluwer Academic Publishers.

Ragin, Charles C. 2008. *Redesigning Social Inquiry: Fuzzy Sets and Beyond*. Chicago: University of Chicago Press.

Ragin, Charles C. 2009. *Redesigning Social Inquiry: Fuzzy Sets and Beyond*. Chicago: University of Chicago Press.

Ragin, Charles C. 2014a. "Comment: Lucas and Szatrowski in Critical Perspective." *Sociological Methodology* 44(1):80–94. doi: 10.1177/0081175014542081.

Ragin, Charles C. 2014b. *The Comparative Method: Moving beyond Qualitative and Quantitative Strategies*. University of California Press.

Ragin, Charles C., and Peer C. Fiss. 2017. *Intersectional Inequality: Race, Class, Test Scores, and Poverty*. Chicago: University of Chicago Press.

Ragin, Charles C., and Benoît Rihoux. 2004. "Qualitative Comparative Analysis (QCA): State of the Art and Prospects." *Qualitative Methods: Newsletter of the American Political Science Association Organized Section on Qualitative Methods* 2(2):21–4.

Rambotti, Simone. 2015. "Recalibrating the Spirit Level: An Analysis of the Interaction of Income Inequality and Poverty and Its Effect on Health." *Social Science & Medicine* 139:123–31. doi: 10.1016/j.socscimed.2015.02.026.

Rambotti, Simone, and Ronald L. Breiger. 2020. "Extreme and Inconsistent: A Case-Oriented Regression Analysis of Health, Inequality, and Poverty." *Socius* 6:1–13. doi: 10.1177/2378023120906064.

Raudenbush, Stephen W., and Anthony S. Bryk. 2002. *Hierarchical Linear Models: Applications and Data Analysis Methods*. Vol. 1. SAGE Publications.

Rihoux, Benoît, and Charles C. Ragin. 2008. *Configurational Comparative Methods: Qualitative Comparative Analysis (QCA) and Related Techniques*. SAGE Publications.

Robette, Nicolas, and Olivier Roueff. 2019. "Cultural Domains and Class Structure: Assessing Homologies and Cultural Legitimacy." pp. 115–34 in *Empirical Investigations of Social Space*, edited by J. Blasius, F. Lebaron, B. Le Roux, and A. Schmitz. Springer Nature Switzerland.

Roscigno, Vincent J., and Randy Hodson. 2004. "The Organizational and Social Foundations of Worker Resistance." *American Sociological Review* 69(1):14–39. doi: 10.1177/000312240406900103.

Rosenberg, Andrew S., Austin J. Knuppe, and Bear F. Braumoeller. 2017. "Unifying the Study of Asymmetric Hypotheses." *Political Analysis* 25(3):381–401. doi: 10.1017/pan.2017.16.

Rosvall, Martin, Jean-Charles Delvenne, Michael T. Schaub, and Renaud Lambiotte. 2019. "Different Approaches to Community Detection." pp. 105–19 in *Advances in Network Clustering and Blockmodeling*. Oxford, UK: Wiley.

Rouanet, Henry, Werner Ackermann, and Brigitte Le Roux. 2000. "The Geometric Analysis of Questionnaires: The Lesson of Bourdieu's La Distinction (Corrected Version Sept. 2004)." *Bulletin de Methodologie Sociologique* 65:5–15.

Rouanet, Henry, Frédéric Lebaron, Viviane Le Hay, Werner Ackermann, and Brigitte Le Roux. 2002. "Régression et Analyse Géométrique Des Données : Réflexions et Suggestions [Regression and Geometric Data Analysis: Reflections and Suggestions]." *Mathématiques et Sciences Humaines / Mathematics and Social Sciences* 40(160):13–45.

Le Roux, Brigitte, and Henry Rouanet. 2004b. *Geometric Data Analysis: From Correspondence Analysis to Structured Data Analysis*. Dordrecht: Kluwer Academic Publishers.

Schmidt-Wellenburg, Christian, and Frédéric Lebaron. 2018. "There Is No Such Thing as 'the Economy'. Economic Phenomena Analysed from a Field-Theoretical Perspective." *Historical Social Research / Historische Sozialforschung* 43(3):7–38.

Schneider, Carsten Q., and Kristin Makszin. 2014. "Forms of Welfare Capitalism and Education-Based Participatory Inequality." *Socio-Economic Review* 12(2):437–62. doi: 10.1093/ser/mwu010.

Schneider, Carsten Q., and Ingo Rohlfing. 2016. "Case Studies Nested in Fuzzy-Set QCA on Sufficiency: Formalizing Case Selection and Causal Inference." *Sociological Methods & Research* 45(3):526–68. doi: 10.1177/0049124114532446.

Schneider, Carsten Q., and Claudius Wagemann. 2012. *Set-Theoretic Methods for the Social Sciences: A Guide to Qualitative Comparative Analysis*. Cambridge University Press.

Schoon, Eric W. 2014. "The Asymmetry of Legitimacy: Analyzing the Legitimation of Violence in 30 Cases of Insurgent Revolution." *Social Forces* 93(2):779–801. doi: 10.1093/sf/sou079.

Schultz, Kenneth A. 1999. "Do Democratic Institutions Constrain or Inform? Contrasting Two Institutional Perspectives on Democracy and War." *International Organization* 53(2):233–66. doi: 10.1162/002081899550878.

Seawright, Jason. 2004. "Qualitative Comparative Analysis Vis-a-Vis Regression." *Qualitative Methods: Newsletter of the American Political Science Association Organized Section on Qualitative Methods* 2(2):14–17.

Seawright, Jason. 2016a. *Multi-Method Social Science: Combining Qualitative and Quantitative Tools*. Cambridge: Cambridge University Press.

Seawright, Jason. 2016b. "The Case for Selecting Cases That Are Deviant or Extreme on the Independent Variable." *Sociological Methods & Research* 45(3):493–525. doi: 10.1177/0049124116643556.

Seawright, Jason, and John Gerring. 2008. "Case Selection Techniques in Case Study Research: A Menu of Qualitative and Quantitative Options." *Political Research Quarterly* 61(2):294–308. doi: 10.1177/1065912907313077.

Sewell, Abigail A. 2015. "Disaggregating Ethnoracial Disparities in Physician Trust." *Social Science Research* 54:1–20. doi: 10.1016/j.ssresearch.2015.06.020.

Shalev, Michael. 2007. "Limits and Alternatives to Multiple Regression in Comparative Research." pp. 261–308 in *Comparative Social Research*, edited by L. Mjøset and T. H. Clausen. Vol. 24. Elsevier.

Skillicorn, David B. 2006. "Social Network Analysis via Matrix Decompositions." pp. 367–91 in *Emergent Information Technologies and Enabling Policies for Counter-Terrorism*, edited by R. L. Popp and J. Yen. Aptima Incorporated, Woburn, Massachusetts, and formerly at Defense Advanced Research Projects Agency (DARPA), USA; The Pennsylvania State University, University Park, Pennsylvania, USA: Wiley Interscience.

Small, Mario Luis. 2011. "How to Conduct a Mixed Methods Study: Recent Trends in a Rapidly Growing Literature." *Annual Review of Sociology* 37(1):57–86. doi: 10.1146/annurev.soc.012809.102657.

Tarrow, Sidney. 1995. "Bridging the Quantitative-Qualitative Divide in Political Science" edited by G. King, R. O. Keohane, and S. Verba. *The American Political Science Review* 89(2):471–74. doi: 10.2307/2082444.

Tashakkori, Abbas, R. Burke Johnson, and Charles Teddlie. 2020. *Foundations of Mixed Methods Research: Integrating Quantitative and Qualitative Approaches in the Social and Behavioral Sciences*. SAGE Publications.

Tashakkori, Abbas, Charles Teddlie, and Charles B. Teddlie. 1998. *Mixed Methodology: Combining Qualitative and Quantitative Approaches*. SAGE Publications.

Ter Braak, Cajo J. F., and Caspar W. N. Looman. 1994. "Biplots in Reduced-Rank Regression." *Biometrical Journal* 36(8):983–1003.

Thiem, Alrik, Michael Baumgartner, and Damien Bol. 2016. "Still Lost in Translation! A Correction of Three Misunderstandings between Configurational Comparativists and Regressional Analysts." *Comparative Political Studies* 49(6):742–74. doi: 10.1177/0010414014565892.

Tong, Christopher. 2019. "Statistical Inference Enables Bad Science; Statistical Thinking Enables Good Science." *The American Statistician* 73(sup1):246–61. doi: 10.1080/00031305.2018.1518264.

Tsang, Michael, Dehua Cheng, and Yan Liu. 2017. "Detecting Statistical Interactions from Neural Network Weights." *arXiv preprint arXiv:1705.04977*.

Vaisey, Stephen. 2007. "Structure, Culture, and Community: The Search for Belonging in 50 Urban Communes." *American Sociological Review* 72(6):851–73. doi: 10.1177/000312240707200601.

Vaisey, Stephen. 2009. "QCA 3.0: The 'Ragin Revolution' Continues." *Contemporary Sociology: A Journal of Reviews* 38(4):308–12. doi: 10.1177/009430610903800403.

Vaisey, Stephen. 2014. "Comment: QCA Works – When Used with Care." *Sociological Methodology* 44(1):108–12. doi: 10.1177/0081175014542083.

Van der Meer, Tom, Manfred Te Grotenhuis, and Ben Pelzer. 2010. "Influential Cases in Multilevel Modeling: A Methodological Comment." *American Sociological Review* 75(1):173–78. doi: 10.1177/0003122409359166.

Vandenberghe, Frédéric. 1999. "'The Real Is Relational': An Epistemological Analysis of Pierre Bourdieu's Generative Structuralism." *Sociological Theory* 17(1):32–67. Retrieved June 11, 2022 (www-jstor-org.ezproxy4.library.arizona.edu/stable/201926?seq=1).

Velleman, Paul F., and Roy E. Welsch. 1981. "Efficient Computing of Regression Diagnostics." *The American Statistician* 35(4):234–42. doi: 10.1080/00031305.1981.10479362.

Vuolo, Mike. 2013. "National-Level Drug Policy and Young People's Illicit Drug Use: A Multilevel Analysis of the European Union." *Drug and Alcohol Dependence* 131(1):149–56. doi: 10.1016/j.drugalcdep.2012.12.012.

Wackerly, Dennis, William Mendenhall, and Richard L. Scheaffer. 2014. *Mathematical Statistics with Applications*. Cengage Learning.

Wasserman, Stanley, and Katherine Faust. 1994. *Social Network Analysis: Methods and Applications*. Vol. 8. Cambridge, NY: Cambridge University Press.

Weller, Nicholas, and Jeb Barnes. 2016. "Pathway Analysis and the Search for Causal Mechanisms." *Sociological Methods & Research* 45(3):424–57. doi: 10.1177/0049124114544420.

White, Harrison, Scott Boorman, and Ronald Breiger. 1976. "Social Structure from Multiple Networks. I. Blockmodels of Roles and Positions." *American Journal of Sociology* 81(4):730–80.

Whyte, William Foote. 1943. *Street Corner Society: The Social Structure of an Italian Slum*. Chicago: University of Chicago Press.

Wilkinson, Richard, and Kate Pickett. 2011. *The Spirit Level: Why Greater Equality Makes Societies Stronger*. Bloomsbury Publishing USA.

Wimmer, Andreas, Lars-Erik Cederman, and Brian Min. 2009. "Ethnic Politics and Armed Conflict: A Configurational Analysis of a New Global Data Set." *American Sociological Review* 74(2):316–37. doi: 10.1177/000312240907400208.

Woolridge, Jeffrey M. 2010. *Econometric Analysis of Cross Section and Panel Data*. Cambridge MA: MIT Press.

Index